Software Development with Go

Cloud-Native Programming using Golang with Linux and Docker

Nanik Tolaram

Apress®

Software Development with Go: Cloud-Native Programming using Golang with Linux and Docker

Nanik Tolaram
Sydney, NSW, Australia

ISBN-13 (pbk): 978-1-4842-8730-9   ISBN-13 (electronic): 978-1-4842-8731-6
https://doi.org/10.1007/978-1-4842-8731-6

Managing Director, Apress Media LLC: Welmoed Spahr
Acquisitions Editor: James Robinson-Prior
Development Editor: James Markham
Coordinating Editor: Gryffin Winkler
Copy Editor: Mary Behr

Cover designed by eStudioCalamar

Cover image designed by Freepik (www.freepik.com)

Distributed to the book trade worldwide by Springer Science+Business Media New York, 1 New York Plaza, Suite 4600, New York, NY 10004-1562, USA. Phone 1-800-SPRINGER, fax (201) 348-4505, e-mail orders-ny@springer-sbm.com, or visit www.springeronline.com. Apress Media, LLC is a California LLC and the sole member (owner) is Springer Science + Business Media Finance Inc (SSBM Finance Inc). SSBM Finance Inc is a **Delaware** corporation.

For information on translations, please e-mail booktranslations@springernature.com; for reprint, paperback, or audio rights, please e-mail bookpermissions@springernature.com.

Apress titles may be purchased in bulk for academic, corporate, or promotional use. eBook versions and licenses are also available for most titles. For more information, reference our Print and eBook Bulk Sales web page at www.apress.com/bulk-sales.

Any source code or other supplementary material referenced by the author in this book is available to readers on GitHub (https://github.com/Apress). For more detailed information, please visit www.apress.com/source-code.

Printed on acid-free paper

I would like to dedicate this book to my late Dad who stood by me and encouraged me to write my very first book when I was 17 years old. To my dearest Mum who always supported me in pursuing my dreams and encouraged me to keep on going no matter what life brings. To my beautiful wife and best friend for allowing me the time to write the book and supporting me in every step of our life. To both my sons, Rahul and Manav, for allowing me to spend time in front of the computer on weekends to chase my dream and passion. Last but not least, to God for giving me this life and opportunity to be where I am in this world.

Table of Contents

About the Author

Nanik Tolaram is a big proponent of open source software with over 20 years of industry experience. He has dabbled in different programming languages like Java, JavaScript, C, and C++. He has developed different products from the ground up while working in start-up companies. He is a software engineer at heart, but he loves to write technical articles and share his knowledge with others. He learned to program with Go during the COVID-19 pandemic and hasn't looked back.

About the Technical Reviewer

Fabio Claudio Ferracchiati is a senior consultant and a senior analyst/developer using Microsoft technologies. He works for BluArancio (www.bluarancio.com). He is a Microsoft Certified Solution Developer for .NET, a Microsoft Certified Application Developer for .NET, a Microsoft Certified Professional, and a prolific author and technical reviewer. Over the past ten years, he's written articles for Italian and international magazines and coauthored more than ten books on a variety of computer topics.

Acknowledgments

Thanks to everyone on the Apress team who helped and guided me so much. Special thanks to James Robinson-Prior who guided me through the writing process and to Nirmal Selvaraj who made sure everything was done correctly and things were on track.

Thanks to the technical reviewers for taking time from their busy schedules to review my book and provide great feedback.

Finally, thanks to you, the reader, for spending time reading this book and spreading the love of Go.

Introduction

Go has been out for more than 10 years, and open source projects were developed using Go. The aim of this book is to show you the way to use Go to write a variety of applications that are useful in cloud-based systems.

Deploying applications into the cloud is a normal process that developers do every day. There are many questions that developers ask themselves about the cloud, like

- How do containers work in a cloud environment?

- How do cloud monitoring applications knows how much memory is left for my virtual machines?

- How can I build a high performance networking server in Linux environment?

- How do I scan code before deploying to the cloud to stop code deployment if it contains related information?

and many other cloud-relevant questions.

The book talk about different topics that are relevant in today's cloud environment. The approach is to explain each topic at a high level and then help you understand it by going through the details with the code. The book uses combination of open source projects hosted in GitHub and sample code. The open source projects chosen are relevant to the topic. You will get a good grasp about the tool and also how the code works internally.

PART I

System Programming

CHAPTER 1

System Calls

Linux provides a lot of features and provides applications access to everything that the operating system has access to. When discussing system calls, most people will turn their attention to using C because it is the most common language to use when interfacing with the operating system.

In this chapter, you will explore what system calls are and how you can program in Go to make system calls. By the end of this chapter, you will have learned the following:

- What a system call looks like in C

- Understanding the sys/unix Go package

- Exploring a project using system calls

If you are using Go for the first time, refer to the online documentation at https://go.dev/doc/install. The online documentation will walk you through the steps to install Go on your local computer. Go through the Go tutorial that the Go documentation provides at https://go.dev/doc/.

Source Code

The source code for this chapter is available from the https://github.com/Apress/Software-Development-Go repository.

© Nanik Tolaram 2023
N. Tolaram, *Software Development with Go*,
https://doi.org/10.1007/978-1-4842-8731-6_1

What Is a System Call?

A system call is the interface provided by the underlying operating system that your application is currently running on. Using this interface, your application can communicate with the operating system to perform an operation. In general, the operating system provides numerous services that applications can take advantage of.

Figure 1-1 shows at a high level how an application uses system calls to request some service operation to the operating system. The user app will make a call to the provided system library, which in this case is the Go library, and it will call the operating system service through the provided interface. Data transfer flows in both directions for the different components.

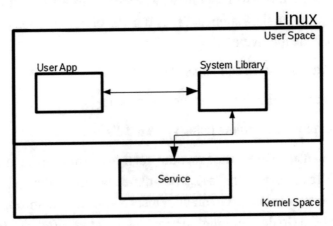

Figure 1-1. *High-level view of a system call*

Operating systems provide a large number of system calls that applications can use. Figure 1-2 shows a snapshot list of system calls. For a complete available Linux system call list, you can visit https://man7.org/linux/man-pages/man2/syscalls.2.html.

The list of system calls that are available as at kernel 5.11 (or in a few cases only on older kernels) is as follows:

System call	Kernel	Notes
_llseek(2)	1.2	
_newselect(2)	2.0	
_sysctl(2)	2.0	Removed in 5.5
accept(2)	2.0	See notes on socketcall(2)
accept4(2)	2.6.28	
access(2)	1.0	
acct(2)	1.0	
add_key(2)	2.6.10	
adjtimex(2)	1.0	
alarm(2)	1.0	
alloc_hugepages(2)	2.5.36	Removed in 2.5.44
arc_gettls(2)	3.9	ARC only
arc_settls(2)	3.9	ARC only

Figure 1-2. *Snapshot of a Linux system call*

C System Call

In this section, you will briefly look at how system calls normally work inside a C program. This will give you an idea of how system calls are done in C compared to how they are done in Go.

You will see a simple example of using a socket to connect to a server and read the response. The code can be found inside the chapter1/c directory. The code creates a socket and uses it to connect to a public website named httpbin.org and print the response it receives to the screen. Listing 1-1 shows the sample code.

Listing 1-1. Sample Code

```
#include<stdio.h>
#include<string.h>
#include<sys/socket.h>
#include<arpa/inet.h>
```

```c
#include<netdb.h>

int main(int argc, char * argv[]) {
 int socket_desc;
 struct sockaddr_in server;
 char * message, server_reply[2000];
 struct hostent * host;
 const char * hostname = "httpbin.org";
 //Create socket
 socket_desc = socket(AF_INET, SOCK_STREAM, 0);
 if (socket_desc == -1) {
   printf("Could not create socket");
 }

 if ((server.sin_addr.s_addr = inet_addr(hostname)) ==
0xffffffff) {
   if ((host = gethostbyname(hostname)) == NULL) {
     return -1;
   }

   memcpy( & server.sin_addr, host -> h_addr, host ->
   h_length);
 }

 server.sin_family = AF_INET;
 server.sin_port = htons(80);

 if (connect(socket_desc, (struct sockaddr * ) & server,
 sizeof(server)) < 0) {
   puts("connect error");
   return 1;
 }
 puts("Connected\n");
 //Send some data
```

```c
message = "GET / HTTP/1.0\n\n";
if (send(socket_desc, message, strlen(message), 0) < 0) {
    puts("Send failed");
    return 1;
}
puts("Data Send\n");
//Receive a reply from the server
if (recv(socket_desc, server_reply, 2000, 0) < 0) {
    puts("recv failed");
}
puts("Reply received\n");
puts(server_reply);
return 0;
}
```

To test the code, make sure you have a C compiler installed in your machine. Follow the instructions outlined on the GCC website to install the compiler and tools (https://gcc.gnu.org/). Use the following command to compile the code:

```
cc sample.c -o sample
```

The code will be compiled to an executable named *sample,* and it can be run by just typing ./sample on the command line. After a successful run, it will print out the following:

```
Connected

Data Send

Reply received

HTTP/1.1 200 OK
```

```
Date: Tue, 01 Mar 2022 10:21:13 GMT
Content-Type: text/html; charset=utf-8
Content-Length: 9593
Connection: close
Server: gunicorn/19.9.0
Access-Control-Allow-Origin: *
Access-Control-Allow-Credentials: true
```

The code sample shows the system call that it uses to resolve the address of httpbin.org to an IP address by using the gethostbyname function. It also uses the connect function to use the newly created socket to connect to the server.

In the next section, you will start exploring Go by using the standard library to write code using system calls.

sys/unix Package

The sys/unix package is a package provided by the Go language that provides a system-level interface to interact with the operating system. Go can run on a variety of operating systems, which means that it provides different interfaces to applications for different operating systems. Complete package documentation can be found at https://pkg.go.dev/golang.org/x/sys/unix. Figure 1-3 shows different system calls in different operating systems, in this case between Darwin and Linux.

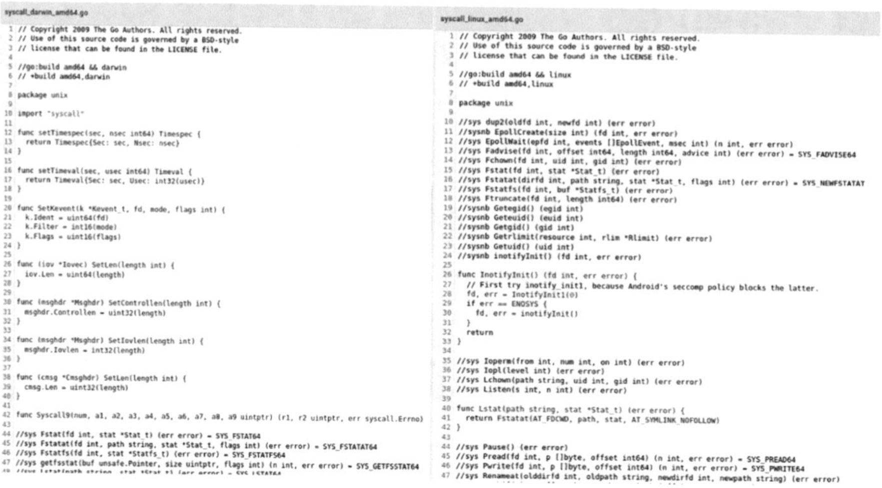

syscall_darwin_amd64.go

```
// Copyright 2009 The Go Authors. All rights reserved.
// Use of this source code is governed by a BSD-style
// license that can be found in the LICENSE file.

//go:build amd64 && darwin
// +build amd64,darwin

package unix

import "syscall"

func setTimespec(sec, nsec int64) Timespec {
  return Timespec{Sec: sec, Nsec: nsec}
}

func setTimeval(sec, usec int64) Timeval {
  return Timeval{Sec: sec, Usec: int32(usec)}
}

func SetKevent(k *Kevent_t, fd, mode, flags int) {
  k.Ident = uint64(fd)
  k.Filter = int16(mode)
  k.Flags = uint16(flags)
}

func (iov *Iovec) SetLen(length int) {
  iov.Len = uint64(length)
}

func (msghdr *Msghdr) SetControllen(length int) {
  msghdr.Controllen = uint32(length)
}

func (msghdr *Msghdr) SetIovlen(length int) {
  msghdr.Iovlen = int32(length)
}

func (cmsg *Cmsghdr) SetLen(length int) {
  cmsg.Len = uint32(length)
}

func Syscall9(num, a1, a2, a3, a4, a5, a6, a7, a8, a9 uintptr) (r1, r2 uintptr, err syscall.Errno)

//sys Fstat(fd int, stat *Stat_t) (err error) = SYS_FSTAT64
//sys Fstatat(fd int, path string, stat *Stat_t, flags int) (err error) = SYS_FSTATAT64
//sys Fstatfs(fd int, stat *Statfs_t) (err error) = SYS_FSTATFS64
//sys getfsstat(buf unsafe.Pointer, size uintptr, flags int) (n int, err error) = SYS_GETFSSTAT64
```

syscall_linux_amd64.go

```
// Copyright 2009 The Go Authors. All rights reserved.
// Use of this source code is governed by a BSD-style
// license that can be found in the LICENSE file.

//go:build amd64 && linux
// +build amd64,linux

package unix

//sys dup2(oldfd int, newfd int) (err error)
//sysnb EpollCreate(size int) (fd int, err error)
//sys EpollWait(epfd int, events []EpollEvent, msec int) (n int, err error)
//sys Fadvise(fd int, offset int64, length int64, advice int) (err error) = SYS_FADVISE64
//sys Fchown(fd int, uid int, gid int) (err error)
//sys Fstat(fd int, stat *Stat_t) (err error)
//sys Fstatat(dirfd int, path string, stat *Stat_t, flags int) (err error) = SYS_NEWFSTATAT
//sys Fstatfs(fd int, buf *Statfs_t) (err error)
//sys Ftruncate(fd int, length int64) (err error)
//sysnb Getegid() (egid int)
//sysnb Geteuid() (euid int)
//sysnb Getgid() (gid int)
//sysnb Getrlimit(resource int, rlim *Rlimit) (err error)
//sysnb Getuid() (uid int)
//sysnb inotifyInit() (fd int, err error)

func InotifyInit() (fd int, err error) {
  // First try inotify_init1, because Android's seccomp policy blocks the latter.
  fd, err = InotifyInit1(0)
  if err == ENOSYS {
    fd, err = inotifyInit()
  }
  return
}

//sys Ioperm(from int, num int, on int) (err error)
//sys Iopl(level int) (err error)
//sys Lchown(path string, uid int, gid int) (err error)
//sys Listen(s int, n int) (err error)

func Lstat(path string, stat *Stat_t) (err error) {
  return Fstatat(AT_FDCWD, path, stat, AT_SYMLINK_NOFOLLOW)
}

//sys Pause() (err error)
//sys Pread(fd int, p []byte, offset int64) (n int, err error) = SYS_PREAD64
//sys Pwrite(fd int, p []byte, offset int64) (n int, err error) = SYS_PWRITE64
//sys Renameat(olddirfd int, oldpath string, newdirfd int, newpath string) (err error)
```

Figure 1-3. *System calls in Linux vs. Darwin*

Listing 1-2 shows how to use system calls using the `sys/unix` package.

Listing 1-2. Go System Call

```
package main

import (
  u "golang.org/x/sys/unix"
  "log"
)

func main() {
  c := make([]byte, 512)

  log.Println("Getpid : ", u.Getpid())
  log.Println("Getpgrp : ", u.Getpgrp())
  log.Println("Getppid : ", u.Getppid())
  log.Println("Gettid : ", u.Gettid())

  _, err := u.Getcwd(c)
```

```
if err != nil {
    log.Fatalln(err)
}

log.Println(string(c))
}
```

The code prints out information that it obtained by calling the following system calls:

Getpid	Obtains the process id of the current running sample app
Getpgrp	Obtains the group process id of the current running app
Getppid	Obtains the parent process id of the current running app
Gettid	Obtains the caller's thread it

Running the app on a Linux machine will result in output something like the following:

```
2022/02/19 21:25:59 Getpid :   12057
2022/02/19 21:25:59 Getpgrp :   12057
2022/02/19 21:25:59 Getpgrp :   29162
2022/02/19 21:25:59 Gettid :   12057
2022/02/19 21:25:59 /home/nanik/
```

The other system call that the application uses is to get the current working directory using the Getcwd function.

System Call in Go

In the previous section, you looked at a simple example of using the sys/unix package. In this section, you will explore more on system calls by looking at an open source project. The project can be found at https://github.com/tklauser/statx. This project works similarly to the stat command in Linux for printing out statistical information about a particular file.

Change your directory to the statx project and compile and run the app as follows:

```
go run statx.go ./README.md
```

You will see output as follows:

```
 File: ./README.md
 Size: 476                  Blocks: 8
IO Block: 4096    regular file
Device: fd01h/64769d        Inode:  2637168
Links:    1
Access: (0644/-rw-r--r--) Uid:    (1000/      nanik)
Gid: (1000/    nanik)
Access: 2022-02-19 18:10:29.919351223 +1100 AEDT
Modify: 2022-02-19 18:10:29.919351223 +1100 AEDT
Change: 2022-02-19 18:10:29.919351223 +1100 AEDT
 Birth: 2022-02-19 18:10:29.919351223 +1100 AEDT
 Attrs: 0000000000000000 (-----....)
```

How does the application get all this information about the file? It obtains the information from the operating system by making a system call. Let's take a look at the code in Listing 1-3.

Listing 1-3. Code Using statx

```
import (

    ....

    "golang.org/x/sys/unix"
)
```

```
....
func main() {
    log.SetFlags(0)
    flag.Parse()

    if len(flag.Args()) < 1 {
        flag.Usage()
        os.Exit(1)
    }
    ....
    for _, arg := range flag.Args() {
        var statx unix.Statx_t
        if err := unix.Statx(unix.AT_FDCWD, arg, flags, mask,
        &statx); err != nil {
    ....
        dev := unix.Mkdev(statx.Dev_major, statx.Dev_minor)
    ....
}
```

As seen in the snippet, the application uses a `unix.Statx` system call and it passes filename and other relevant arguments. The system call is provided as part of the `golang.org/x/sys/unix` package, which is declared as follows:

```
func Statx(dirfd int, path string, flags int, mask int,
stat *Statx_t) (err error)
```

Declaration and documentation of the `Statx` function system call can be found in the following link: `https://pkg.go.dev/golang.org/x/sys/unix`. Going through the documentation, there is not much information about the parameters. As an alternative, you can take a look at the same system call defined for Linux, which can be found at `https://man7.org/linux/man-pages/man2/statx.2.html`. Figure 1-4 shows information about the different parameters that the function call accepts and what they mean.

```
Invoking statx():
```
To access a file's status, no permissions are required on the file itself, but in the case of **statx()** with a pathname, execute (search) permission is required on all of the directories in *pathname* that lead to the file.

statx() uses *pathname*, *dirfd*, and *flags* to identify the target file in one of the following ways:

An absolute pathname
> If *pathname* begins with a slash, then it is an absolute pathname that identifies the target file. In this case, *dirfd* is ignored.

A relative pathname
> If *pathname* is a string that begins with a character other than a slash and *dirfd* is **AT_FDCWD**, then *pathname* is a relative pathname that is interpreted relative to the process's current working directory.

A directory-relative pathname
> If *pathname* is a string that begins with a character other than a slash and *dirfd* is a file descriptor that refers to a directory, then *pathname* is a relative pathname that is interpreted relative to the directory referred to by *dirfd*. (See **openat(2)** for an explanation of why this is useful.)

By file descriptor
> If *pathname* is an empty string and the **AT_EMPTY_PATH** flag is specified in *flags* (see below), then the target file is the one referred to by the file descriptor *dirfd*.

flags can be used to influence a pathname-based lookup. A value for *flags* is constructed by ORing together zero or more of the following constants:

Figure 1-4. *Linux statx*

On successful return from calling the unix.Statx function, the application processes the information that is inside the statx variable to extract information. The variable is of type Statx_t, which is defined as follows in the sys/unix package. The struct contains a fair amount of data pertaining to the file that the application has access to. Using this information, the application will print out information such as file size, type of file, user id, and group id.

```
type Statx_t struct {
    Mask                uint32
    Blksize             uint32
    Attributes          uint64
    Nlink               uint32
    Uid                 uint32
    Gid                 uint32
    Mode                uint16
    _                   [1]uint16
    Ino                 uint64
    Blocks              uint64
    Attributes_mask uint64
    Atime               StatxTimestamp
    ...
    Dev_major           uint32
    Dev_minor           uint32
    ...
}
```

Summary

In this chapter, you learned what system calls are and how to write a simple application to interface with the operating system by using the sys/unix package. You dug deeper into system calls by looking at an open source project to learn how it uses the system calls to provide statistical information about a particular file.

In the next chapters, you will explore system calls more and you will look at various ways to interface with the operating system using Go.

## CHAPTER 2

System Calls Using Go

In this chapter, you will explore writing applications that perform system-level operations using system calls. The operating system provides a lot of ways for applications to extract information and perform operations. You will look at the different ways to extract system-level information and use both the Go standard library and system files.

In this chapter, you will learn the following:

- How to use `syscall` packages

- How to understand and read ELF format files

- How to use the `/sys` filesystem

- How to write a simple application to read disk statistics

Source Code

The source code for this chapter is available from the `https://github.com/Apress/Software-Development-Go` repository.

© Nanik Tolaram 2023
N. Tolaram, *Software Development with Go*,
https://doi.org/10.1007/978-1-4842-8731-6_2

Syscall Package

The syscall package is the standard library provided by Go that provides function calls that interface with the log-level operating system. The following are some of the functionalities provided by the package:

- Change directory

- Duplicate file descriptor

- Get current working directory

- ...and many more

syscall Application

Let's take the existing application from Chapter 1 and convert it to use the syscall package. The app can be seen inside the chapter2/syscalls directory. Open terminal and run the sample as follows:

```
go run main.go
```

You will see the following output:

```
2022/07/17 19:20:42 Getpid :  23815
2022/07/17 19:20:42 Getpgrp :  23712
2022/07/17 19:20:42 Getpgrp :  23712
2022/07/17 19:20:42 Gettid :  23815
2022/07/17 19:20:42 /home/nanik/go/chapter2/syscal
```

The sample code uses system calls to get information about itself such as the process id assigned by the operating system for itself, the parent id, and others. The following shows how it uses the syscall package:

```
package main

import (
```

```go
    "log"
    s "syscall"
)

func main() {
    ...

    log.Println("Getpid : ", s.Getpid())
    ...

    _, err := s.Getcwd(c)


    ...
}
```

The code is the same except for replacing the golang.org/x/sys/unix package with the syscall package, while the function call remains the same.

Figure 2-1 shows the comparison between the sys/unix and syscall packages. As you can see, there are functions providing the same functionality available in both packages.

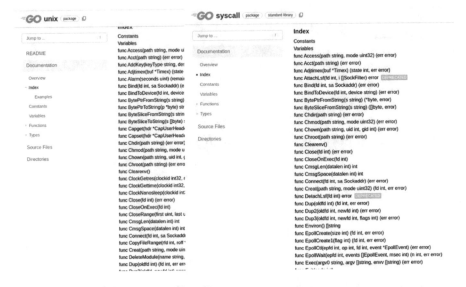

Figure 2-1. *sys/unix vs. syscall*

Checking Disk Space

You are going to take a look at an example application that can be found inside the chapter2/diskspace directory. The application uses the syscall package to obtain hard disk information such as free space, total space, and such.

Open terminal and run the sample as follows:

```
go run main.go
```

You will see the following output:

```
Total Disk Space : 460.1 GB
Total Disk Used  : 322.4 GB
Total Disk Free  : 137.7 GB
```

The output shows in gigabytes the total size of the drive, total amount of disk used, and total amount of disk free. The following code snippet shows how the disk information is obtained using the syscall package:

```
func main() {
  var statfs = syscall.Statfs_t{}
  var total uint64
  var used uint64
  var free uint64
  err := syscall.Statfs("/", &statfs)
  if err != nil {
    fmt.Printf("[ERROR]: %s\n", err)
  } else {
    total = statfs.Blocks * uint64(statfs.Bsize)
    free = statfs.Bfree * uint64(statfs.Bsize)
    used = total - free
  }

  ...
}
```

As seen in the above code snippet, the application uses the syscall. Statfs function call to get information about the path. In this case, it's the root directory. The result is populated into the statfs variable, which is of type Statfs_t. The Statfs_t struct declaration looks like the following:

```
type Statfs_t struct {
  Type    int64
  Bsize   int64
  Blocks  uint64
  Bfree   uint64
  Bavail  uint64
  Files   uint64
  Ffree   uint64
```

```
Fsid     Fsid
Namelen  int64
Frsize   int64
Flags    int64
Spare    [4]int64
}
```

Webserver with syscall

Let's take a look at another example using the `syscall` package, which can be found inside the `chapter2/webserversyscall` directory. The sample code is a web server that uses the `syscall` package to create a socket connection.

Open terminal and run the sample as follows:

```
go run main.go
```

You will see the following output:

```
2022/07/17 19:27:49 Listening on  127.0.0.1 : 8888
```

The web server is now ready to accept connection on port 8888. Open your browser and type in `http://localhost:8888`. You will get a response in your browser: *Server with syscall*

The following code snippet shows the function that takes care of starting up the server that listens on port 8888:

```
func startServer(host string, port int) (int, error) {
    fd, err := syscall.Socket(syscall.AF_INET, syscall.SOCK_
    STREAM, 0)
    if err != nil {
        log.Fatal("error (listen) : ", err)
    }
```

```
sa := &syscall.SockaddrInet4{Port: port}
addrs, err := net.LookupHost(host)
...
for _, addr := range addrs {
...
}
...
return fd, nil
}
```

The code performs the following process:

- Creates a socket

- Binds a socket to port 8888

- Listens for an incoming request

The code use syscall.Socket to create a socket. Once it is able to create a socket, it will bind it to the specified port 8888 by calling syscall.Bind, as shown in the following code snippet:

```
for _, addr := range addrs {
  ...
  if err = syscall.Bind(fd, srv); err != nil {
     log.Fatal("error (bind) : ", err)
  }
}
```

On successful completion of the binding process, the code starts listening for incoming requests, as shown here:

```
if err = syscall.Listen(fd, syscall.SOMAXCONN); err != nil {
  log.Fatal("error (listening) : ", err)
} else {
  log.Println("Listening on ", host, ":", port)
}
```

The syscall.Listen is called, passing syscall.SOMAXCONN as the parameter. This instructs the operating system that the code wants to have the maximum queue allocated to take care of pending connections when they happen. Now the server is ready to accept connections.

The next part of the code accepts and processes incoming requests, which can be seen in the following code snippet:

```
for {
  cSock, cAddr, err := syscall.Accept(fd)

  if err != nil {
    ...
  }

  go func(clientSocket int, clientAddress syscall.Sockaddr) {
    err := syscall.Sendmsg(clientSocket, []byte(message),
    []byte{}, clientAddress, 0)
    ...
    syscall.Close(clientSocket)
  }(cSock, cAddr)
}
```

The code uses syscall.Accept to start accepting incoming requests, as can be seen in the for{} loop. On every accepted request, the code processes the request by processing it in a separate go routine. This allows the server to be able to process incoming requests without being blocked.

ELF Package

The standard library provides different packages that can be used to interact with different parts of the operating system. In the previous sections, you looked at interacting on a system level by using the different standard library packages. In this section, you will look at the debug/elf package.

This package provides interfaces for applications to interact with ELF files. ELF stands for the Executable Linkable Format, which means that an ELF file can be an executable or object file that is used for linking processes to create an executable file. I will not go into detail on ELF; more information can be found at `https://linux.die.net/man/5/elf`.

High-Level ELF Format

ELF is a common standard file format for executable files, object code, shared libraries, and core dumps; it is cross platform. Figure 2-2 shows at high level the structure of an ELF file.

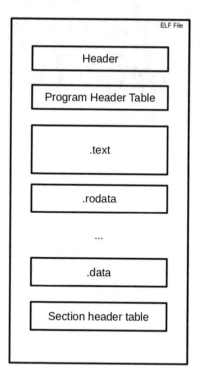

Figure 2-2. *ELF file structure*

Figure 2-3 shows output of the header section of a sample application compiled on my local machine.

```
ELF Header:
  Magic:    7f 45 4c 46 02 01 01 00 00 00 00 00 00 00 00 00
  Class:                              ELF64
  Data:                               2's complement, little endian
  Version:                            1 (current)
  OS/ABI:                             UNIX - System V
  ABI Version:                        0
  Type:                               EXEC (Executable file)
  Machine:                            Advanced Micro Devices X86-64
  Version:                            0x1
  Entry point address:                0x45e020
  Start of program headers:           64 (bytes into file)
  Start of section headers:           456 (bytes into file)
  Flags:                              0x0
  Size of this header:                64 (bytes)
  Size of program headers:            56 (bytes)
  Number of program headers:          7
  Size of section headers:            64 (bytes)
  Number of section headers:          23
  Section header string table index: 3
```

Figure 2-3. *ELF file header section*

Dump Example

In this section, you will take a look at an open source project named GoPlay, which is hosted at https://github.com/n4ss/GoPlay. It can also be found inside the chapter2/GoPlay directory. This is a simple app that dumps the contents of a Go ELF executable file. You will look at how the application uses the Go library to read the ELF file

Compile the GoPlay application to create an executable using the following command:

```
go build main.go
```

Now compile GoPlay and run it as follows:

```
./goplay -action=dump -filename=./goplay
```

You are instructing GoPlay to dump the contents of the goplay executable, which will give you output something like the following:

```
Tracing program : "[path]goplay".
Action : "dump".
DynStrings:
Symbols:
        go.go
        runtime.text
        cmpbody
        countbody
        memeqbody
        indexbody
        indexbytebody
        gogo
        callRet
        gosave_systemstack_switch
        setg_gcc
        aeshashbody
        debugCall32
        debugCall64

        ....
        runtime.(*cpuProfile).addNonGo
        ....
         _cgo_init
         runtime.mainPC
         go.itab.syscall.Errno,error
         runtime.defaultGOROOT.str
         runtime.buildVersion.str
         type.*
         runtime.textsectionmap
     ....
```

Let's start analyzing how the code works and what system calls it is
using to get what information out from the executable file.

```go
func main() {
    ....
        file, err := os.Stat(*filename)
    ....
        f, err := os.Open(*filename)
    ....
        switch *action {
    ....
        case "dump": os.Exit(dump_elf(*filename))
        }
    } else {
        goto Usage
    }
    ....
}
```

On startup, the application uses the os.Stat system call to check
whether the executable file specified as the parameter exists and opens
it using os.Open if it does exist. Once open, it will use the function dump_
elf(..) to dump the file contents. The following is a snippet of the function:

```go
func dump_elf(filename string) int {
    file, err := elf.Open(filename)
    if err != nil {
        fmt.Printf("Couldn't open file : \"%s\" as an ELF.\n")
        return 2
    }
    dump_dynstr(file)
    dump_symbols(file)
    return 0
}
```

The function uses another system call named elf.Open, which is available inside the debug/elf package. This is similar to the os.Open function but with the additional functionality that the opened file is prepared to be read as an ELF file. On returning from calling elf.Open, the returned file variable will be populated with information about the internals of the ELF file.

Once the file is open, it calls dump_symbols to dump the file contents. The dump_symbols function dumps all symbols information from the file, which is made available by calling the file.Symbols() function. The application just prints the Name field.

```go
func dump_symbols(file *elf.File) {
    fmt.Printf("Symbols:\n")
    symbols, _ := file.Symbols()
    for _, e := range symbols {
        if !strings.EqualFold(e.Name, "") {
            fmt.Printf("\t%s\n", e.Name)
        }
    }
}
```

The following is the struct definition of the Symbol struct. As you can see, it contains useful information.

```go
type Symbol struct {
    Name         string
    Info, Other  byte
    Section      SectionIndex
    Value, Size  uint64
```

```
// Version and Library are present only for the
dynamic symbol
  // table.
  Version string
  Library string
}
```

The other function called to dump ELF information is dump_dynstr:

```
func dump_dynstr(file *elf.File) {
  fmt.Printf("DynStrings:\n")
  dynstrs, _ := file.DynString(elf.DT_NEEDED)
  ...
  dynstrs, _ = file.DynString(elf.DT_SONAME)
  ...
  dynstrs, _ = file.DynString(elf.DT_RPATH)
  ...
  dynstrs, _ = file.DynString(elf.DT_RUNPATH)
  ...
}
```

This function is used to obtain certain parts of the ELF file, which are passed as parameters when calling the file.DynString function. For example, when calling

```
dynstrs, _ = file.DynString(elf.DT_SONAME)
```

the code will get information about the shared library name of the file.

/sys Filesystem

In this section, you will look at a different way of reading system-level information. You will not use a function to read system information; rather, you will use system directories that are made available by the operating system for user applications.

The directory that you want to read is the /sys directory, which is a virtual filesystem containing device drivers, device information, and other kernel features. Figure 2-4 shows what the /sys directory contains on a Linux machine.

```
dr-xr-xr-x   13 root root    0 Feb  8 17:25 .
drwxr-xr-x   18 root root 4096 Nov 27 23:06 ..
drwxr-xr-x    2 root root    0 Feb  8 17:25 block
drwxr-xr-x   50 root root    0 Feb  8 17:25 bus
drwxr-xr-x   81 root root    0 Feb  8 17:25 class
drwxr-xr-x    4 root root    0 Feb  8 17:25 dev
drwxr-xr-x   26 root root    0 Feb  8 17:25 devices
drwxr-xr-x    5 root root    0 Feb  8 17:25 firmware
drwxr-xr-x    8 root root    0 Feb  8 17:25 fs
drwxr-xr-x    2 root root    0 Feb  8 17:25 hypervisor
drwxr-xr-x   16 root root    0 Feb  8 17:25 kernel
drwxr-xr-x  249 root root    0 Feb  8 17:25 module
drwxr-xr-x    3 root root    0 Feb  8 17:25 power
```

Figure 2-4. Inside the /sys directory

Reading AppArmor

Some of the information that is provided by Linux inside the /sys directory is related to AppArmor (short for Application Armor). What is AppArmor? It is a kernel security module that gives system administrators the ability to restrict application capabilities with a profile. This gives system administrators the power to select which resources a particular application can have access to. For example, a system administrator can define Application A to have network access or raw socket access, while Application B does not have access to network capabilities.

Let's look at an example application to read AppArmor information from the /sys filesystem, specifically whether AppArmor is enabled and whether it is enforced. The following is the sample code that can be found inside the chapter2/apparmor directory:

```
import (
    "fmt"
```

```go
    ...
)
const (
  appArmorEnabledPath = "/sys/module/apparmor/parameters/
                         enabled"
  appArmorModePath    = "/sys/module/apparmor/parameters/mode"
)
func appArmorMode() (mode string) {
  content, err := ioutil.ReadFile(appArmorModePath)
  ...
  return strings.TrimSpace(string(content))
}

func appArmorEnabled() (support bool) {
  content, err := ioutil.ReadFile(appArmorEnabledPath)
  ...
  return strings.TrimSpace(string(content)) == "Y"
}

func main() {
  fmt.Println("AppArmor mode : ", appArmorMode())
  fmt.Println("AppArmor is enabled : ", appArmorEnabled())
}
```

Since the code is accessing a system filesystem, you must run it using root. Compile the code and run it as follows:

```
sudo ./apparmor
```

The code reads the information from the directory using the standard library ioUtil.ReadFile, which is just like reading a file, so it's simpler than using the function calls that you looked at in the previous sections.

Summary

In this chapter, you looked at using system calls to interface with the operating system. You looked at using the syscall standard library that provides a lot of function calls to interface with the operating system and wrote a sample application to print out disk space information. You looked at how the debug/elf standard library is used to read Go ELF file information. Lastly, you looked at the /sys filesystem to extract information that you want to read to understand whether the operating system supports AppArmor.

CHAPTER 3

Accessing proc File System

In Chapter 2, you looked at the /sys filesystem in Linux and wrote a simple app to extract information from it. In this chapter, you are going to take a look at another system directory called /proc. The /proc directory is also known as procfs, and it contains useful information about processes that are currently running. The kernel uses it as an information center for all related processes.

In this chapter, you will learn how to do the following:

- Look at the different information available inside procfs

- Write an application to read procfs

- Use an open source library to interface with procfs

Source Code

The source code for this chapter is available from the https://github.com/Apress/Software-Development-Go repository.

© Nanik Tolaram 2023
N. Tolaram, *Software Development with Go*,
https://doi.org/10.1007/978-1-4842-8731-6_3

Peeking Inside procfs

In this section, you will look at procfs and see what it contains. Use the following command in your terminal to view what is available inside the /proc directory:

```
ls /proc -la
```

You will see output like the following:

```
dr-xr-xr-x 423 root        root        0 Jul 17 17:55 .
drwxr-xr-x  20 root        root     4096 May 25 13:21 ..
dr-xr-xr-x   9 root        root        0 Jul 17 17:55 1
dr-xr-xr-x   9 root        root        0 Jul 17 17:56 10
dr-xr-xr-x   9 nanik       nanik       0 Jul 17 18:02 10023
dr-xr-xr-x   9 nanik       nanik       0 Jul 17 18:02 10057
dr-xr-xr-x   9 nanik       nanik       0 Jul 17 18:02 10075
dr-xr-xr-x   9 root        root        0 Jul 17 17:56 101

...
-r--r--r--   1 root        root        0 Jul 17 17:56
                                                    execdomains
-r--r--r--   1 root        root        0 Jul 17 17:56 fb
-r--r--r--   1 root        root        0 Jul 17 17:55
                                                    filesystems
dr-xr-xr-x   5 root        root        0 Jul 17 17:56 fs
-r--r--r--   1 root        root        0 Jul 17 17:56
                                                    interrupts
-r--r--r--   1 root        root        0 Jul 17 17:56 iomem
-r--r--r--   1 root        root        0 Jul 17 17:56 ioports
dr-xr-xr-x  59 root        root        0 Jul 17 17:56 irq
-r--r--r--   1 root        root        0 Jul 17 17:56
                                                    kallsyms
-r--r--r--   1 root        root        0 Jul 17 17:56 keys
```

-r--r--r--	1 root	root	0 Jul 17 17:56 key-users
-r--------	1 root	root	0 Jul 17 17:56 kmsg
-r--------	1 root	root	0 Jul 17 17:56 kpagecgroup
-r--------	1 root	root	0 Jul 17 17:56 kpagecount
...			
dr-xr-xr-x	5 root	root	0 Jul 17 17:56 sysvipc
lrwxrwxrwx	1 root	root	0 Jul 17 17:55 thread-self -> 17987/ task/17987
-r--------	1 root	root	0 Jul 17 17:56 timer_list
dr-xr-xr-x	6 root	root	0 Jul 17 17:56 tty
-r--r--r--	1 root	root	0 Jul 17 17:55 uptime
-r--r--r--	1 root	root	0 Jul 17 17:56 version
-r--------	1 root	root	0 Jul 17 17:56 vmallocinfo
-r--r--r--	1 root	root	0 Jul 17 17:56 vmstat
-r--r--r--	1 root	root	0 Jul 17 17:56 zoneinfo

The output contains a lot of numerical directories. These directories correspond to the process id of applications running in the system, and inside these directories is more detailed information about the corresponding process, such as the command used to run the process, memory maps to executables and library files, and more.

Let's take a look at one of the processes that is running on my system. I picked the process id that is allocated for the Goland IDE. In this case, the process id is 4280. Table 3-1 shows the information from inside /proc/4280.

Table 3-1. *Information from* /proc/4280

Directory	Content
/proc/4280/ cmdline	/bin/sh./goland.sh
/proc/4280/ cgroup	14:misc:/ 13:rdma:/ 11:hugetlb:/ 10:net_prio:/ 9:perf_event:/ 8:net_cls:/ 7:freezer:/ 6:devices:/ 4:blkio:/ 3:cpuacct:/ 2:cpu:/ 1:cpuset:/ 0::/user.slice/user-1000.slice/user@1000.service/app.slice/app-org.gnome. Terminal.slice/vte-spawn-9c827742-8e1f-42d8-bb25-7911712b0d8.scope

(continued)

Table 3-1. (continued)

Directory	Content
/proc/4280/ mountinfo	24 31 0:22 / /sys rw,nosuid,nodev,noexec,relatime shared:7 - sysfs sysfs rw ... 27 26 0:24 / /dev/pts rw,nosuid,noexec,relatime shared:3 - devpts devpts rw, gid=5,mode=620,ptmxmode=000 28 31 0:25 / /run rw,nosuid,nodev,noexec,relatime shared:5 - tmpfs tmpfs rw, size=1607888k,mode=755,inode64 ...

As you can see from the table, there is much information that can be extracted that is relevant to the process id 4280. This information gives us better visibility about the application, resources the application uses, user and group information, and more.

Reading Memory Information

In the previous section, you learned what procfs is all about and looked at some of the process information that can be viewed. You looked at extracting the information by going into the /proc directory and using standard tools like ls and cat to view file and directory content.

In this section, you are going to write a simple application to read system memory information from procfs. The sample code can be found inside the chapter3/readingmemory directory. Run the application using the following command:

```
go run main.go
```

You will see output like the following:

```
MemTotal = 32320240 KB, MemFree = 3260144 KB, MemUsed =
29060096 KB
MemTotal = 32320240 KB, MemFree = 3146556 KB, MemUsed =
29173684 KB
MemTotal = 32320240 KB, MemFree = 3074524 KB, MemUsed =
29245716 KB
MemTotal = 32320240 KB, MemFree = 3068300 KB, MemUsed =
29251940 KB
MemTotal = 32320240 KB, MemFree = 3264940 KB, MemUsed =
29055300 KB
MemTotal = 32320240 KB, MemFree = 3269584 KB, MemUsed =
29050656 KB
MemTotal = 32320240 KB, MemFree = 3270340 KB, MemUsed =
29049900 KB
```

The application continuously prints memory information (total memory, free memory, and used memory) in kilobytes of the local device. Let's look at the code to understand how it works.

```go
func main() {
  sampler := &sampler{
     rate: 1 * time.Second,
  }
  ...

  for {
     select {
     case sampleSet := <-sampler.sample:
        ...
        fmt.Printf("total = %v KB, free = %v KB, used =
        %v KB\n",
           s.total, s.free, s.used)
     }
   }
}
```

On startup, the code initializes the Sampler struct and goes into a loop waiting on the data to be made available from SampleSetChan. Once the data arrives, it prints out the memory information into the console.

The data sampling code that collects the data and sends it to the channel is seen below. The StartSampling function spins off a Go routine that calls GetMemSample to extract the memory information and sleep after sending the data to the SampleSetChan channel.

```go
func (s *sampler) start() *sampler {
   ...
```

```go
go func() {
    for {
        var ss sample
        ss.memorySample = getMemorySample()
        s.sample <- ss
        time.Sleep(s.rate)
    }
}()
...
}
```

The crux of reading the memory information can be seen in the following GetMemSample function:

```go
func getMemorySample() (samp memory) {
    ...
    contents, err := ioutil.ReadFile(memInfo)
    if err != nil {
        return
    }

    reader := bufio.NewReader(bytes.NewBuffer(contents))
    for {
        line, _, err := reader.ReadLine()
        if err == io.EOF {
            break
        }
        ...
        if ok && len(fields) == 3 {
            ...
            switch fieldName {
            case "total:":
                samp.total = val
```

```
        case "free:":
            samp.free = val
        }
      }
   }
   ...
}
```

The memory information is collected from the /proc/meminfo directory. The collected data is parsed and only values that it is interested in are stored, namely total memory, free memory, and calculated value of memory used.

This is how the raw data looks like when reading the /proc/meminfo directory:

```
MemTotal:        32320240 kB
MemFree:           927132 kB
MemAvailable:     5961720 kB
...
HugePages_Total:        0
HugePages_Free:         0
HugePages_Rsvd:         0
HugePages_Surp:         0
Hugepagesize:        2048 kB
Hugetlb:                0 kB
...
```

Peeking Network Information

In this section, you will now look at network information that can be extracted out from procfs. There is a directory named /proc/net/sockstat that looks like the following in raw format:

```
sockets: used 3229
TCP: inuse 49 orphan 0 tw 82 alloc 64 mem 90
UDP: inuse 28 mem 139
UDPLITE: inuse 0
RAW: inuse 0
FRAG: inuse 0 memory 0
```

Table 3-2 explains the meaning of the different fields shown in the raw information above

Table 3-2. */proc/net data breakdown*

Sockets	Used	Total number of all protocol sockets used
TCP	inuse	Total number of TCP sockets listening
	orphan	Total number of TCP sockets that do not belong to any process (a.k.a. orphans)
	tw	Total number of TCP sockets that are time waiting or waiting to be closed
	alloc	Total number of TCP sockets that have been allocated
	mem	Total number of pages allocated to TCP
UDP	inuse	The number of UDP sockets in use
	mem	Total number of pages allocated to UDP
UDPLITE	inuse	Total number of Lightweight UDP in use
RAW	inuse	Total number of *raw* protocols in use
FRAG	inuse	Number of IP segments used
	memory	Total amount of memory in KB allocated for fragmentation reassembly

Now that you have a good idea of what the different values mean, let's take a look at how to extract this information using Go. The sample code is inside the chapter3/sockstat directory. Open terminal and run the code using the following command:

```
go run main.go
```

Figure 3-1 shows the output.

UDP INUSE	UDP MEM	SOCKETS USED	TCP MEM	TCP INUSE	TCP ORPHAN	TCP TW	TCP ALLOC
29	148	3.2K	91	50	0	69	65

Figure 3-1. *sockstat sample output*

Let's explore the code to understand what it is doing. When the app starts up, it opens the /proc/net/sockstat directory. On success, the code reads and parses it to the format suitable for displaying to the console.

```
const (
  ...
  netstat = "/proc/net/sockstat"
)

  ...


func main() {
  fs, err := os.Open(netstat)
  ...
  m := make(map[string]int64)
  for {
     line, err := readLine(reader)
     if bytes.HasPrefix(line, []byte(sockets)) ||
        bytes.HasPrefix(line, []byte(tcp)) ||
```

```
        bytes.HasPrefix(line, []byte((udp))) {
        idx := bytes.Index(line, []byte((colon)))
        ...
    }
    ...
}
...
}
```

As you can see, it is straightforward to write an application to read system-level information from procfs. To write an application to read procfs, the following is the information you will need to know beforehand:

- In what directory is the required information located?

- Do you need root access to access the information?

- How will you parse the raw data properly and handle data parsing issues?

Using the procfs Library

You now understood what kind of information available inside the /proc directory and you've also seen how to write code and parse the information. In this section, you are going to take a look at an open source library that provides access to different information available in the /proc directory. The project can be found at https://github.com/jandre/procfs.

Code Sample

Open your terminal and change to the chapter3/jandreprocfs directory and run the code using the following command:

```
go run main.go
```

You will see output that looks like Figure 3-2

```
   1415 | /usr/libexec/goa-daemon                        | /home/nanik
. . .
 334864 | /home/nanik/Downloads/procfs                   | /home/nanik/Downloads
. . .
   2712 | /usr/bin/nautilus                              | /home/nanik
   1970 | /usr/bin/ibus-daemon                           | /home/nanik
   1982 | /usr/libexec/ibus-portal                       | /home/nanik
. . .
   2788 | /usr/bin/gnome-disks                           | /home/nanik
   1974 | /usr/libexec/ibus-memconf                      | /home/nanik
   1402 | /usr/libexec/gvfs-gphoto2-volume-monitor       | /home/nanik
   1426 | /usr/libexec/goa-identity-service              | /home/nanik
. . .
```

Figure 3-2. *Output running procfs sample code*

The following code snippet uses the `jandre/procfs` library to read the information:

```
package main

import (
  "github.com/jandre/procfs"
  ...
)

func main() {
  processes, _ := procfs.Processes(false)
  table := tablewriter.NewWriter(os.Stdout)

  for _, p := range processes {
     table.Append([]string{strconv.Itoa(p.Pid), p.Exe, p.Cwd})

  }
  table.Render()
}
```

The sample code is simpler than the previous code that you looked at in the previous sections. It uses the `procfs.Processes(..)` function call to obtain all the current processes.

Inside the procfs Library

Let's take a look a bit deeper into the library to investigate what exactly it is doing. You are going to dive into the following procfs.Processes(..) function call. The Processes function call inside the library looks like the following:

```
func Processes(lazy bool) (map[int]*Process, error) {
   ...
   files, err := ioutil.ReadDir("/proc")
   if err != nil {
      return nil, err
   }

   ...

   fetch := func(pid int) {
      proc, err := NewProcess(pid, lazy)
      if err != nil {
         ...
         done <- nil
      } else {
         done <- proc
      }
   }

   todo := len(pids)

   for _, pid := range pids {
      go fetch(pid)
   }

   ...
   for ;todo > 0; {
```

```
    proc := <-done
    todo--
    if proc != nil {
        processes[proc.Pid] = proc
    }
}

return processes, nil
}
```

At a high level, Figure 3-3 shows what the function is actually doing.

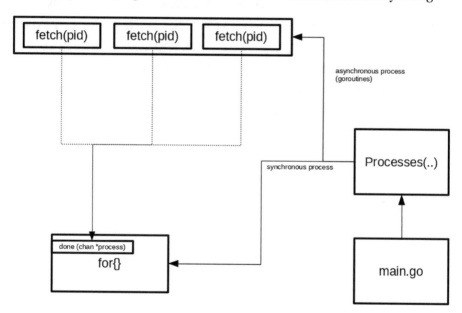

Figure 3-3. *Processes(..) function flow*

The function reads processes information from the /proc directory, and it traverses through it by reading each process information in a separate Go routine that calls the fetch(pid) function. The function extracts and parses information of the process id that it is assigned. Once collected, it passes into the channel that the Processes(..) function is waiting on; in this case, it is called the done channel.

All the heavy lifting of opening and traversing through the /proc directory including parsing the results is taken care of by the library. The application can just focus on the output that it receives.

Summary

In this chapter, you looked at the /proc file system and learned about the system information that applications have access to. You looked at sample code to read information from inside the /proc directory that is related to the network and memory on the device. You also learned that the bulk of the code that needs to be written when extracting system information is in terms of reading and parsing the information. You also looked at an open source library that can provide functionality in reading the /proc directory that performs all the heavy lifting, leaving you to focus on writing simpler code to read all the system information that you need.

PART II

Containers

CHAPTER 4

Simple Containers

In this chapter, you will look at using Go to explore the container world.
You will look at different container-related projects to get a better
understanding about containers and some of the technologies they
use. There are many different aspects of containers such as security,
troubleshooting, and scaling container registries. This chapter will give you
an understanding of the following topics:

- The Linux namespace

- Understanding cgroups and rootfs

- How containers use rootfs

You will explore different open source projects to understand how
containers work and how tools such as Docker actually work.

Linux Namespace

In this section, you will look at namespaces, which are key components in
running containers on your local or cloud environment. Namespaces are
features that are only available in the Linux kernel, so everything that you
will read here is relevant to the Linux operating system.

A namespace is a feature provided by the Linux kernel for applications
to use, so what actually is it? It is used to create an isolated environment for
processes that you want to run with their own resources.

© Nanik Tolaram 2023
N. Tolaram, *Software Development with Go*,
https://doi.org/10.1007/978-1-4842-8731-6_4

Figure 4-1 shows a representation of each isolated namespace that is running applications with its own network. Each application that is running inside a namespace cannot access anything outside its own namespace. For example, App1 cannot access App2 resources. If for some reason App1 crashes, it will not bring down the other applications, nor it will bring down the Linux host. Think of a namespace as an island to run applications; it can provide anything you need for the applications to run on without disturbing the other surrounding islands.

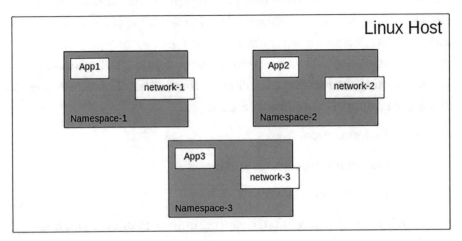

Figure 4-1. *Linux namespace*

You can create namespaces using tools that are already available in the Linux system. One of the tools you are going to experiment with is called *unshare*. It is a tool that allows users to create namespaces and run applications inside that namespace.

Before you run unshare, let's take a look my local host machine compared to when I run the app using unshare. We will compare the following:

- The applications that are running in the host machine compared to when we run them inside a namespace

- The available network interface in a host machine compared to when inside the namespace

To list running applications on my local Linux machine, I use the command ps.

```
ps au
```

The following is a snippet of the list of applications that are currently running on my local machine:

```
USER          PID %CPU %MEM    VSZ   RSS TTY        STAT
START    TIME COMMAND
...
nanik        2551   0.0  0.0  231288     4 tty2       SNl+ May09
0:00 /usr/libexec/gnome-session-binary --systemd --session=pop
nanik        6418   0.0  0.0  21644   712 pts/0     S<s  May09
0:00 bash
nanik        8594   0.0  0.0  22820     8 pts/2     S<s  May09
0:00 bash
nanik        9828   0.0  0.0  22516  4300 pts/3     S<s+ May09
0:03 bash
...
nanik      295802  0.0  0.0 1716900 6408 pts/7     S<l+ May11
2:18 docker run -p 6379:6379 redis
nanik      511876  0.0  0.0  21288    24 pts/6     S<s  May13
0:00 bash
nanik      642244  0.0  0.0  21420     8 pts/8     S<s+ May14
0:00 bash
...
root      1368986 0.0  0.0  25220   108 pts/3     T<   May19
0:00 sudo gedit /etc/hosts
```

To look at the available network interface on local machine, use the command ip.

```
ip link
```

It shows the following interfaces:

```
1: lo: <LOOPBACK,UP,LOWER_UP> mtu 65536 qdisc noqueue state
UNKNOWN mode DEFAULT group default qlen 1000
    link/loopback 00:00:00:00:00:00 brd 00:00:00:00:00:00
2: enp4s0: <NO-CARRIER,BROADCAST,MULTICAST,UP> mtu 1500 qdisc
fq_codel state DOWN mode DEFAULT group default qlen 1000
    link/ether 88:a4:c2:a4:85:ac brd ff:ff:ff:ff:ff:ff
3: wlp0s20f3: <BROADCAST,MULTICAST,UP,LOWER_UP> mtu 1500 qdisc
noqueue state UP mode DORMANT group default qlen 1000  link/
ether xx:xx:xa:xx:xx:xx brd   xx:xx:xx:xx:xx:xx
...
5: docker0: <BROADCAST,MULTICAST,UP,LOWER_UP> mtu 1500 qdisc
noqueue state UP mode DEFAULT group default
    link/ether xx:xx:xa:xx:xx:xx brd ff:ff:ff:ff:ff:ff
...
447: thebridge: <BROADCAST,MULTICAST> mtu 1500 qdisc noop state
DOWN mode DEFAULT group default
    link/ether xx:xx:xa:xx:xx:xx brd ff:ff:ff:ff:ff:ff
```

As you can see, there are many processes running in the local host machine and there are many network interfaces.

Run the following command to create a namespace and run bash inside the namespace as the application:

```
unshare --user --pid --map-root-user --cgroup --mount-proc --
net --uts --fork bash
```

It will look like Figure 4-2.

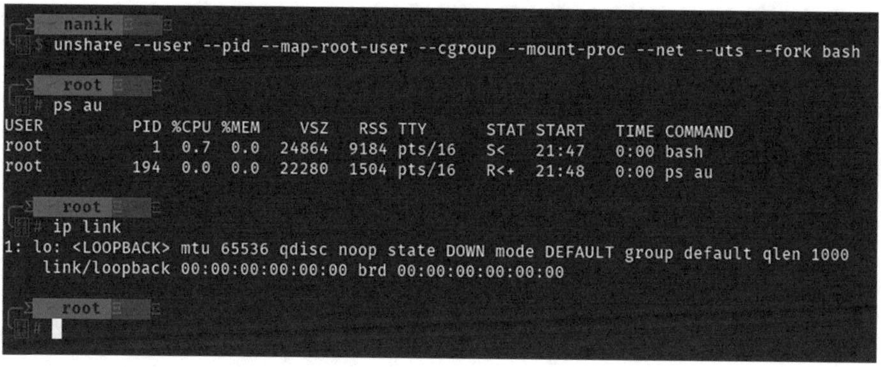

Figure 4-2. *Running unshare*

Inside the new namespace, as seen in Figure 4-2, it will only display two processes and one network interface (local interface). This shows that the namespace is isolating access to the host machine.

You have looked at using unshare to create namespaces and run bash as an application isolated in its own namespace. Now that you have a basic understanding of namespaces, you will explore another piece of the puzzle called cgroups in the next section.

cgroups

cgroups stands for control groups, which is a feature provided by the Linux kernel. Namespaces, which we discussed in the previous section, go hand in hand with cgroups. Let's take a look at what cgroups contains. cgroups gives users the ability to limit certain resources such as the CPU and memory network allocated for a particular process or processes. Host machines resources are finite, and if you want to run multiple processes in separate namespaces, you want to allocate resources across different namespaces.

cgroups resides inside the /sys/fs/cgroup directory. Let's create a subdirectory inside the main cgroup directory and take a peek inside it. Run the following command to create a directory using root:

```
sudo mkdir /sys/fs/cgroup/example
```

List the directories inside the newly created directory using the following command:

```
sudo ls /sys/fs/cgroup/example -la
```

You will see output that looks like the following:

```
-r--r--r--  1 root root 0 May 24 23:06 cgroup.controllers
-r--r--r--  1 root root 0 May 24 23:06 cgroup.events
-rw-r--r--  1 root root 0 May 24 23:06 cgroup.freeze
...
-rw-r--r--  1 root root 0 May 24 23:06 cgroup.type
-rw-r--r--  1 root root 0 May 24 23:06 cpu.idle
-rw-r--r--  1 root root 0 May 24 23:06 cpu.max
-rw-r--r--  1 root root 0 May 24 23:06 cpu.max.burst
-rw-r--r--  1 root root 0 May 24 23:06 cpu.pressure
-rw-r--r--  1 root root 0 May 24 23:06 cpuset.cpus
-r--r--r--  1 root root 0 May 24 23:06 cpuset.cpus.effective
-rw-r--r--  1 root root 0 May 24 23:06 cpuset.cpus.partition
-rw-r--r--  1 root root 0 May 24 23:06 cpuset.mems
-r--r--r--  1 root root 0 May 24 23:06 cpuset.mems.effective
...
-rw-r--r--  1 root root 0 May 24 23:06 io.max
...
-rw-r--r--  1 root root 0 May 24 23:06 memory.low
-rw-r--r--  1 root root 0 May 24 23:06 memory.max
-rw-r--r--  1 root root 0 May 24 23:06 memory.min
-r--r--r--  1 root root 0 May 24 23:06 memory.numa_stat
```

```
-rw-r--r-- 1 root root 0 May 24 23:06 memory.oom.group
-rw-r--r-- 1 root root 0 May 24 23:06 memory.pressure
...
```

The directories that you see are actually the configurations that you can set values relevant to the resources that you want to allocate for a particular process. Let's take a look at an example.

You will run a tool called stress (https://linux.die.net/man/1/stress), which you need to install to your local machine. If you are using Ubuntu, you can use the command

```
sudo apt install stress
```

Open a terminal and run the stress tool as follows. The application will run for 60 seconds using one core and consuming 100% of CPU usage.

```
stress --cpu 1 --timeout 60
```

Open another terminal and run the following command to obtain the process id of the stress application:

```
top
```

On my local machine, the process id is 2185657, as shown in Figure 4-3.

```
top - 23:23:16 up 15 days,  6:40,  1 user,  load average: 0.84, 0.95, 0.90
Tasks: 448 total,   3 running, 441 sleeping,   3 stopped,   1 zombie
%Cpu(s): 13.9 us,  0.3 sy,  0.2 ni, 84.7 id,  0.0 wa,  0.0 hi,  1.0 si,  0.0 st
MiB Mem : 15702.0 total,    394.7 free,  11856.2 used,   3451.1 buff/cache
MiB Swap:  4095.5 total,    861.1 free,   3234.4 used.   1911.0 avail Mem

    PID USER      PR  NI    VIRT    RES    SHR S  %CPU  %MEM     TIME+ COMMAND
2185657 nanik     15  -5    3684    112      0 R 100.0   0.0   0:03.68 stress
   2668 nanik     15  -5 8020184   1.8g  37156 S  12.3  11.6  1479:00 gnome-shell
   2131 nanik     15  -5 1946352  95548  39116 S   5.0   0.6 681:11.04 Xorg
   6370 nanik     15  -5  797936  60808  21944 S   2.7   0.4  13:30.04 gnome-terminal-
```

Figure 4-3. *Output of top*

Now insert the value of the process id into the cgroups directory as follows:

```
sudo echo "200000 1000000" > /sys/fs/cgroup/example/cpu.max
sudo echo "2185657" > /sys/fs/cgroup/example/cgroup.procs
```

The command allocates 20% of the CPU usage for all processes inside the example cgroups, and for this example, the stress application process id is marked as part of the example cgroups. If you have your terminal running top open, you will see that the stress application will now only consume 20% instead of 100%.

This example shows that by applying cgroups to processes, you can restrict the amount of resource it is consuming based on how you want to allocate it.

You looked at cgroups (control groups) in this section and learned how to allocate resources to processes. In the next section, you will learn about rootfs, which you must understand because it is a crucial component in understanding containers.

rootfs

In this section, you will explore rootfs and how it is applied in containers. First, let's understand what rootfs actually is. rootfs stands for root filesystem, which simply means it is the filesystem containing all the basic necessary files required to boot the operating system. Without the correct rootfs, the operating system will not boot up and no application can run.

rootfs is required so that the operating system can allow other file systems to be mounted, which includes configuration, essential startup processes and data, and other filesystems that are located in other disk partitions. The following shows the minimal directories found in a rootfs:

```
/bin
/sbin
```

```
/etc
/root
/lib
/lib/modules
/dev
/tmp
/boot
/mnt
/proc
/usr
/var,
/home
```

To run an application inside a container requires rootfs, which allows the application to run like how it runs in a normal system. Let's take a look at what a minimal rootfs actually looks like. Head over to www.alpinelinux.org/downloads/ to download the Alpine rootfs. Alpine is a very well-known Linux distribution that is used widely when creating containers because of its small image size.

Download the rootfs file from the "Mini Root Filesystem" section as shown in Figure 4-4. If you are using an x86 processor, download the x86_64 file.

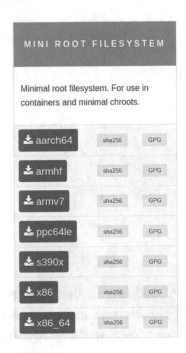

Figure 4-4. Mini root filesystem

Once downloaded, copy the file into a separate directory. In my case, the file is called alpine-minirootfs-3.15.4-x86_64.tar.gz and it is copied into the /home/nanik/play/rootfs directory. Use the following command to extract it:

```
gunzip ./alpine-minirootfs-3.15.4-x86_64.tar.gz
tar -xvf ./alpine-minirootfs-3.15.4-x86_64.tar
```

The following is the output of the extracted file:

```
drwxr-xr-x 19 nanik nanik    4096 Apr  5 02:06 ./
drwxrwxr-x  3 nanik nanik    4096 May 28 18:46 ../
drwxr-xr-x  2 nanik nanik    4096 Apr  5 02:06 bin/
drwxr-xr-x  2 nanik nanik    4096 Apr  5 02:06 dev/
drwxr-xr-x 16 nanik nanik    4096 Apr  5 02:06 etc/
```

```
drwxr-xr-x  2 nanik nanik  4096 Apr  5 02:06 home/
drwxr-xr-x  7 nanik nanik  4096 Apr  5 02:06 lib/
drwxr-xr-x  5 nanik nanik  4096 Apr  5 02:06 media/
drwxr-xr-x  2 nanik nanik  4096 Apr  5 02:06 mnt/
drwxr-xr-x  2 nanik nanik  4096 Apr  5 02:06 opt/
dr-xr-xr-x  2 nanik nanik  4096 Apr  5 02:06 proc/
drwx------  2 nanik nanik  4096 Apr  5 02:06 root/
drwxr-xr-x  2 nanik nanik  4096 Apr  5 02:06 run/
drwxr-xr-x  2 nanik nanik  4096 Apr  5 02:06 sbin/
drwxr-xr-x  2 nanik nanik  4096 Apr  5 02:06 srv/
drwxr-xr-x  2 nanik nanik  4096 Apr  5 02:06 sys/
drwxrwxr-x  2 nanik nanik  4096 Apr  5 02:06 tmp/
drwxr-xr-x  7 nanik nanik  4096 Apr  5 02:06 usr/
drwxr-xr-x 12 nanik nanik  4096 Apr  5 02:06 var/
```

The following output shows what the different directories contain:

```
.
├── bin
│     ├── arch -> /bin/busybox
...
├── dev
├── etc
...
│     ├── modprobe.d
...
├── home
...
├── sbin
│     ├── acpid -> /bin/busybox
│     ├── adjtimex -> /bin/busybox
...
```

```
├── srv
├── sys
├── tmp
├── usr
│   ├── bin
│   │   ├── [ -> /bin/busybox
│   │   ├── [[ -> /bin/busybox
...
│   │   └── yes -> /bin/busybox
│   ├── lib
│   │   ├── engines-1.1
...
│   │   └── modules-load.d
│   ├── local
│   │   ├── bin
...
│       ├── man
│       ├── misc
│       └── udhcpc
│           └── default.script
├── var
│   ├── cache
│   ├── empty
│   ├── lib
```

Now that you have a good idea of what rootfs is all about and what it contains, you will explore further in the next section how to put everything together into rootfs and run an application like how it normally runs as a container.

Gontainer Project

So far you have looked at how to create the different things that are required to run an application in isolation: namespaces, cgroups and configuring rootfs. In this section, you will look at a sample app that will put everything together and run an application inside its own namespace. In other words, you are going to run the application as a container. The code can be checked out from https://github.com/nanikjava/gontainer.

Make sure you download and extract the rootfs as explained in section "rootFS." Once the rootfs has been extracted to your local machine, change the directory to the gotainer directory and compile the project using the following command:

```
go build
```

Once compiled, you will get an executable called gotainer. Run the application using the following command:

```
sudo ./gontainer --chrt "[rootfs directory]]" run sh
```

The command will run the sh command, which is the native bash command for the Alpine distro in a container. Replace [rootfs directory] with the directory containing the uncompressed Alpine roofs. For example, in my machine, it is /home/nanik/play/rootfs. The full command for my local machine is

```
sudo ./gontainer --chrt "/home/nanik/play/rootfs" run sh
```

You will get the prompt /usr # and you'll able to execute any normal Linux commands. Figure 4-5 shows some of the commands executed inside gotainer.

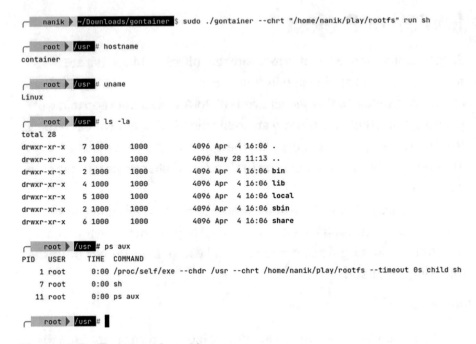

Figure 4-5. *Gotainer in action*

Let's take a look at the code to understand how the whole thing works. There is only one file called gontainer.go. As you saw earlier, the way you run the app is by supplying the argument run sh, which is processed by the main() function shown here:

```go
func main() {
  // outline cleanup tasks
  wg.Add(1)

  ...

  // actual program
  switch args[0] {
  case "run":
    go run()
```

```
    ...
}
```

The function run() that takes care of running the application specified
with the parameter run is shown here:

```
func run() {
  defer cleanup()
  infof("run as [%d] : running %v", os.Getpid(), args[1:])

  lst := append(append(flagInputs, "child"), args[1:]...)
  infof("running proc/self/exe %v", lst)
  if timeout > 0 {
    ctx, cancel := context.WithTimeout(context.Background(),
    timeout)
    defer cancel()
    runcmd = exec.CommandContext(ctx, "/proc/self/
    exe", lst...)
  } else {
    runcmd = exec.Command("/proc/self/exe", lst...)
  }
  runcmd.Stdin = os.Stdin
  runcmd.Stdout = os.Stdout
  runcmd.Stderr = os.Stderr
  runcmd.SysProcAttr = &syscall.SysProcAttr{
    Cloneflags:   syscall.CLONE_NEWUTS | syscall.CLONE_NEWPID
    | syscall.CLONE_NEWNS,
    Unshareflags: syscall.CLONE_NEWNS,
  }
  runcmd.Run()
}
```

You can see that the code is using /proc/self/exe, so what is this? The Linux manual at https://man7.org/linux/man-pages/man5/ proc.5.html says

/proc/self

> When a process accesses this magic symbolic link, it resolves to the process's own /proc/[pid] directory.

/proc/[pid]/exe

> Under Linux 2.2 and later, this file is a symbolic link containing the actual pathname of the executed command. This symbolic link can be dereferenced normally; attempting to open it will open the executable.

The explanation clearly states that using /proc/self/exe means you are spawning the currently running app, so this means that the run() function is running itself as a separate process, passing in the parameter in lst.

The function uses exec.Command to run /proc/self/exe, passing the variable as lst, which contains the following command:

```
--chdr /usr --chrt /home/nanik/play/roofs/ --timeout 0s
child sh
```

Let's explore what the arguments passed to the application are telling the application to do. The init() function declares the following flags that it can receive as arguments:

```
func init() {
  pflag.StringVar(&chroot, "chrt", "", "Where to chroot to.
  Should contain a linux filesystem. Alpine is recommended.
  GONTAINER_FS environment is default if not set")
  pflag.StringVar(&chdir, "chdr", "/usr", "Initial chdir
  executed when running container")
```

```
pflag.DurationVar(&timeout, "timeout", 0, "Timeout before
ending program. If 0 then never ends")
...
infof("flaginputs: %v", flagInputs)
}
```

Table 4-1 explains the mapping of the argument passed via 1st.

Table 4-1. *Mapping Arguments*

Format	Explanation
--chdr /usr	Initial chdir executed when running container
--chrt /home/nanik/ play/roofs/	Where to chroot to
--timeout 0s	Timeout before ending program. If 0, then it never ends.
sh	The app to run once the rootfs is up and running

The only parameter not shown in the table is the child parameter, which is not processed. The child parameter will be processed by the main() function by executing the function child() in goroutine, as shown in the following code snippet:

```
func main() {
  // outline cleanup tasks
  ...
  // actual program
  switch args[0] {
  ...
  case "child":
    go child()
  ...
}
```

The child() function does all the heavy lifting of running the new process in a container-like environment. The following shows the code of the child() function:

```
func child() {
  defer cleanup()
  infof("child as [%d]: chrt: %s,  chdir:%s", os.Getpid(),
  chroot, chdir)
  infof("running %v", args[1:])
  must(syscall.Sethostname([]byte("container")))
  must(syscall.Chroot(chroot), "error in 'chroot ", chroot+"'")
  syscall.Mkdir(chdir, 0600)

  // initial chdir is necessary so dir pointer is in chroot dir
  when proc mount is called
  must(syscall.Chdir("/"), "error in 'chdir /'")
  must(syscall.Mount("proc", "proc", "proc", 0, ""), "error in
  proc mount")
  must(syscall.Chdir(chdir), "error in 'chdir ", chdir+"'")
  if timeout > 0 {
      ctx, cancel := context.WithTimeout(context.Background(),
      timeout+time.Millisecond*50)
      defer cancel()
      cntcmd = exec.CommandContext(ctx, args[1], args[2:]...)
  } else {
      cntcmd = exec.Command(args[1], args[2:]...)
  }

  cntcmd.Stdin = os.Stdin

  ...
```

```
    must(cntcmd.Run(), fmt.Sprintf("run %v return error",
    args[1:]))
    syscall.Unmount("/proc", 0)
}
```

Table 4-2 explains what each section of code is doing. Ignore the must function call as this is an internal function call that checks the return value of each system call.

Table 4-2. *Code Explanations*

Code	Description
must(syscall.Sethostname([] byte("container")))	Specifies the hostname of the container
must(syscall.Chdir("/"), "error in 'chdir /'")	Performs chroot using the specific rootfs (in this example, it's /home/nanik/play/ rootfs)
must(syscall.Chdir(chdir), "error in 'chdir ", chdir+"'")	Changes directory to the specified location
must(cntcmd.Run(), fmt. Sprintf("run %v return error", args[1:]))	Runs the specified argument (in this example, it's sh)

The following code snippet specifies to the operating system to use the standard in/out and error for the application that is executed:

```
...
cntcmd.Stdin = os.Stdin
cntcmd.Stdout = os.Stdout
cntcmd.Stderr = os.Stderr
...
```

Once `cntcmd.Run()` is completed and the prompt shows up, it means that you are running inside the container, isolated from the host operating system.

Summary

In this chapter, you explored the different parts required to run an application inside a container: namespaces, cgroups, and rootfs. You experimented with the different available Linux tools to create namespaces and configured resources for particular namespaces.

You also explored rootfs, which is a key component to run the operating system, thus allowing applications to run. Finally, you looked at a sample project that shows how to use the different components together inside Go by using the Alpine rootfs.

CHAPTER 5

Containers with Networking

In Chapter 4, you learned about the different features of the Linux kernel used for containers. You also explored namespaces and how they help applications isolate from other processes. In this chapter, you will focus solely on the network namespace and understand how it works and how to configure it.

The network namespace allows applications that run on their own namespaces to have a network interface that allows running processes to send and receive data to the host or to the Internet. In this chapter, you will learn how to do the following:

- Create your own network namespace

- Communicate with the host

- Use network space in Go

Source Code

The source code for this chapter is available from the https://github. com/Apress/Software-Development-Go repository.

© Nanik Tolaram 2023
N. Tolaram, *Software Development with Go*,
https://doi.org/10.1007/978-1-4842-8731-6_5

Network Namespace

In Chapter 4, you looked at namespaces, which are used to create a virtual isolation for an application, which is one of the key ingredients in running applications inside a container. The network namespace is another isolation feature that applications need because it allows them to communicate with the host or the Internet.

Why is the network namespace important?

Looking at Figure 5-1, you can see that there are two different applications running on a single host in different namespaces and each of the namespaces has their own network namespace.

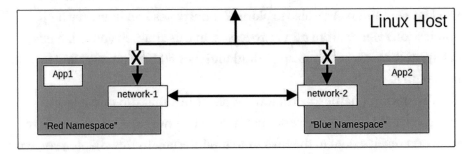

Figure 5-1. *Network namespaces*

The applications are allowed to talk to each other, but they are not allowed to talk to the host and vice versa. This not only makes the applications more secure, but also it makes the application easier to maintain because it does not need to worry about services outside the host.

Using a network namespace requires a few things to be configured properly in order for the application to use it. Figure 5-2 shows the different things that are needed.

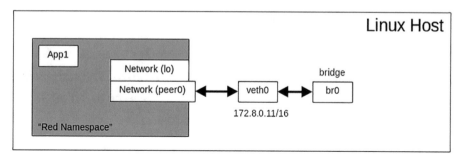

Figure 5-2. *Virtual networks*

Let's take a look at them individually:

Network (lo)	In your computer, you normally access servers that are running locally using *localhost*. This inside the network namespace is also configured the same; it is known as *lo*.
Network (peer0)	This is known as a peer name, and it is configured for the namespace that will communicate with traffic outside the namespace. As shown in Figure 5-2, it communicates with veth0.
veth0	This is called a virtual ethernet and it is configured in the host computer. The virtual ethernet, or in this case veth0, communicates between the host and the namespace.
br0	This is a virtual switch. It's also known as a bridge. Any network attached to the bridge can communicate with the others. In this case, there is only one virtual ethernet (veth0) but if there was another virtual ethernet, they could communicate with each other.

Now that you have a good understanding of the different things that need to be configured in a network namespace, in the next section you will explore using a Linux tool to play around with network namespaces.

Setting Up with the ip Tool

In this section, you will look at setting up two different network namespaces and each will be assigned its own IP address. The script will use the standard Linux tool called *ip*. If you don't have the tool installed on your machine, use the following command to install it:

```
sudo apt-get install -y iproute OR
sudo apt-get install -y iproute2
```

The script will set up the network namespaces to allow them to access each other but they cannot communicate with any external services. The script can be found inside the chapter5/ns directory. Change to this directory and execute it as follows (make sure you run it as root):

```
sudo ./script.sh
```

You will get output that looks like the following:

```
...
64: virt0: <NO-CARRIER,BROADCAST,MULTICAST,UP,LOWER_UP> mtu
1500 qdisc pfifo_fast state DOWN mode DEFAULT group default
qlen 1000
...
66: virt1: <BROADCAST,MULTICAST,UP,LOWER_UP> mtu 1500 qdisc
pfifo_fast state UNKNOWN mode DEFAULT group default qlen 1000
...
PING 10.0.0.1 (10.0.0.1) 56(84) bytes of data.
64 bytes from 10.0.0.1: icmp_seq=1 ttl=64 time=0.069 ms
64 bytes from 10.0.0.1: icmp_seq=2 ttl=64 time=0.052 ms
...

--- 10.0.0.1 ping statistics ---
5 packets transmitted, 5 received, 0% packet loss, time 3999ms
rtt min/avg/max/mdev = 0.044/0.053/0.069/0.009 ms
```

```
PING 10.0.0.1 (10.0.0.1) 56(84) bytes of data.
64 bytes from 10.0.0.1: icmp_seq=1 ttl=64 time=0.060 ms
64 bytes from 10.0.0.1: icmp_seq=2 ttl=64 time=0.044 ms
...

--- 10.0.0.1 ping statistics ---
5 packets transmitted, 5 received, 0% packet loss, time 3999ms
rtt min/avg/max/mdev = 0.044/0.053/0.060/0.006 ms
PING 10.0.0.10 (10.0.0.10) 56(84) bytes of data.
64 bytes from 10.0.0.10: icmp_seq=1 ttl=64 time=0.031 ms
64 bytes from 10.0.0.10: icmp_seq=2 ttl=64 time=0.035 ms
...

--- 10.0.0.10 ping statistics ---
5 packets transmitted, 5 received, 0% packet loss, time 3999ms
rtt min/avg/max/mdev = 0.031/0.037/0.047/0.005 ms
PING 10.0.0.10 (10.0.0.10) 56(84) bytes of data.
64 bytes from 10.0.0.10: icmp_seq=1 ttl=64 time=0.070 ms
64 bytes from 10.0.0.10: icmp_seq=2 ttl=64 time=0.070 ms
...

--- 10.0.0.10 ping statistics ---
5 packets transmitted, 5 received, 0% packet loss, time 3999ms
rtt min/avg/max/mdev = 0.043/0.058/0.070/0.013 ms
PING 10.0.0.11 (10.0.0.11) 56(84) bytes of data.
64 bytes from 10.0.0.11: icmp_seq=1 ttl=64 time=0.070 ms
64 bytes from 10.0.0.11: icmp_seq=2 ttl=64 time=0.042 ms
...

--- 10.0.0.11 ping statistics ---
5 packets transmitted, 5 received, 0% packet loss, time 3999ms
rtt min/avg/max/mdev = 0.042/0.057/0.070/0.010 ms
```

```
PING 10.0.0.11 (10.0.0.11) 56(84) bytes of data.
64 bytes from 10.0.0.11: icmp_seq=1 ttl=64 time=0.032 ms
...
```

The script creates two different namespaces called ns1 and ns2, assigning virtual networks to both of them, as explained in the previous section. The virtual networks are assigned IP addresses 10.0.0.10 and 10.0.0.11, and both networks are connected to each other via a bridge that is assigned IP address 10.0.0.1.

Let's go through the script to understand what it is doing. The following snippet creates two network namespaces labeled ns1 and ns2:

```
ip netns add ns1
ip netns add ns2
```

Once the namespace has been set up, it will set up a local network interface inside the namespace.

```
ip netns exec ns1 ip link set lo up
ip netns exec ns1 ip link

ip netns exec ns2 ip link set lo up
ip netns exec ns2 ip link
```

Now, you need to create a network bridge and assign 10.0.0.1 as its IP address.

```
ip link add br0 type bridge
ip link set br0 up
# setup bridge IP
ip addr add 10.0.0.1/8 dev br0
```

Once the bridge has been set up, the script will link the virtual networks to the network namespaces and also link them to the bridge. This will link all the different virtual networks together through the bridge. The script will assign the different IP address to the virtual networks.

```
# setup virtual ethernet and link it to namespace
ip link add v0 type veth peer name virt0
ip link set v0 master br0
ip link set v0 up
ip link set virt0 netns ns1
# bring up the virtual ethernet
ip netns exec ns1 ip link set virt0 up
# print out info about the network link
ip netns exec ns1 ip link

# setup virtual ethernet and link it to namespace
ip link add v1 type veth peer name virt1
ip link set v1 master br0
ip link set v1 up
ip link set virt1 netns ns2
# bring up the virtual ethernet
ip netns exec ns2 ip link set virt1 up
# print out info about the network link
ip netns exec ns2 ip link

# Set IP address to the different virtual interfaces
ip netns exec ns1 ip addr add 10.0.0.10/8 dev virt0
ip netns exec ns2 ip addr add 10.0.0.11/8 dev virt1
```

The last step that the script will do is route traffic between the bridge. This will allow traffic to flow through the ns1 and ns2 namespaces.

```
# register the bridge in iptables to allow forwarding
iptables -I FORWARD -i br0 -o br0 -j ACCEPT
```

Once the script has run successfully, you will see the routing information using the following command:

```
iptables  -v --list FORWARD  --line-number
```

You will see the output shown below. The output shows that bridge br0 has been registered into the routing table to allow traffic through.

```
Chain FORWARD (policy DROP 53 packets, 4452 bytes)
num      pkts bytes target                    prot opt in
out       source              destination
1       4    336 ACCEPT                       all  -- br0
br0       anywhere            anywhere
2       53  4452 DOCKER-USER                  all  -- any
any       anywhere            anywhere
3       53  4452 DOCKER-ISOLATION-STAGE-1 all  -- any
any       anywhere            anywhere
4       0     0 ACCEPT                        all  -- any     docker0
anywhere  anywhere            ctstate RELATED, ESTABLISHED
5       0     0 DOCKER                        all  -- any
docker0   anywhere            anywhere
6       0     0 ACCEPT                        all  -- docker0
!docker0  anywhere            anywhere
7       0     0 ACCEPT                        all  -- docker0
docker0   anywhere            anywhere
```

After executing the script, you can remove the br0 routing information by using the following command. Replace the value 1 with the chain number you obtained when running the above command to print out the routing information.

```
iptables  -v --delete FORWARD  1
```

You just learned how to set up two network namespaces and allow traffic flow between the two of them using a Linux tool. In the next section, you will see how to set up network namespaces in a Go program, similar to what tools like Docker do.

Containers with Networks

In this section, you will look at a small project that provides Docker-like functionality. The project will be similar to the tool we discussed in Chapter 4, but this tool creates network namespaces to allow the container to have network capability. The project can be checked out from https://github.com/nanikjava/container-networking.

Check out the project and compile it as follows:

```
go build -o cnetwork
```

Once compiled, execute the following command to run it as an Alpine container:

```
sudo ./cnetwork run alpine /bin/sh
```

You will see output that looks like the following:

```
2022/06/05 12:59:11 Cmd args: [./cnetwork run alpine /bin/sh]
2022/06/05 12:59:11 New container ID: 20747aa00a4d
2022/06/05 12:59:11 Downloading metadata for alpine:latest,
please wait...
2022/06/05 12:59:13 imageHash: e66264b98777
2022/06/05 12:59:13 Checking if image exists under
another name...
2022/06/05 12:59:13 Image doesn't exist. Downloading...
2022/06/05 12:59:16 Successfully downloaded alpine
2022/06/05 12:59:16 Uncompressing layer to: /var/lib/gocker/
images/e66264b98777/4a973e6cf97f/fs
2022/06/05 12:59:16 Image to overlay mount: e66264b98777
2022/06/05 12:59:16 Cmd args: [/proc/self/exe setup-netns
20747aa00a4d]
2022/06/05 12:59:16 Cmd args: [/proc/self/exe setup-veth
20747aa00a4d]
```

```
2022/06/05 12:59:16 Cmd args: [/proc/self/exe child-mode --img=
e66264b98777 20747aa00a4d /bin/sh]
/ #
```

You will see a prompt (/#) to enter a command inside the container.
Try using the ifconfig command that will print out the configured
network interface.

```
/ # ifconfig
```

On my local machine, the output looks like the following:

```
lo        Link encap:Local Loopback
          inet addr:127.0.0.1  Mask:255.0.0.0
          inet6 addr: ::1/128 Scope:Host
          UP LOOPBACK RUNNING  MTU:65536  Metric:1
          RX packets:0 errors:0 dropped:0 overruns:0 frame:0
          TX packets:0 errors:0 dropped:0 overruns:0 carrier:0
          collisions:0 txqueuelen:1000
          RX bytes:0 (0.0 B)  TX bytes:0 (0.0 B)

veth1_7ea0e6 Link encap:Ethernet  HWaddr 02:42:4C:66:FD:FE
          inet addr:172.29.69.160  Bcast:172.29.255.255
Mask:255.255.0.0
          inet6 addr: fe11::11:4c11:fe11:fdfe/64 Scope:Link
          UP BROADCAST RUNNING MULTICAST  MTU:1500  Metric:1
          RX packets:19 errors:0 dropped:0 overruns:0 frame:0
          TX packets:6 errors:0 dropped:0 overruns:0 carrier:0
          collisions:0 txqueuelen:1000
          RX bytes:2872 (2.8 KiB)  TX bytes:516 (516.0 B)
```

As you can see, the virtual ethernet network has been configured with
IP address 172.29.69.160. The bridge configured on the host looks like the
following when you run ifconfig on the host:

```
...
gocker0: flags=4163<UP,BROADCAST,RUNNING,MULTICAST>  mtu 1500
        inet 172.29.0.1  netmask 255.255.0.0  broadcast
        172.29.255.255
        inet6 fe80::5851:6bff:fe0e:1768  prefixlen 64  scopeid
        0x20<link>
        ether ce:cc:2c:e2:9e:97  txqueuelen 1000  (Ethernet)
        RX packets 61  bytes 4156 (4.1 KB)
        RX errors 0  dropped 0  overruns 0  frame 0
        TX packets 110  bytes 15864 (15.8 KB)
        TX errors 0  dropped 0 overruns 0  carrier
        0  collisions 0
...
veth0_7ea0e6: flags=4163<UP,BROADCAST,RUNNING,MULTICA
ST>  mtu 1500
        inet6 fe80::e8a3:faff:fed2:2ee9  prefixlen 64  scopeid
        0x20<link>
        ether ea:a3:fa:d2:2e:e9  txqueuelen 1000  (Ethernet)
        RX packets 11  bytes 866 (866.0 B)
        RX errors 0  dropped 0  overruns 0  frame 0
        TX packets 46  bytes 7050 (7.0 KB)
        TX errors 0  dropped 0 overruns 0  carrier
        0  collisions 0
...
```

The gocker0 bridge is configured with IP 172.29.0.1 and you can ping it from the container.

Let's test the network communication between the container and the host. Open terminal and run the following command:

```
sudo ./cnetwork run alpine /bin/sh
```

Once the container is up and running, get the IP address of the container by using the following command:

```
ip addr show
```

Once you get the IP address of your container, run the following command in the container:

```
nc -l -p 4000
```

The container is now ready to accept a connection on port 4000. Open another terminal window from your host machine and run the following command:

```
nc <container_ip_address> 4000
```

Type in anything on your terminal window and the container will output your type. You will see something like Figure 5-3.

Figure 5-3. *Communication between container and host*

Let's take a look at the code to understand how the application is able to do all this inside Go. The application performs a two-step execution process. The first step is setting up the bridge and virtual networks, and the second step is setting up the network namespaces, setting up the different configurations of the virtual networks, and executing the container inside the namespace.

Let's take a look at the first step of creating the bridge and virtual networks, as shown here:

```go
func setupGockerBridge() error {
  linkAttrs := netlink.NewLinkAttrs()
  linkAttrs.Name = "gocker0"
  gockerBridge := &netlink.Bridge{LinkAttrs: linkAttrs}
  if err := netlink.LinkAdd(gockerBridge); err != nil {
    return err
  }
  addr, _ := netlink.ParseAddr("172.29.0.1/16")
  netlink.AddrAdd(gockerBridge, addr)
  netlink.LinkSetUp(gockerBridge)
  return nil
}
```

The function sets up a new bridge by creating a new netlink.Bridge, which contain network bridge information that is populated with the name gocker0 and is assign the IP address 172.29.0.1.

Once it successfully sets up the bridge, it will set up the virtual ethernet that is called inside the initContainer(..) function, as shown here:

```go
func initContainer(mem int, swap int, pids int, cpus float64,
src string, args []string) {
  ...
  if err := setupVirtualEthOnHost(containerID); err != nil {
    log.Fatalf("Unable to setup Veth0 on host: %v", err)
  }
  ...
}
```

The setupVirtualEthOnHost(..) function is shown here:

```go
unc setupVirtualEthOnHost(containerID string) error {
  veth0 := "veth0_" + containerID[:6]
  veth1 := "veth1_" + containerID[:6]
  linkAttrs := netlink.NewLinkAttrs()
  linkAttrs.Name = veth0
  veth0Struct := &netlink.Veth{
     LinkAttrs:         linkAttrs,
     PeerName:          veth1,
     PeerHardwareAddr: createMACAddress(),
  }
  if err := netlink.LinkAdd(veth0Struct); err != nil {
     return err
  }
  netlink.LinkSetUp(veth0Struct)
  gockerBridge, _ := netlink.LinkByName("gocker0")
  netlink.LinkSetMaster(veth0Struct, gockerBridge)

  return nil
}
```

The function creates two virtual networks labeled veth0_xxx and veth1_xxx. The *xxx* represents the generated container id, so in my case it looks like veth0_7ea0e6. The new virtual network will be given a generated MAC address by calling createMACAddress() and will be linked to the newly created gocker0 bridge.

Now that the bridge and virtual networks have been set up, the application will set up the network namespace, configure the container's virtual network, and run the container, which is performed by initContainer(..).

```go
func initContainer(mem int, swap int, pids int, cpus float64,
src string, args []string) {
```

```
...
prepareAndExecuteContainer(mem, swap, pids, cpus,
containerID, imageShaHex, args)
...
}
```

The prepareAndExecuteContainer(..) function takes care of few things, as shown in the following snippet:

```
func prepareAndExecuteContainer(mem int, swap int, pids int,
cpus float64,
  containerID string, imageShaHex string, cmdArgs []string) {

  cmd := &exec.Cmd{
      Path:   "/proc/self/exe",
      Args:   []string{"/proc/self/exe", "setup-netns",
      containerID},
      ...
  }
  cmd.Run()

  cmd = &exec.Cmd{
      Path:   "/proc/self/exe",
      Args:   []string{"/proc/self/exe", "setup-veth",
      containerID},
      ...
  }
  cmd.Run()
  ...
  opts = append(opts, "--img="+imageShaHex)
  args := append([]string{containerID}, cmdArgs...)
  args = append(opts, args...)
  args = append([]string{"child-mode"}, args...)
```

```
cmd = exec.Command("/proc/self/exe", args...)
...
cmd.SysProcAttr = &unix.SysProcAttr{
    Cloneflags: unix.CLONE_NEWPID |
        unix.CLONE_NEWNS |
        unix.CLONE_NEWUTS |
        unix.CLONE_NEWIPC,
}
doOrDie(cmd.Run())
}
```

The function runs itself again (via the /proc/self/exe way),
passing the parameters setup-ns and setup-veth. These two functions
perform the network namespace (setupNetNetworkNamespace) and
virtual ethernet setup, (setupContainerNetworkInterfaceStep1 and
setupContainerNetworkInterfaceStep2).

```
func setupNewNetworkNamespace(containerID string) {
    _ = createDirsIfDontExist([]string{getGockerNetNsPath()})
    ...
    if err := unix.Setns(fd, unix.CLONE_NEWNET); err != nil {
        log.Fatalf("Setns system call failed: %v\n", err)
    }
}

func setupContainerNetworkInterfaceStep1(containerID string) {
    ...
    veth1 := "veth1_" + containerID[:6]
    veth1Link, err := netlink.LinkByName(veth1)
    ...
    if err := netlink.LinkSetNsFd(veth1Link, fd); err != nil {
```

```
      log.Fatalf("Unable to set network namespace for veth1:
      %v\n", err)
   }
}

func setupContainerNetworkInterfaceStep2(containerID string) {
   ...
   if err := unix.Setns(fd, unix.CLONE_NEWNET); err != nil {
      log.Fatalf("Setns system call failed: %v\n", err)
   }

   veth1 := "veth1_" + containerID[:6]
   veth1Link, err := netlink.LinkByName(veth1)
   if err != nil {
      log.Fatalf("Unable to fetch veth1: %v\n", err)
   }
   ...
   route := netlink.Route{
      Scope:     netlink.SCOPE_UNIVERSE,
      LinkIndex: veth1Link.Attrs().Index,
      Gw:        net.ParseIP("172.29.0.1"),
      Dst:       nil,
   }
   ...
}
```

Once all the network setup is done, it calls itself again, passing in child-mode as the parameter, which is performed by the following code snippet:

```
...
case "child-mode":
  fs := flag.FlagSet{}
```

```
fs.ParseErrorsWhitelist.UnknownFlags = true
...
execContainerCommand(*mem, *swap, *pids, *cpus, fs.Args()[0],
*image, fs.Args()[1:])
...
```

Once all setup is done, the final step is to set up the container by calling execContainerCommand(..) to allow the user to execute the command inside the container.

In this section, you learned the different steps involved in setting up virtual networks for a container. The sample application used in this section performs operations such as downloading images, setting up rootfs, setting up network namespaces, and configuring all the different virtual networks required for a container.

Summary

In this chapter, you learned about virtual networks that are used inside containers. You went through the steps of configuring network namespaces along with virtual networks manually using a Linux tool called ip. You looked at configuring iptables to allow communication to happen between the different network namespaces.

After understanding how to configure a network namespace with virtual networks, you looked at a Go example of how to configure virtual networks in a container. You went through the different functions that perform different tasks that are required to configure the virtual networks for a container.

CHAPTER 6

Docker Security

This chapter, you will look at seccomp profiles, one of the security features provided by Docker, which use the seccomp feature built into the Linux kernel. Standalone Go applications can also implement seccomp security without using Docker, and you will look at how to do this using the seccomp library.

You will also look at how Docker communicates using sockets by writing a proxy that listens to Docker communication. This is super useful to know because it gives you a better idea of how to secure Docker in your infrastructure.

Source Code

The source code for this chapter is available from the `https://github.com/Apress/Software-Development-Go` repository.

seccomp Profiles

seccomp is short for secure computing mode. It is a feature that is available inside the Linux operating system. Linux as an operating system provides this feature out of the box, which means that it is ready to be used. What is it actually? It is a security feature that allows applications to make only certain system calls, and this can be configured per application. As a developer, you can specify what kind of restriction you want to put in place

© Nanik Tolaram 2023
N. Tolaram, *Software Development with Go*,
https://doi.org/10.1007/978-1-4842-8731-6_6

so, for example, application A can only make system calls to read and write text files but it cannot make any other system calls, while application B can only make network system calls but can't read or write files. You will look at how to do this in the application and how to make restrictions when running the application as a Docker container.

This kind of restriction provides more security for your infrastructure because you don't want an application to run on your infrastructure without any restrictions. seccomp, when used with Docker containers, provides more layers of security for the host operating system because it can be configured to allow certain system call access to applications that are currently running inside the container.

In order to use seccomp, first you must check whether your operating system supports it. Open your terminal and run the following command:

```
grep CONFIG_SECCOMP= /boot/config-$(uname -r)
```

If your operating supports seccomp, you will get the following output:

```
CONFIG_SECCOMP=y
```

If your Linux operating system does not support seccomp, you can install it using the package manager of your operating system. For example, in Ubuntu, you can install it using the following command:

```
sudo apt install seccomp
```

In the next section, you'll see examples of how to use seccomp in a sample application.

libseccomp

In order to use the seccomp security feature inside the application, you must install the library. In this case, the library is called libseccomp (https://github.com/seccomp/libseccomp). Not all distros install the libseccomp by default, so you need to install it using your operating system package manager. In Ubuntu, you can install it by using the following command:

```
sudo apt  install libseccomp-dev
```

Now that the default seccomp library has been installed, you can start using it in your application. Run the sample application that is inside the chapter6/seccomp/libseccomp directory as follows:

```
go run main.go
```

You will get output as follows:

```
2022/07/05 22:11:34 Starting app
2022/07/05 22:11:34 Directory /tmp/NjAZmQrt created
successfully
2022/07/05 22:11:34 Trying to get current working directory
2022/07/05 22:11:34 Current working directory is: <your_
current_directory>
```

The code run by creating a temporary directory and reading the current directory using a system call is shown here:

```
package main
...
func main() {
  ...

  dirPath := "/tmp/" + randomString(8)
  if err := syscall.Mkdir(dirPath, 0600); err != nil {
```

```
    ...
  }
  ...
  wd, err := syscall.Getwd()
  if err != nil {
    ...
  }
  ...
}
```

What's so special about the code? There is nothing special in what the code is doing. What's special is the way you configured seccomp inside the sample code. The code uses a Go library called libseccomp-golang, which can be found at github.com/seccomp/libseccomp-golang.

The libseccomp-golang library is a Go binding library for the native seccomp library, which you installed in the previous section. You can think of the library as a wrapper to the C seccomp library that can be used inside the Go program. The library is used inside an application to configure itself, specifying what system calls it is allowed to make.

So why do you want to do this? Well, say you are working in a multiple-team environment and you want to make sure that the code written can only perform system calls that are configured internally. This will remove the possibility of introducing code that makes system calls that are not allowed in the configuration. Doing so will introduce an error and crash the application.

Looking at the snippet sample code, you can see the following allowable system calls, declared as string of an array in the whitelist variable:

```
var (
  whitelist   = []string{"getcwd", "exit_group",
  "rt_sigreturn", "mkdirat", "write"})
```

The listed system calls are the system calls that are required by the application. You will see later what happens if the code makes a system call that is not configured. The function configureSeccomp() is responsible for registering the defined system calls with the library.

```go
func configureSeccomp() error {
  ...
  filter, err = seccomp.NewFilter(seccomp.ActErrno)
  ...
  for _, name := range whitelist {
    syscallID, err := seccomp.GetSyscallFromName(name)
    if err != nil {
      return err
    }
    err = filter.AddRule(syscallID, seccomp.ActAllow)
    if err != nil {
      return err
    }
  }
  ...
}
```

The first thing the function does is create a new filter by calling seccomp.NewFilter(..), passing in the action (seccomp.ActErrno) as parameter. The parameter specifies the action to be taken when the application calls system calls that are not allowed. In this case, you want it to return an error number.

Once it creates a new filter, it will loop through the whitelist system calls by first obtaining the correct system call id calling seccomp. GetSyscallFromName(..) and registering the id to the library using the filter.AddRule(..) function. The parameter seccomp.ActAllow specifies that the id is the system calls the application is allowed to make. On completion of the configureSeccomp() function, the application is configured to allow only the calls that have been white-listed.

The system calls that the application makes are simple. Create a file using the following snippet:

```
func main() {
  ...
  if err := syscall.Mkdir(dirPath, 0600); err != nil {
    return
  }
  ...
}
```

Get the current working directory using the following system call:

```
func main() {
  ...
  wd, err := syscall.Getwd()
  if err != nil {
    ...
  }
  ...
}
```

The question that pops up now is, what will happen if the application makes a system call that it is not configured for? Let's modify the code a bit. Change the whitelist variable as follows:

```
var (
  whitelist = []string{
    "exit_group", "rt_sigreturn", "mkdirat", "write",
  }
  ...
)
```

This removed getcwd from the list. Now run the application. You will get an error as follows:

```
...
2022/07/05 22:53:06 Failed getting current working directory:
invalid argument -
```

The code fails to make the system call to get the current working directory and returns an error. You can see that removing the registered system call from the list stops the application from functioning properly. In the next section, you will look at using seccomp for applications that run as containers using Docker.

Docker seccomp

Docker provides seccomp security for applications running in a container without having to add security inside the code. This is done by specifying the seccomp file when running the container. Open the file chapter6/dockerseccomp/seccomp.json to see what it looks like:

```json
{
    "defaultAction": "SCMP_ACT_ERRNO",
    "architectures": [
        "SCMP_ARCH_X86_64"
    ],
    "syscalls": [
        {
            "names": [
                "arch_prctl",
                ...
                "getcwd"
            ],
            "action": "SCMP_ACT_ALLOW"
```

```
        }
    ]
}
```

The syscalls section outlines the different system calls that are permitted inside the container. Let's build a docker container using the Dockerfile inside the chapter6/dockerseccomp directory. Open your terminal and change the directory to chapter6/dockerseccomp and run the following command:

```
docker build -t docker-seccomp:latest -f Dockerfile .
```

This will build the sample main.go inside that directory and package it into a container. Executing docker images shows the following image from your local repository:

```
REPOSITORY                     TAG           IMAGE ID
CREATED          SIZE
...
docker-seccomp                 latest        4cebeb0b7fce
47 hours ago     21.3MB
...
gcr.io/distroless/base-debian10    latest a5880de4abab
52 years ago     19.2MB
```

You now have container called docker-seccomp. Test the container by running it as follows:

```
docker run  docker-seccomp:latest
```

You will get the same output as when you run the sample in a terminal:

```
2022/07/07 12:04:12 Starting app
```

```
2022/07/07 12:04:12 Directory /tmp/QPRNrGAA created
successfully
2022/07/07 12:04:12 Trying to get current working directory
2022/07/07 12:04:12 Current working directory is: /
```

The container works as expected, which is great. Now let's add some restrictions into the container for the app using seccomp. To run a container with a seccomp restriction, use the following command. In this example, the seccomp file is chapter6/dockerseccomp/seccomp.json. Open terminal and run the following command:

```
docker run --security-opt="no-new-privileges" --security-opt
seccomp=<directory_of_chapter6>/dockerseccomp/seccomp.json
docker-seccomp:latest
```

This will execute the container and you will get the same output as previously. The reason why you are able to run the container without any problem even after adding seccomp is because the seccomp.json contains all the necessary permitted syscalls for the container.

Let's remove some syscalls from seccomp.json. You have another file called problem_seccomp.json that has removed mkdirat and getcwd from the allowable syscall list. Run the following from your terminal:

```
docker run --security-opt="no-new-privileges" --security-opt
seccomp=<directory_of_chapter6>/dockerseccomp/problem_seccomp.
json docker-seccomp:latest
```

The container will not run successfully, and you will get the following output:

```
2022/07/07 12:12:18 Starting app
2022/07/07 12:12:18 Failed creating directory: operation not
permitted
```

You have successfully run the container, applying restricted syscalls for the application.

In the next section, you will look at building a Docker proxy to listen to the Docker communication to understand how Docker actually works in terms of receiving a command and responding to it.

Docker Proxy

Docker comprises two main components: the client tool, which is normally called *docker* when you run from your terminal, and the server where it runs as a server/daemon and listens for incoming commands. The Docker client communicates with the server using what is known as socket, which is an endpoint that passes data between different processes. Docker uses what is known as a non-networked socket, which is mostly used for local machine communication and is called a Unix domain socket (or IPC socket).

Docker by default uses Unix socket /var/run/docker.sock to communicate between client and server, as shown in Figure 6-1.

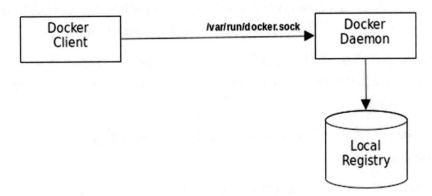

Figure 6-1. *Docker communication /var/run/docker.sock*

In this section, you will look at sample code of how to intercept the communication between Docker client and server. You will step through the code to understand what it is actually doing and how it is performed. The code is inside the `chapter6/docker-proxy` directory. Run it on your terminal as follows:

```
go run main.go
```

You will get the following output when it runs successfully:

```
2022/07/09 11:59:04 Listening on /tmp/docker.sock for Docker
commands
```

The proxy is now ready and listening on `/tmp/docker.sock` for messages to use Docker so that it goes through the proxy and sets the `DOCKER_HOST` environment variable. The `DOCKER_HOST` variable is used by the Docker command line tool to know which Unix socket to use to send the commands.

For example, to use the proxy to print out the list of running containers, use the following command on your terminal:

```
DOCKER_HOST=unix:///tmp/docker.sock docker ps
```

On the terminal that is running the proxy, you will see the Docker output in JSON format. On my local machine, the output look as follows:

```
2022/07/09 16:33:02 [Request] : HEAD /_ping HTTP/1.1
Host: docker
User-Agent: Docker-Client/20.10.9 (linux)

2022/07/09 16:33:02 [Request] : GET /v1.41/containers/json
HTTP/1.1
Host: docker
User-Agent: Docker-Client/20.10.9 (linux)

2022/07/09 16:33:02 [Response] : [
```

```
{
  "Id": "56f68f7cafb7e5f8b1b1f6263ac6b26f4d47b7a0653684221
  2d577ddf1910a11",
  "Names": [
    "/redis"
  ],
  "Image": "redis",
  "ImageID": "sha256:bba24acba395b778d9522a1adf5f0d6bba3
  e6094b2d298e71ab08828b880a01b",
  "Command": "docker-entrypoint.sh redis-server",
  "Created": 1657331859,
  ...
},
{
  "Id": "2ab2942c2591dcd8eba883a1d57f1183a1d99bafb60be8f
  17edf8794e9295e53",
  "Names": [
    "/postgres"
  ],
  "Image": "postgres",
  "ImageID": "sha256:1ee973e26c6564a04b427993f47091cd3ae
  4d5156fbd46d331b17a8e7ab45d39",
  "Command": "docker-entrypoint.sh postgres",
  "Created": 1657331853,
  ...
}
]
```

The proxy prints out the request from the Docker client and the response from the Docker server into the console. The Docker command line still prints out as normal and the output look as follows:

CONTAINER ID	IMAGE	COMMAND	CREATED		
STATUS	PORTS				NAMES
56f68f7cafb7	redis	"docker-entrypoint.s..."	4 hours ago		
Up 4 hours	0.0.0.0:6379->6379/tcp, :::6379->6379/tcp				redis
2ab2942c2591	postgres	"docker-entrypoint.s..."	4 hours ago		
Up 4 hours	0.0.0.0:5432->5432/tcp, :::5432->5432/tcp				postgres

As you can see, the response that the Docker client receives is in the JSON format and it contains a lot of information. Now let's dig into the code to understand how things work internally.

Figure 6-2 shows the command flow from client to proxy to Docker server. The communication from the Docker client passes through the proxy before reaching the Docker daemon.

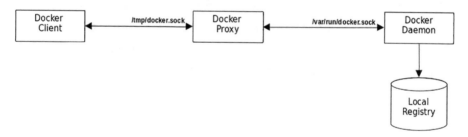

Figure 6-2. *Docker communication using a proxy*

The following snippet shows the code that listens to the socket /tmp/docker.sock:

```
func main() {
  in := flag.String("in", proxySocket, "Proxy docker socket")
  ...

  sock, err := net.Listen("unix", *in)
```

```
if err != nil {
    log.Fatalf("Error : %v", err)
}
...
}
```

The code uses the net.Listen(..) function passing in the parameter unix. The unix parameter indicates to the function that the requested socket is a non-networked Unix socket, which is handled differently internally in the net library.

Once the socket has been initialized successfully, the code will create a socket handler that will take care of processing the incoming request and outgoing response. This is performed by the function ServeHTTP, which is the function of the handler struct. The following snippet shows the declaration of the handler and calling http.Serve to inform the library of the handler that the socket sock will be using. The handler is created, passing in dsocket to be populated into the socket variable.

```
func main() {
    ...
    dhandler := &handler{dsocket}
    ...
    err = http.Serve(sock, dhandler)
    ...
}
```

With the socket ready to accept connections, the function ServeHTTP takes care of processing the request and response for all traffic. The first thing the function does is create a separate connection to the Docker socket.

```
func (h *handler) ServeHTTP(response http.ResponseWriter,
request *http.Request) {
```

```
conn, err := net.DialUnix(unix, nil, &net.UnixAddr{h.
socket, unix})
if err != nil {
    writeError(response, errCode, err)
    return
}
...
}
```

The net.DialUnix(..) function creates a Unix socket using the h.socket value as the socket name; in this sample code, the value is var/run/docker.sock. The connection object returned by this function will be used as a bridge by the code to pass back and forth the request and response.

The code will *forward* the incoming request to the Docker socket, as shown in the following snippet:

```
func (h *handler) ServeHTTP(response http.ResponseWriter,
request *http.Request) {
    ...
    err = request.Write(conn)
    ...
}
```

The request.Write(..) function forwards the incoming request to the original Docker socket that is pointed by the conn variable. Once the request is sent, the code needs to get a http/Response struct in order to read the response reply from the Docker socket. This is done in the following code snippet:

```
func (h *handler) ServeHTTP(response http.ResponseWriter,
request *http.Request) {
    ...
```

```
resp, err := http.ReadResponse(bufio.NewReader(conn),
request)
if err != nil {
    writeError(response, errCode, err)
    return
}
...
}
```

The resp variable now contains the response from the original Docker socket and it will extract the relevant information and forward it back to the caller response stored inside the response object, as shown in the following code snippet:

```
func (h *handler) ServeHTTP(response http.ResponseWriter,
request *http.Request) {
    ...
    response.WriteHeader(resp.StatusCode)

    reader := bufio.NewReader(resp.Body)
    for {
        line, _, err := reader.ReadLine()
        ...
        // write the response back to the caller
        response.Write(line)
        ...
    }
}
```

In the next section, you will look at how to configure your Dockerfile to minimize the container attack surface.

Container Attack Surface

Building applications for cloud environments requires building the application as a container image, which requires creating Dockerfiles. This section will show how to minimize risk when creating Docker images for Go applications.

The main thing to remember when building a Docker image is the final image that the application will be running on. The rule of thumb is to use the bare minimum base image to host your application. In the Docker world, the bare minimum base image is *scratch*. More detailed information about the scratch image can be found at https://hub.docker.com/_/scratch.

The sample Dockerfile that uses the scratch image can be found inside the chapter6/dockersecurity directory. Open terminal and change to the chapter6/dockersecurity directory and build the image as follows:

```
docker build -t sample:latest  .
```

Once it's successfully built, you will get output in your terminal as shown:

```
Step 1/14 : FROM golang:1.18 as build
 ---> 65b2f1fa535f
Step 2/14 : COPY ./main.go .
 ---> 5164c620eaff
...
Step 10/14 : FROM scratch
 --->
...
Successfully built 1a977f4b1cec
Successfully tagged sample:latest
```

Run the newly created Docker image using the following command:

```
docker run sample:latest
```

You will get output that looks like the following:

```
2022/07/09 10:06:42 Hello, from inside Docker image
2022/07/09 10:06:42 Build using Go version  go1.18.2
```

The sample Dockerfile uses the scratch image, as shown in the following snippet:

```
FROM golang:1.18 as build
...
RUN go build -trimpath -v -a -o sample -ldflags="-w -s"
RUN useradd -u 12345 normaluser

FROM scratch
...
ENTRYPOINT ["/sample"]
```

In using the scratch image, you have minimized the attack surface of your container because this image does not have a lot of applications installed like other Docker images (example: Ubuntu, Debian, etc.).

Summary

In this chapter, you learned about Docker security. The first thing you looked at is seccomp and why it is useful. You looked at the sample code and how to restrict a Go application using sec. You looked at setting up libseccomp, which allows you to apply restrictions to your application as to what system calls it can make.

The next thing you looked at using the libseecomp-golang library in your application and how to apply system call restrictions inside your code. Applying restriction inside code is good, but it will be hard to keep changing this code once it is running in production, so you looked at using seccomp profiles when running Docker containers.

Lastly, you looked at a Docker proxy to intercept and understand the communication between a Docker client and server. You also dove into the proxy code to understand how the proxy works in forwarding requests and responses. Finally, you looked briefly at the best way to reduce container attack surface by writing a Dockerfile to use the scratch base image.

PART III

Application Security

CHAPTER 7

Gosec and AST

In this chapter, you will look at AST (abstract syntax tree) and learn what it is about and why it is useful. You will learn AST by looking at the different examples in this chapter to understand the conversion of Go source code to AST. You will also learn about an open source security code analysis tool called gosec. This tool uses AST to perform code static analysis and you will see how this is performed by the tool.

Source Code

The source code for this chapter is available from the `https://github.com/Apress/Software-Development-Go` repository.

Abstract Syntax Tree

Abstract syntax tree (also known as syntax tree) is a tree representation of the structure of the source code written in a programming language. When you write code in Go and you compiled the code, the compiler will first convert the source code internally into a data structure representing the code. This data structure will be used by the compiler as an intermediate representation and it will go through several stages before it produces machine code. Figure 7-1 shows at a high level the different steps that compiler does when compiling code.

© Nanik Tolaram 2023
N. Tolaram, *Software Development with Go*,
https://doi.org/10.1007/978-1-4842-8731-6_7

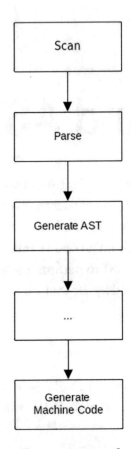

Figure 7-1. *Stages of compiling source code*

Let's take a quick peek at what AST looks like in comparison to the original code. Figure 7-2 shows the comparison between the original Go code and when it is converted into AST during the compilation process.

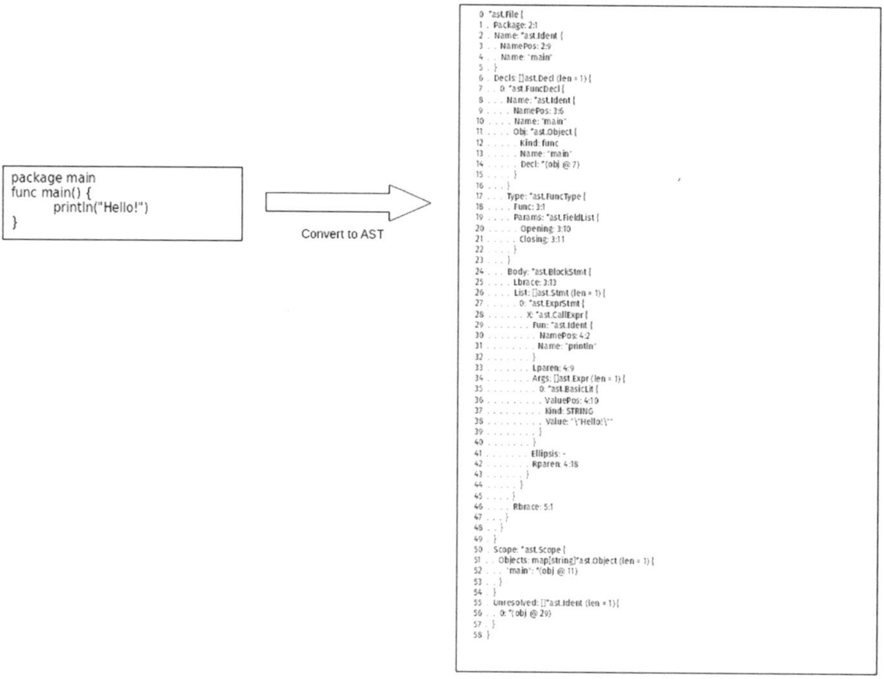

Figure 7-2. *Original code vs. AST*

To the normal eye, the AST looks like a bunch of text, but for the compiler it is very helpful because the data structure allows it to go through different parts of the code to check for errors, warnings, and many other things.

Go provides a built-in module that makes it easy for applications to convert source code into AST, and this module is used by tools like golanci-lint (github.com/golangci/golangci-lint) for reading and linting Go source code.

What does the AST data structure look like? Figure 7-3 shows a brief view of the AST structure.

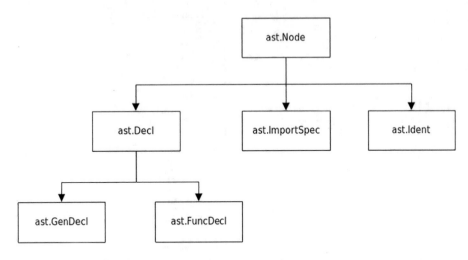

Figure 7-3. *AST structure*

Table 7-1 briefly explains the different structures.

Table 7-1. *Different Structures*

Ast.Node	This is the main interface that others must implement

ast.FuncDecl	The structure representing the declaration-like function, such as
	func myfunc(){
	}

ast.GenDecl	The structure representing a generic declaration, such as var x = "a string"
ast. ImportSpec	The structure representing an import declaration, such as import "go/token"

There are many real world use cases that benefit from using AST:

- **Code generators**: This kind of application requires the use of AST to generate source code.

- **Static code analyzer**: Tools such as gosec, which will be discussed in this chapter, use AST extensively to read source code and identify security issues.

- **Code coverage**: This kind of tool requires AST to measure an application's test coverage and uses AST to perform its operation.

Modules

The modules that you will be using in this chapter are go/parser and go/ast. The godocs can be found respectively at https://pkg.go.dev/go/parser and https://pkg.go.dev/go/ast. Each module provide different functions, as explained here:

- go/parser: This module provides parsing capability to Go source files. The provided input can be from a string or from a filename. The result of the parsing is an AST structure of the source file.

- go/ast: The returned value after parsing a source file is of type go/ast, and this module allows applications to traverse through the different AST structures of the source files. This module provides the AST data structure that the application will work with.

In the next section, it will be clearer how the AST works when you look at different examples.

Sample Code

You will explore different samples in this section using the different Go AST modules. The examples will give you a good idea of how to use the different AST modules and what can be done with the AST results.

Inspecting

Run the code inside the chapter7/samplecode/inspecting folder as follows:

```
go run main.go
```

You will get the following output:

```
2:9:    id: p
3:7:    id: c
3:11:   bl: 1.0
4:5:    id: X
4:9:    id: f
4:11:   bl: 3.14
4:17:   bl: 2
4:21:   id: c
```

The code creates an AST data structure for the code that is provided when calling the AST function and filters out the declared constant and variables. Let's go through the sample code to understand what each part of the code does.

The code declares a variable named src that contains the source code. It's simple Go code containing const and var declarations. Successfully parsing the source code will return a type of ast.File. The ast.File contains the AST data structure of the code that the code will use to traverse through.

```
package main
```

```
import (
   ...
)

func main() {
  src := `
package p
const c = 1.0
var X = f(3.14)*2 + c
`
  fset := token.NewFileSet()
  f, err := parser.ParseFile(fset, "", src, 0)
  ...
}
```

The ast.File is declared inside go/ast module that is declared as follows:

```
type File struct {
  Doc          *CommentGroup
  Package      token.Pos
  Name         *Ident
  Decls        []Decl
  Scope        *Scope
  Imports      []*ImportSpec
  Unresolved   []*Ident
  Comments     []*CommentGroup
}
```

The code then uses the ast.Inspect(..) function that traverses through the AST data structure and calls the function that is declared. The simple function passed as a parameter to ast.Inspect(..) checks what

kind of ast.Node it receives, filtering out only ast.BasicLint and ast.
Ident. The ast.Node refers here is the same as we discussed in Figure 7-2.

```
package main

import (
  ...
)

func main() {
 ...

  ast.Inspect(f, func(n ast.Node) bool {
     var s string
     switch x := n.(type) {
     case *ast.BasicLit:
        s = "bl: " + x.Value
     case *ast.Ident:
        s = "id: " + x.Name
     }
     if s != "" {
        fmt.Printf("%s:\t%s\n", fset.Position(n.Pos()), s)
     }
     return true
  })
}
```

The ast.Inspect(..) is the main function provided by the go/ast
module that is used in traversing through the AST tree in Go. Table 7-2
explains the ast.BasicLint and ast.Ident.

Table 7-2. *ast.BasicLint and ast.Ident*

ast. BasicLint	Represents nodes of the basic type, which is the value of the variable or constant declared
ast.Ident	Represents an identifier. This is defined clearly in the Go language specification (https://go.dev/ref/spec#Identifiers)

Parsing a File

The sample code in this section creates an AST data structure of the main.go that prints out the different module names that are imported, the function names declared in the code, and the line number for the return statement. The code can be found inside chapter7/samplecode/parsing directory. Run the sample in terminal as follows:

```
go run main.go
```

You will see the following output:

```
2022/07/02 16:28:05 Imports:
2022/07/02 16:28:05    "fmt"
2022/07/02 16:28:05    "go/ast"
2022/07/02 16:28:05    "go/parser"
2022/07/02 16:28:05    "go/token"
2022/07/02 16:28:05    "log"
2022/07/02 16:28:05 Functions:
2022/07/02 16:28:05    main
2022/07/02 16:28:05 return statement found in line 36:
2022/07/02 16:28:05 return statement found in line 39:
```

The sample uses the same parser.ParseFile(..) and ast. Inspect(..) functions as shown here:

```
package main
```

```
import (
  ...
)

func main() {
  ...
  f, err := parser.ParseFile(fset, "./main.go", nil, 0)
  ...
  ast.Inspect(f, func(n ast.Node) bool {
     ret, ok := n.(*ast.ReturnStmt)
     if ok {
        ...
     }

     return true
  })
}
```

The function inside ast.Inspect(..) only prints nodes that are of type ast.ReturnStmt that represent return statements; anything else is ignored. The other functions that it uses to print out import information are shown here:

```
package main

import (
  ...
)

func main() {
  ...
  f, err := parser.ParseFile(fset, "./main.go", nil, 0)
  ...
  log.Println("Imports:")
```

```
  for _, i := range f.Imports {
    log.Println(" ", i.Path.Value)
  }
  ...
}
```

The returned value from ParseFile is ast.File and one of the fields in that structure is Imports, which contains all the imports declared in the source code. The code range loops through the Imports field and prints out the import name to the console. The code also prints out the declared function name, which is done by the following code:

```
func main() {
  ...
  for _, f := range f.Decls {
    fn, ok := f.(*ast.FuncDecl)
    ...
    log.Println(" ", fn.Name.Name)
  }
}
```

The Decls field contains all the declarations found in the source code and it filters out only the ast.FuncDecl type containing the function declaration.

You have looked at different AST example code and should now have a better understanding how to use it and what information you can get out of it. In the next section, you will look at how AST is used in an open source security project.

gosec

The gosec project is an open source tool (https://github.com/securego/gosec) that provides security static code analysis. The tool provides a set of secure code best practices for the Go language, and it scans your source code to check if there is any code that breaks those rules.

Use the following command to install it if you are using Go 1.16 and above:

```
go install github.com/securego/gosec/v2/cmd/gosec@latest
```

Once installed, open your terminal and change the directory to chapter7/samplecode and execute the following command:

```
gosec  ./...
```

The tool will scan your sample code recursively and print out the message on the console.

```
[gosec] 2022/07/02 17:00:11 Including rules: default
...
Results:
...
 - G104 (CWE-703): Errors unhandled. (Confidence: HIGH,
Severity: LOW)
    22:
 > 23:            ast.Print(fset, f)
    24: }

Summary:
  Gosec  : dev
  Files  : 3
  Lines  : 105
  Nosec  : 0
  Issues : 1
```

The tool scans through all the .go files inside the directory recursively and, after completing the parsing and scanning process, prints out the final result. In my directory, it found one issue, which is labeled as G104. The tool is able to perform the code analysis by using the go/ast module similar to these examples.

Inside gosec

Figure 7-4 shows at a high level how gosec works.

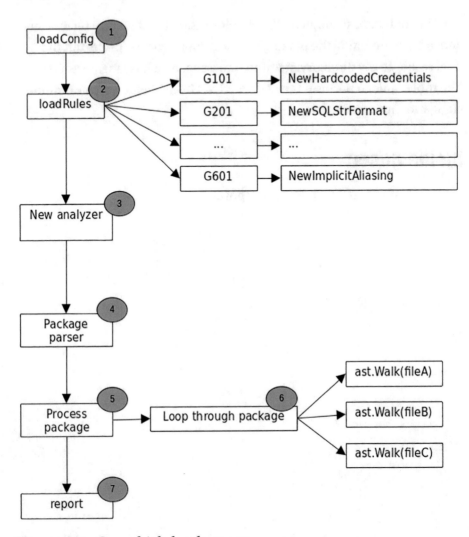

Figure 7-4. *Gosec high-level process*

The tool loads up rules (step 1) that have been defined internally. These rules define functions that are called to check the code being processed. This is discussed in detail in the next section.

Once the rules have been loaded, it proceeds to process the directory given as parameter and recursively gets all the .go files that are found (step 4). This is performed by the following code (helpers.go):

```go
func PackagePaths(root string, excludes []*regexp.Regexp)
([]string, error) {
  ...
  err := filepath.Walk(root, func(path string, f os.FileInfo,
  err error) error {
    if filepath.Ext(path) == ".go" {
      path = filepath.Dir(path)
      if isExcluded(filepath.ToSlash(path), excludes) {
        return nil
      }
      paths[path] = true
    }
    return nil
  })
  ...

  result := []string{}
  for path := range paths {
    result = append(result, path)
  }
  return result, nil
}
```

The PackagePaths(..) function uses the path/filepath Go internal module to traverse through the directory to collect all the different directories that contain .go source. After successfully collecting all the directory names, it calls the Process(..) function (analyzer.go) shown here:

```go
func (gosec *Analyzer) Process(buildTags []string, packagePaths
...string) error {
  ...
  for _, pkgPath := range packagePaths {
    pkgs, err := gosec.load(pkgPath, config)
    if err != nil {
      gosec.AppendError(pkgPath, err)
    }
    for _, pkg := range pkgs {
      if pkg.Name != "" {
        err := gosec.ParseErrors(pkg)
        if err != nil {
          return fmt.Errorf("parsing errors in pkg %q: %w",
          pkg.Name, err)
        }
        gosec.Check(pkg)
      }
    }
  }
  sortErrors(gosec.errors)
  return nil
}
```

This function calls the gosec.load(..) function to collect all the different .go source code found inside the directory using another Go module called golang.org/x/tools.

```go
func (gosec *Analyzer) load(pkgPath string, conf *packages.
Config) ([]*packages.Package, error) {
  abspath, err := GetPkgAbsPath(pkgPath)
  ...   conf.BuildFlags = nil
  pkgs, err := packages.Load(conf, packageFiles...)
```

```
  if err != nil {
    return []*packages.Package{}, fmt.Errorf("loading files
    from package %q: %w", pkgPath, err)
  }
  return pkgs, nil
}
```

The last step, once all the filenames are collected, is to loop through the files and call ast.Walk.

```
func (gosec *Analyzer) Check(pkg *packages.Package) {
  ...
  for _, file := range pkg.Syntax {
    fp := pkg.Fset.File(file.Pos())
    ...
    checkedFile := fp.Name()
    ...
    gosec.context.PassedValues = make(map[string]interface{})
    ast.Walk(gosec, file)
    ...
  }
}
```

The ast.Walk is called with two parameters: gosec and file. The gosec is the receiver that will be called by the AST module, while the file parameter passes the file information to AST.

The gosec receiver implements the Visit(..) function that will be called by AST module when nodes are obtained. The Visit(..) function of the tool can be seen here:

```
func (gosec *Analyzer) Visit(n ast.Node) ast.Visitor {
  ...
  for _, rule := range gosec.ruleset.RegisteredFor(n) {
```

```
    ...
    issue, err := rule.Match(n, gosec.context)
    if err != nil {
        ...
    }
    if issue != nil {
        ...
    }
  }
  return gosec
}
```

The Visit(..) function calls the rules that were loaded in step 2 by calling the Match(..) function, passing in the ast.Node. The rule source checks whether the ast.Node fulfills certain conditions for that particular rule or not.

The last step, 7, is to print out the report it obtains from the different rules executed.

Rules

The tool defines rules that are basically Go code that validates the ast. Node to check if it fulfills certain conditions. The function that generates the rules is seen here (inside rulelist.go):

```
func Generate(trackSuppressions bool, filters ...RuleFilter)
RuleList {
  rules := []RuleDefinition{
      {"G101", "Look for hardcoded credentials",
      NewHardcodedCredentials},

      ...
```

```
   {"G601", "Implicit memory aliasing in RangeStmt",
    NewImplicitAliasing},
 }
 ...
 return RuleList{ruleMap, ruleSuppressedMap}
}
```

The rule is defined by specific code, description and the function name. Looking at G101, you can see that the function name is NewHardCodedCredentials, which is defined as follows:

```
package rules

import (
  ...
)

 ...

func (r *credentials) Match(n ast.Node, ctx *gosec.Context)
(*gosec.Issue, error) {
  switch node := n.(type) {
  case *ast.AssignStmt:
     return r.matchAssign(node, ctx)
  ...
  }
  ...
}

func NewHardcodedCredentials(id string, conf gosec.Config)
(gosec.Rule, []ast.Node) {
   ...

  return &credentials{
```

```
    pattern:             regexp.MustCompile(pattern),
    entropyThreshold: entropyThreshold,
    ...
    MetaData: gosec.MetaData{
        ID:          id,
        What:        "Potential hardcoded credentials",
        Confidence: gosec.Low,
        Severity:    gosec.High,
    },
  }, []ast.Node{(*ast.AssignStmt)(nil), (*ast.ValueSpec)(nil),
(*ast.BinaryExpr)(nil)}
}
```

The NewHardcodedCredentials function initializes all the different parameters that it needs to process the node. The rule has a Match(..) function that is called by gosec when it processes the AST data structure for each file that it processes.

Summary

In this chapter, you looked at what an abstract syntax tree is and what it looks like. Go provides modules that make it easy for applications to work with the AST data structure. This opens up the possibility of writing tools like static code analysers like the open source project gosec.

The sample code provided for this chapter shows how to use AST for simple things like calculating the number of global variables and printing out the package name from the import declaration. You also looked in depth at the gosec tool to understand how it uses AST to provide secure code analysis by going through the different parts of the source code.

CHAPTER 8

Scorecard

In this chapter, you will look at an open source security tool called Scorecard. Scorecard provides security metrics for projects you are interested in. The metrics will give you visibility on the security concerns that you need to be aware of regarding the projects.

You will learn how to create GitHub tokens using your GitHub account. The tokens are needed by the tool to extract public GitHub repository information. You will walk through the steps of installing and using the tool. To understand the tool better, you will look at the high-level flow of how the tool works and also at how it uses the GitHub API.

One of the key takeaways of this chapter is how to use the GitHub API and the information that can be extracted from repositories hosted on GitHub. You will learn how to use GraphQL to query repository data from GitHub using an open source library.

Source Code

The source code for this chapter is available from the `https://github.com/Apress/Software-Development-Go` repository.

What Is Scorecard?

Scorecard is an open source project that analyzes your project's dependencies and gives ratings about them. The tool performs several

© Nanik Tolaram 2023
N. Tolaram, *Software Development with Go*,
https://doi.org/10.1007/978-1-4842-8731-6_8

checks that can be configured depending on your needs. The checks
are associated with software security and are assigned a score of 0 to 10.
The tool shows whether dependencies in your project are safe and also
provides other security checks such as your GitHub configuration, license
checking, and many other useful checks.

The project maintainer runs the tool every day, scanning through
thousands of GitHub repositories and scoring them. The score results are
publicly available in BigQuery, as shown in Figure 8-1.

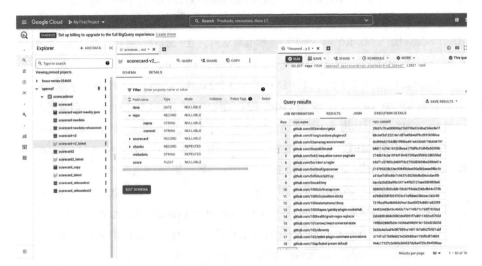

Figure 8-1. *Scorecard public dataset in BigQuery*

To access the public dataset, you need to have a Google (Gmail)
account. Open your browser and type in the following address: `http://
console.cloud.google.com/bigquery`. Once the Google Cloud page
loads, click Add Data ➤ Pin a Project ➤ Enter project name, as shown in
Figure 8-2, for the project name *openssf* and you will see dataset displayed
on the left side of your screen.

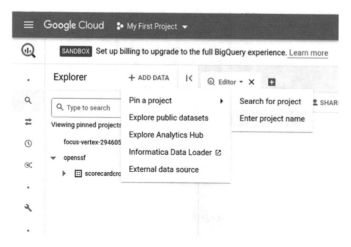

Figure 8-2. *Add the openssf project*

In the next section, you will look at setting up the GitHub token key so that you can use it to scan the GitHub repository of your choice.

Setting Up Scorecard

Scorecard requires a GitHub token key to scan the repository. The reason behind this is the rate limit imposed by GitHub for unauthenticated requests. Let's walk through the following steps to create a token key in GitHub.

1. Go to your GitHub repository (in my case, `https://
    github.com/nanikjava`) and click the top right icon,
    as shown in Figure 8-3, to access the profile page by
    clicking the *Settings* menu.

Figure 8-3. *Accessing the Settings menu*

2. Once you are on the Profile page, shown in Figure 8-4, click *Developer settings.*

Figure 8-4. *Menu on Profile page*

3. You will be brought into the apps page, as shown in Figure 8-5. Click the *Personal access tokens* link.

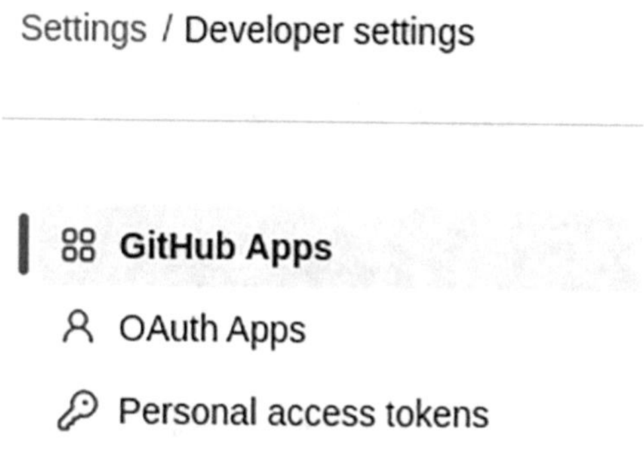

Settings / **Developer settings**

⊞ **GitHub Apps**

⣿ OAuth Apps

⚿ Personal access tokens

Figure 8-5. *Apps page*

4. Once you are inside the tokens page, shown in
    Figure 8-6, click *Generate new token.*

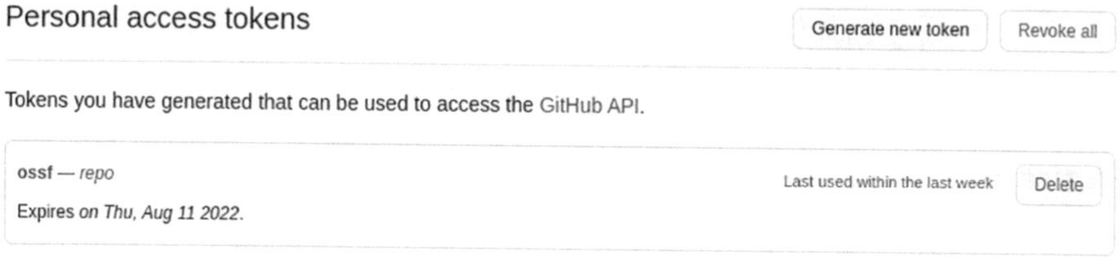

Personal access tokens   Generate new token   Revoke all

Tokens you have generated that can be used to access the GitHub API.

ossf — *repo*   Last used within the last week   Delete
Expires on Thu, Aug 11 2022.

Figure 8-6. *Tokens page*

5. You will see the new personal token page,
    shown in Figure 8-7. Fill in the *Note* textbox with
    information about what the token is used for and
    set the expiration to whatever you want. Finally, in
    the *Select scopes* section, select the *repo* tickbox;
    this will automatically select the reset of the repo
    permissions that fall under it. Once done, scroll
    down and click the *Generate token* button.

New personal access token

Personal access tokens function like ordinary OAuth access tokens. They can be used in: HTTPS, or can be used to authenticate to the API over Basic Authentication.

Note

testossf

What's this token for?

Expiration *

30 days   ↕   The token will expire on Thu, Aug 11 2022

Select scopes

Scopes define the access for personal tokens. Read more about OAuth scopes.

☑ **repo**	Full control of private repositories
☑ repo:status	Access commit status
☑ repo_deployment	Access deployment status
☑ public_repo	Access public repositories
☑ repo:invite	Access repository invitations
☑ security_events	Read and write security events

Figure 8-7. *Generate a new token page*

6. Once the token has been generated, you will see a
    screen like Figure 8-8 showing the new token. Copy
    the token and paste it somewhere on your editor so
    you can use it for the next section.

Figure 8-8. *Token successfully generated*

In the next section, you will use the token you generated to build and run Scorecard.

Running Scorecard

Download the tool from the project GitHub repository. For this chapter, you'll use v4.4.0; the binary can be downloaded from `https://github.com/ossf/scorecard/releases/tag/v4.4.0`. Once you download the archive file, unzip it to a directory on your local machine.

Execute Scorecard to check it's working.

```
/directory/scorecard help
```

You will see the following output in your console:

```
A program that shows security scorecard for an open source
software.

Usage:
  ./scorecard --repo=<repo_url> [--checks=check1,...]
[--show-details]
or ./scorecard --{npm,pypi,rubgems}=<package_name>
[--checks=check1,...] [--show-details] [flags]
  ./scorecard [command]

...


Flags:
    ...

Use "./scorecard [command] --help" for more information about a
command.
```

Now that Scorecard is working on your machine, let's use the token you generated in the previous section to scan a repository. For this example, you will scan the github.com/ossf/scorecard repository. Open terminal and executed the following command:

```
GITHUB_AUTH_TOKEN=<github_token> /directory_of_scorecard/
scorecard --repo=github.com/ossf/scorecard
```

Replace <github_token> with your GitHub token. The tool will take a bit of time to run because it is scanning and doing checks on the GitHub repository. Once complete, you will see output something like Figure 8-9.

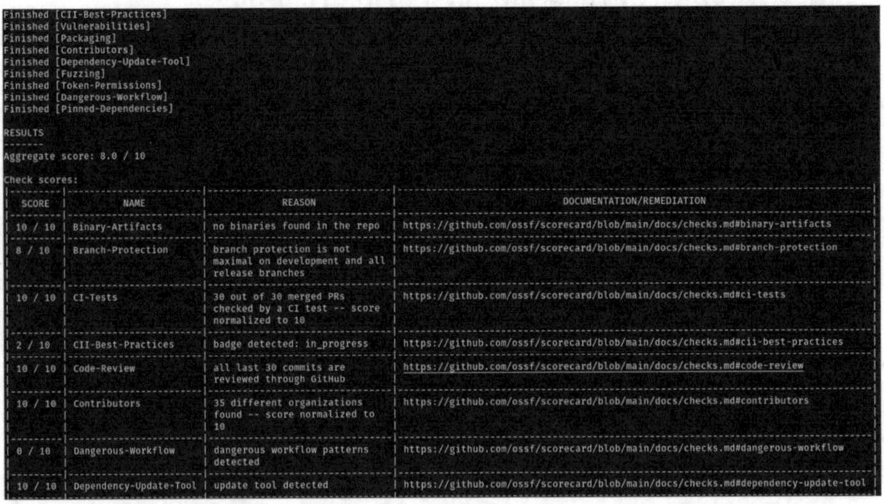

Figure 8-9. *Scorecard output*

You have successfully run the tool to scan a GitHub repository and received an output with a high score of 8.0. A higher score indicates that the repository is doing all the right things as per the predefined checks in the tool.

In the next section, you will further explore the tool to understand how it works and go through code for different parts of the tool.

High-Level Flow

In this section, you will go in depth to understand what the tool is doing and look at code from the different parts of the tool. In digging through the code, you will uncover new things that can be used when designing your own application. First, let's take a high-level look at the process of the tool, as shown in Figure 8-10.

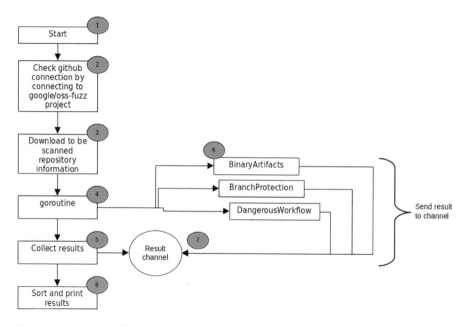

Figure 8-10. *High-level flow*

Use this diagram as a reference when you read the different parts of the application along with the code. The first thing that the tool does when it starts up is check whether it is able to use the provided token to access GitHub. It is hard-coded to test GitHub connectivity by accessing the github.com/google/oss-fuzz repository (step 2). This is shown in the following code snippet (checker/client.go):

```
func GetClients(...) (
```

```
  ...
) {
  ...

  ossFuzzRepoClient, errOssFuzz := ghrepo.
  CreateOssFuzzRepoClient(ctx, logger)
  ...
}

func CreateOssFuzzRepoClient(ctx context.Context, logger *log.
Logger) (clients.RepoClient, error) {
  ossFuzzRepo, err := MakeGithubRepo("google/oss-fuzz")
  ...
  return ossFuzzRepoClient, nil
}
```

The code continues after successfully connecting to the GitHub repository by assigning the connection to different GitHub handlers. These handlers use the connection to get different information from the repository (step 3) that will be used to perform security checks. The code for the handler assignment is as follows (clients/githubrepo/client.go):

```
func (client *Client) InitRepo(inputRepo clients.Repo,
commitSHA string) error {
  ...

  // Sanity check.
  repo, _, err := client.repoClient.Repositories.Get(client.
  ctx, ghRepo.owner, ghRepo.repo)
  if err != nil {
    return sce.WithMessage(sce.ErrRepoUnreachable, err.
    Error())
  }
```

```
client.repo = repo
client.repourl = &repoURL{
    owner:            repo.Owner.GetLogin(),
    ...
    commitSHA:        commitSHA,
}

client.tarball.init(client.ctx, client.repo, commitSHA)

// Setup GraphQL.
client.graphClient.init(client.ctx, client.repourl)

client.contributors.init(client.ctx, client.repourl)

...

client.webhook.init(client.ctx, client.repourl)

client.languages.init(client.ctx, client.repourl)
    return nil
}
```

Figure 8-11 outlines the subset of GitHub handlers that use the different GitHub connections.

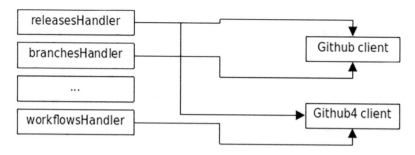

Figure 8-11. *GitHub handlers using GitHub connections*

Once the handlers are initialized successfully with the GitHub connections, the main part of the tool kicks in (step 4). The tool spawns a goroutine that executes the security checks one by one using the information that is downloaded using the GitHub connection. The code that executes the goroutine is as follows (pkg/scorecard.go):

```
func RunScorecards(ctx context.Context,
    ...
) (ScorecardResult, error) {
    ...
    resultsCh := make(chan checker.CheckResult)
    go runEnabledChecks(ctx, repo, &ret.RawResults, checksToRun,
    repoClient, ossFuzzRepoClient,
        ciiClient, vulnsClient, resultsCh)

    ...
    return ret, nil
}
```

Figure 8-12 shows a subset of different security checks that are performed on the GitHub repository.

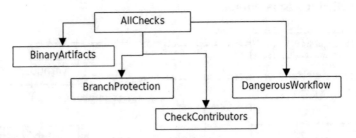

Figure 8-12. *Security checks*

The runEnabledChecks(...) code snippet is shown next. The function executes each check that has been configured (step 6). On completion, the results are passed back via the resultsCh channel (step 7).

```
func runEnabledChecks(...
  resultsCh chan checker.CheckResult,
) {
  ...
  wg := sync.WaitGroup{}
  for checkName, checkFn := range checksToRun {
    checkName := checkName
    checkFn := checkFn
    wg.Add(1)
    go func() {
      defer wg.Done()
      runner := checker.NewRunner(
        checkName,
        repo.URI(),
        &request,
      )

      resultsCh <- runner.Run(ctx, checkFn)
    }()
  }
  wg.Wait()
  close(resultsCh)
}
```

The final step of the tool is collecting, formatting, and scoring the results (step 8). The output depends on the configuration as it can be configured to be displayed on the console (default) or to a file. The code snippet is shown here (scorecard/cmd/root.go):

```
func rootCmd(o *options.Options) {
  ...
  repoResult, err := pkg.RunScorecards(
    ctx,
```

```
    ...
)
if err != nil {
    log.Panic(err)
}
repoResult.Metadata = append(repoResult.Metadata,
o.Metadata...)

sort.Slice(repoResult.Checks, func(i, j int) bool {
    return repoResult.Checks[i].Name < repoResult.
    Checks[j].Name
})

...
resultsErr := pkg.FormatResults(
    o,
    &repoResult,
    checkDocs,
    pol,
)
...
}
```

One thing that you learn from the tool is the usage of the GitHub API. The tool is used extensively by the GitHub API to perform checks by downloading information about the repository and checking that information using the predefined security checks. You are now going to take a look at how to use the GitHub API to do some GitHub exploration.

GitHub

Anyone who works with software knows about GitHub and has used it one way or another. You can find most kinds of open source software in GitHub and it is hosted freely. It has become the go-to destination for anyone who dabbles in software.

GitHub provides an API that allows external tools to interact with the services. The API opens up unlimited potential for developers to access the GitHub service to build tools that can provide value for their organization. This allows the proliferation of third-party solutions (free and paid) to be made available to the general public. The Scorecard project in this chapter is one of the tools made possible because of the GitHub API.

GitHub API

There are two kinds of GitHub APIs: REST and GraphQL (https://docs. github.com/en/graphql). There are different projects that implement both APIs, which you will look at a bit later.

The REST-based API offers access like a normal HTTP call. For example, using your own browser you can type in the following address:

https://api.github.com/users/test

You will see the following JSON response in your browser:

```
{
  "login": "test",
  "id": 383316,
  "node_id": "MDQ6VXNlcjM4MzMxNg==",
  "avatar_url": "https://avatars.githubusercontent.com/
  u/383316?v=4",
  "gravatar_id": "",
  "url": "https://api.github.com/users/test",
```

```
  "html_url": "https://github.com/test",
  ...
  "created_at": "2010-09-01T10:39:12Z",
  "updated_at": "2020-04-24T20:58:44Z"
}
```

You are seeing information about a username called *test* that is registered in GitHub. You can try to use your own GitHub username and you will see details about yourself. Let's get the list of repositories for a particular organization. Type in the following in your browser address:

```
https://api.github.com/orgs/golang/repos
```

The address will send the list of repositories that are listed under a particular organization hosted publicly on GitHub. In the example, you want to get the list of repositories hosted under the Golang organization. You will get the following response:

```
[
  {
    "id": 1914329,
    "node_id": "MDEwOlJlcG9zaXRvcnkxOTE0MzI5",
    "name": "gddo",
    "full_name": "golang/gddo",
    "private": false,
    "owner": {
      "login": "golang",
      "id": 4314092,
      ...
    },
    "html_url": "https://github.com/golang/gddo",
    "description": "Go Doc Dot Org",
    "fork": false,
```

```
    ...
    "license": {
      ...
    },
    ...
    "permissions": {
      ...
    }
  },
  { ... }
]
```

The response is in JSON format. The information you are seeing is the same when you visit the Golang project page at https://github.com/golang. The GitHub documentation at https://docs.github.com/en/rest provides a complete list of REST endpoints that are accessible.

Using the API in a Go application requires you to convert the different endpoints to a function that you can use in your application, which is time consuming, so for this you can use a Go open source library from https://github.com/google/go-github. Let's run the example of using this library, which can be found inside the chapter8/simple folder. Open your terminal and run it as follows:

```
go run main.go
```

You will get the following output:

```
2022/07/16 18:43:43 {
  "id": 23096959,
  "node_id": "MDEwOlJlcG9zaXRvcnkyMzA5Njk10Q==",
  "owner": {
    "login": "golang",
    "id": 4314092,
```

```json
  ...
},
"name": "go",
"full_name": "golang/go",
"description": "The Go programming language",
"homepage": "https://go.dev",
...
"organization": {
  "login": "golang",
  "id": 4314092,
  ...
},
"topics": [
  "go",
  ...
],
...
"license": {
  ...
},
...
}
```

The sample uses the library to get information about a particular repository, http://github.com/golang/go, which is shown in the following code snippet:

```go
package main

import (
  ...
  "github.com/google/go-github/v38/github"
)
```

```
func main() {
  client := github.NewClient(&http.Client{})

  ctx := context.Background()
  repo, _, err := client.Repositories.Get(ctx, "golang", "go")

  ...

  log.Println(string(r))
}
```

The application starts off by initializing the library by calling github. NewClient(..) and passing in http.Client, which is used to make an HTTP call to GitHub. The library package github.com/google/go-github/ v38/github provides all the different functions required. In the example, you use Repositories.Get(..) to obtain information about a particular repository (golang) project (go).

Looking at the library source code (github.com/google/go-github/ v38/github/repos.go), you can see that it is performing a similar call to what is defined in the documentation at https://docs.github.com/en/ rest/repos/repos#get-a-repository.

```
func (s *RepositoriesService) Get(ctx context.Context, owner,
repo string) (*Repository, *Response, error) {
  u := fmt.Sprintf("repos/%v/%v", owner, repo)
  req, err := s.client.NewRequest("GET", u, nil)
  if err != nil {
     return nil, nil, err
  }
  ...
  return repository, resp, nil
}
```

You get the same response using `https://api.github.com/repos/` `golang/go` in your browser.

The other API that is provided by GitHub is called the GraphQL API (`https://docs.github.com/en/graphql`) and it is very different from the REST API. It is based on GraphQL (`https://graphql.org/`), which the website describes as follows:

GraphQL is a query language for APIs and a runtime for fulfilling those queries with your existing data. GraphQL provides a complete and understandable description of the data in your API, gives clients the power to ask for exactly what they need and nothing more, makes it easier to evolve APIs over time, and enables powerful developer tools.

Normally, when using REST API in order to get different kinds of data, you need to get it from different endpoints. Once all of the data is collected, you need to construct them into one structure. GraphQL makes it simple: you just have to define what repository data you want, and it will return the collection of data you requested as one single collection.

This will become clearer when you look at the sample application provided. Open your terminal and run the sample inside `chapter8/` `graphql`. Run it as follows:

```
GITHUB_TOKEN=<your_github_token> go run main.go
```

You need to use the GitHub token you created previously in the section "Setting Up Scorecard." On a successful run, you will get the following (the output will differ because the data is obtained from GitHub in real time, which will have changed by the time you run this sample):

```
2022/07/16 19:39:00 Total number of fork :   15116
2022/07/16 19:39:00 Total number of labels :   10
```

2022/07/16 19:39:00 ----------------------------------
2022/07/16 19:39:00 Issue title - cmd/cgo: fails with gcc 4.4.1
2022/07/16 19:39:00 Issue title - net: LookupHost is returning
odd values and crashing net tests
2022/07/16 19:39:00 Issue title - Problem with quietgcc
2022/07/16 19:39:00 Issue title - Segmentation fault on OS X
10.5 386 for "net" test
2022/07/16 19:39:00 Issue title - HTTP client&server tests
fail. DNS_ServerName and URL_Target strings conjoined into
nonsense.
2022/07/16 19:39:00 Issue title - all.bash segfault
2022/07/16 19:39:00 Issue title - Crash when running tests, no
tests matching.
2022/07/16 19:39:00 Issue title - go-mode.el breaks when
editing empty file
2022/07/16 19:39:00 Issue title - I have already used the name
for *MY* programming language
2022/07/16 19:39:00 Issue title - throw: index out of range
during all.bash
2022/07/16 19:39:00 ----------------------------------
2022/07/16 19:39:00 Commit author (dmitshur), url (https://
github.com/dmitshur)
2022/07/16 19:39:00 Commit author (eaigner), url (https://
github.com/eaigner)
2022/07/16 19:39:00 Commit author (nordicdyno), url (https://
github.com/nordicdyno)
2022/07/16 19:39:00 Commit author (minux), url (https://github.
com/minux)
2022/07/16 19:39:00 Commit author (needkane), url (https://
github.com/needkane)

```
2022/07/16 19:39:00 Commit author (nigeltao), url (https://
github.com/nigeltao)
2022/07/16 19:39:00 Commit author (nigeltao), url (https://
github.com/nigeltao)
2022/07/16 19:39:00 Commit author (h4ck3rm1k3), url (https://
github.com/h4ck3rm1k3)
2022/07/16 19:39:00 Commit author (trombonehero), url (https://
github.com/trombonehero)
2022/07/16 19:39:00 Commit author (adg), url (https://github.
com/adg)
```

The output shows the information that is obtained from GitHub from the http://github.com/golang/go repository as the first 10 issues, first 10 comments, and 10 first labels. This kind of information is very useful and you will see as you walk through the code, which is performed easily by using the GraphQL API.

The main part of the GraphQL API is the query that the sample passes to the GitHub endpoint, which looks like the following:

```
query ($name: String!, $owner: String!) {
  repository(owner: $owner, name: $name) {
    createdAt
    forkCount
    labels(first: 5) {
      edges {
        node {
          name
        }
      }
    }
    issues(first: 5) {
      edges {
```

```
      node {
        title
      }
    }
  }
  commitComments(first: 10) {
    totalCount
    edges {
      node {
        author {
          url
          login
        }
      }
    }
  }
 }
}
```

The query basically describes to GitHub the repository information that you are interested in. It starts off by defining that the query will pass in two parameters ($name and $owner) and the top level of the information that you want is a repository. Inside the repository, you specified that you want the following:

- createdAt

- forkCount

- labels (the first 10 labels)

- issues (the first 10 issues)

- commitComments (the first 10 comments)

GitHub provides a GraphQL tool for creating and testing GraphQL, which you will look at in the next section. The GraphQL cannot be used as is inside your code so you need to convert it into a Go struct, as shown in the following snippet:

```
type graphqlData struct {
  Repository struct {
    CreatedAt githubv4.DateTime
    ForkCount githubv4.Int
    Labels     struct {
      Edges []struct {
        Node struct {
            Name githubv4.String
        }
      }
    } `graphql:"labels(first: $labelcount)"`
    Issues struct {
      Edges []struct {
        Node struct {
            Title githubv4.String
        }
      }
    } `graphql:"issues(first: $issuescount)"`
    CommitComments struct {
      TotalCount githubv4.Int
      Edges      []struct {
        Node struct {
          Author struct {
            URL   githubv4.String
            Login githubv4.String
          }
        }
      }
```

```
        }
    } `graphql:"commitComments(first: $commitcount)"`
  } `graphql:"repository(owner: $owner, name: $name) "`
  RateLimit struct {
      Cost *int
  }
}
```

The strict definition uses data types that are defined in the library (e.g., `githubv4.String`, `githubv4.Int`, etc.).

Once you have defined the GraphQL definition, you use the GraphQL library. In this case, you use the open source library hosted in `https://github.com/shurcooL/githubv4`, as shown here:

```
func main() {
  ...

  data := new(graphqlData)
  vars := map[string]interface{}{
      "owner":        githubv4.String("golang"),
      "name":         githubv4.String("go"),
      "labelcount":   githubv4.Int(10),
      "issuescount":  githubv4.Int(10),
      "commitcount":  githubv4.Int(10),
  }
  if err := graphClient.Query(context.Background(), data,
  vars); err != nil {
      log.Fatalf(err.Error())
  }
  log.Println("Total number of fork : ", data.Repository.
  ForkCount)
  ...
}
```

The code initializes the `graphqlData` struct that will be populated with the information received from GitHub by the library and then it makes the call to GitHub using the `graphClient.Query(..)` function, passing in the newly created struct and variables defined. The variables defined in `vars` contain the value that will be passed to GitHub as the parameter of the GraphQL.

Once the `.Query(..)` function returns successfully, you can use the returned data populated inside the data variable and print it out to the console.

In the next section, you will look at how to use GitHub Explorer to work with GraphQL.

GitHub Explorer

GitHub Explorer is a web-based tool provided by GitHub to allow developers to query GitHub repositories for information. The tool is available from `https://docs.github.com/en/graphql/overview/explorer`. You must sign in with your GitHub account before using the tool. Once access has been granted, you will see Explorer, as shown in Figure 8-13.

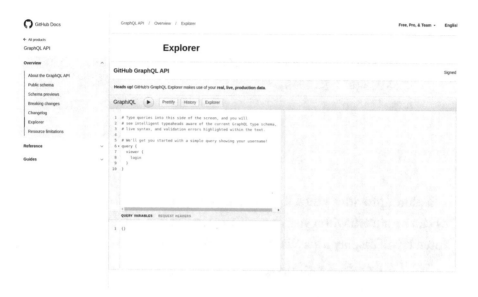

Figure 8-13. *GitHub Explorer*

Once you are logged in, try the following GraphQL and click the run
button.

```
{
  repository(owner: "golang", name: "go") {
    createdAt
    diskUsage
    name
  }
}
```

It queries GitHub for repository http://github.com/golang/go to
extract creation date, total disk usage, and the name of the project. You will
get response as follows:

```
{
```

```
  "data": {
    "repository": {
      "createdAt": "2014-08-19T04:33:40Z",
      "diskUsage": 310019,
      "name": "go"
    }
  }
}
```

Explorer provides quick tips of what data you can add to the query. This can be shown when you create a new line inside the query and hit Alt + Enter. It will display a scrollable tooltip like in Figure 8-14.

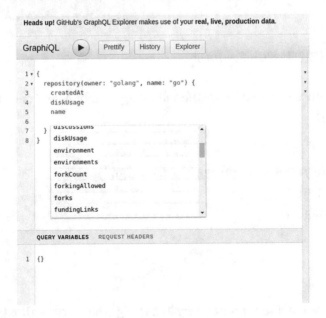

Figure 8-14. *Smart tool tip*

For more reading on the different data that can be extracted using GraphQL, refer to the queries documentation at https://docs.github.com/en/graphql/reference/queries.

Summary

In this chapter, you looked at an open source project called Scorecard that provides security metrics for projects hosted on GitHub. The project measures the security of a project on a scale of 0-10 and this can also be used for projects stored locally. The major benefit of the tool is the public availability of data for projects that have been scanned by the tool. This data is useful for developers because it gives them information and insights on the security metrics of projects they are planning to use.

You also looked at how the tool works and learned how to use the GitHub API to extract repository information to perform predefined security checks.

You learned in detail about the different availability of the GitHub APIs, which are REST and GraphQL. You looked at the sample code to understand how to use each of these APIs to extract information from a GitHub repository. Finally, you explore the GitHub Explorer to understand how to construct GraphQL queries for performing query operations on GitHub.

PART IV

Networking

CHAPTER 9

Simple Networking

In this chapter, you will learn how to write networking code using Go. You will understand how to write client and server code for the TCP and UDP protocols. You will also look at writing a network server that can process requests concurrently using goroutines. By the end of the chapter, you will know how to do the following:

- Write a network client for TCP and UDP

- Write a network server for TCP and UDP

- Use goroutines to process requests

- Load test a network server

Source Code

The source code for this chapter is available from the `https://github.com/Apress/Software-Development-Go` repository.

TCP Networking

In this section, you will explore creating TCP applications using the standard Go network library. The code that you will write is both TCP client and server.

© Nanik Tolaram 2023
N. Tolaram, *Software Development with Go*,
https://doi.org/10.1007/978-1-4842-8731-6_9

TCP Client

Let's start by writing a TCP client that connects to a particular HTTP server, in this case google.com, and prints out the response from the server. The code can be found inside the chapter9/tcp/simple directory. Run it as follows:

```
go run main.go
```

When the code runs, it will try to connect to the google.com server and print out the web page returned to the console, as shown in the output here:

```
HTTP/1.0 200 OK
Date: Sun, 05 Dec 2021 10:27:46 GMT
Expires: -1
Cache-Control: private, max-age=0
Content-Type: text/html; charset=ISO-8859-1
P3P: CP="This is not a P3P policy! See g.co/p3phelp for
more info."
Server: gws
X-XSS-Protection: 0
X-Frame-Options: SAMEORIGIN
Set-Cookie: 1P_JAR=2021-12-05-10; expires=Tue, 04-Jan-2022
10:27:46 GMT; path=/; domain=.google.com; Secure
Set-Cookie:
...
Accept-Ranges: none
Vary: Accept-Encoding

<!doctype html>
...
```

The app uses the net package from the standard library and it uses a TCP connection specified in the following code:

```
conn, err := net.Dial("tcp", t)
if err != nil {
    panic(err)
}
```

Here is the code that connects to the server:

```
package main
...
const (
  host = "google.com"
  port = "80"
)

func main() {
  t := net.JoinHostPort(host, port)

  conn, err := net.Dial("tcp", t)
  if err != nil {
      panic(err)
  }

  ...
}
```

The code uses the net.Dial(..) function to connect to google.com on port 80 using a TCP connection. Once it successfully connects, it sends the HTTP protocol to the server to tell the server that it is requesting the index page, as shown here:

```
func main() {
  ...
```

```
req := "GET / \r\nHost: google.com\r\nConnection:
close\r\n\r\n"
conn.Write([]byte(req))
...
}
```

Once it receives the response, it prints the output on the console, as shown in this code snippet:

```
...

func main() {
  ...
  connReader := bufio.NewReader(conn)
  scanner := bufio.NewScanner(connReader)

  for scanner.Scan() {
    fmt.Printf("%s\n", scanner.Text())
  }

  if err := scanner.Err(); err != nil {
    fmt.Println("Scanner error", err)
  }
}
```

Now that you understand how to write a TCP client, in the next section you will learn how to write a TCP server.

TCP Server

In this section, you will write a TCP server that listens to port 3333 on your local machine. The server will print out what it received and send a response back. The code is inside the tcp/server directory, and it can be run as follows:

```
go run main.go
```

You will get output as follows:

```
2022/03/05 22:51:19 Listening on port 3333
```

Use the nc (network connect) tool to connect to the server, as shown here:

```
nc localhost 3333
```

Once connected, enter any text and press Enter. You will get a response back. The following is an example. I typed in *This is a test* and it came back with a response of *Message received of length : 15.*

```
This is a test
Message received of length : 15
```

Let's take a look at the code. The first thing you will look at how the code waits and listens on port 3333, as shown in the following code snippet:

```go
func main() {
  t := net.JoinHostPort("localhost", "3333")
  l, err := net.Listen("tcp", t)

  ...

  for {
    conn, err := l.Accept()
    if err != nil {
      log.Println("Error accepting: ", err.Error())
      os.Exit(1)
    }
    go handleRequest(conn)
  }
}
```

The code uses the Accept function of the Listener object, which is returned when calling the net.Listen(..) function. The Accept function waits until it receives a connection.

When the client is connected successfully, the code proceeds by calling the handleRequest function in a separate goroutine. Having requests processed in a separate goroutine allows the application to process requests concurrently.

The handling of the request and the sending of the response is taken care of inside the handleRequest function, as shown in the following snippet:

```
func handleRequest(conn net.Conn) {
  ...
  len, err := conn.Read(buf)
  ...
  conn.Write([]byte(fmt.Sprintf("Message received of length :
  %d", len)))
  conn.Close()
}
```

The code reads the data sent by the client using the Read(..) function of the connection and writes the response back using the Write(..) function of the same connection.

Because the code uses a goroutine, the TCP server is able to process multiple client requests without any blocking issues.

UDP Networking

In this section, you will look at writing network applications using the UDP protocol.

UDP Client

In this section, you will write a simple UDP application that communicates with a quote-of-the-day(qotd) server that returns a string quote and prints it out to the console. The following link provides more information about the qotd protocol and the available public servers: `www.gkbrk.com/wiki/qotd_protocol/`. The sample code connects to the server `djxms.net` that listens on port 17.

The code can be found inside the `chapter9/udp/simple` directory, and it can be run as follows:

```
go run main.go
```

Every time you run the application you will get different quotes. In my case, one was the following:

> "Man can climb to the highest summits, but he cannot dwell there long."
>
> George Bernard Shaw (1856-1950)

Let's take a look at the different parts of the application and understand what it is doing. The qotd function contains the following snippet. It uses `net.ResolveUDPAddr(..)` from the standard library to connect to the server and return a `UDPAddr` struct.

```
udpAddr, err := net.ResolveUDPAddr("udp", s)
if err != nil {
  println("Error Resolving UDP Address:", err.Error())
  os.Exit(1)
}
```

The library does a lookup to ensure that the provided domain is valid, and this is done by doing a DNS lookup. On encountering error, it will return a non-nil for the `err` variable.

Stepping through the net.ResolveUDPAddr function inside the standard library shown in Figure 9-1, you can see that the DNS lookup for the domain returns more than one IP address, but only the first IP address is populated in the returned UDPAddr struct.

sock.go

```
⦿ ⦿ ✿ —   🔲 udpsock.go ×
dProjects/syst  71      // parameters.
                72      func ResolveUDPAddr(network, address string) (*UDPAddr, error) {   ad
                73          switch network {
                74          case "udp", "udp4", "udp6":
                75          case "": // a hint wildcard for Go 1.0 undocumented behavior
                76              network = "udp"
                77          default:
                78              return nil, UnknownNetworkError(network)
                79          }
                80          addrs, err := DefaultResolver.internetAddrList(context.Backgroun(
                81          if err != nil {
                82              return nil, err
                83          }
                84          return addrs.forResolve(network, address).(*UDPAddr), nil
                85      }
                86
                87      // UDPConn is the implementation of the Conn and PacketConn interfac(
```

ResolveUDPAddr(network string, address string) (*UDPAddr, error)

Variables

- ⓟ network = {string} "udp"
- ⓟ address = {string} "djxmmx.net:17"
- ≡ err = {error} nil
- ∨ ≣ addrs = {net.addrList} len:5, cap:8
  - ∨ ≡ 0 = {net.Addr | *net.UDPAddr}
    - > ⓕ IP = {net.IP} 68.228.188.226
    - ⓕ Port = {int} 17
    - ⓕ Zone = {string} ""
  - ∨ ≡ 1 = {net.Addr | *net.UDPAddr}
    - > ⓕ IP = {net.IP} 104.9.242.101
    - ⓕ Port = {int} 17
    - ⓕ Zone = {string} ""
  - ∨ ≡ 2 = {net.Addr | *net.UDPAddr}
    - > ⓕ IP = {net.IP} 23.28.179.206
    - ⓕ Port = {int} 17
    - ⓕ Zone = {string} ""
  - > ≡ 3 = {net.Addr | *net.UDPAddr}
  - > ≡ 4 = {net.Addr | *net.UDPAddr}

Figure 9-1. Multiple IPs from ResolveUDPAddr

Once udpAddr is successfully populated, it is used when calling net. DialUDP. The function call opens a socket connection to the server using the IP address that is provided inside udpAddr

```
conn, err := net.DialUDP("udp", nil, udpAddr)
```

In this section, you learned how to connect a UDP server using the standard library. In the next section, you will learn more on how to write a UDP server.

UDP Server

In this section, you will explore further and write a UDP server using the standard library. The server listens on port 3000 and prints out what is sent by the client. The code can be found inside the chapter9/udp/server directory, and it can be run as follows:

```
go run main.go
```

The sample prints out the following on the console:

```
2022/03/05 23:51:32 Listening [::]:3000
```

On a terminal window, use the nc command to connect to port 3000.

```
nc -u localhost 3000
```

Once the nc tool runs, enter any text and you will see it printed in the server's terminal. Here is an example of how it looked on my machine:

```
2022/03/05 23:51:32 Listening [::]:3000
2022/03/05 23:51:36 Received: nanik from [::1]:41518
2022/03/05 23:51:44 Received: this is a long letter from
[::1]:41518
```

Let's explore how the code works. The following snippet sets up the UDP server using the net.ListenUDP function:

```
...

func main() {
  conn, err := net.ListenUDP("udp", &net.UDPAddr{
    Port: 3000,
    IP:   net.ParseIP("0.0.0.0"),
  })
  ...
}
```

The function call returns a UDPConn struct that is used to read and write to the client. After the code successfully creates a UDP server connection, it starts listening to read data from it, as shown here:

```
...
func main() {
  ...
  for {
    message := make([]byte, 512)
    l, u, err := conn.ReadFromUDP(message[:])
    ...
    log.Printf("Received: %s from %s\n", data, u)
  }
}
```

The code uses the ReadFromUDP(..) function of the UDP connection to read the data that is sent by the client to print it out to the console.

Concurrent Servers

In the previous section, you wrote a UDP server but one of the things that is lacking is its ability to process multiple UDP client requests. Writing a UDP server that can process multiple requests is different from normal TCP. The way to structure the application is to spin off multiple goroutines to listen on the same connection and let each goroutine take care of processing the request. The code can be found inside the udp/concurrent directory. Let's take a look at what it is doing differently compared to the previous UDP server implementation.

The following snippet shows the code spinning off multiple goroutines to listen to the UDP connection:

```
...
func main() {
  addr := net.UDPAddr{
    Port: 3333,
  }
  connection, err := net.ListenUDP("udp", &addr)
  ...
  for i := 0; i < runtime.NumCPU(); i++ {
    ...
    go listen(id, connection, quit)
  }
  ...
}
```

The number of goroutine runs depends on the result returned from runtime.NumCPU(). The goroutine use the listen function, which is shown in the following snippet:

```
func listen(i int, connection *net.UDPConn, quit chan
struct{}) {
```

```
buffer := make([]byte, 1024)
for {
    _, remote, err := connection.ReadFromUDP(buffer)
    if err != nil {
        break
    }

    ...

}
...
}
```

Now that the listen function is run as several goroutines, it waits on an incoming UDP request by calling the ReadFromUDP function. When an incoming UDP request is detected, one of the running goroutines processes it.

Load Testing

In this section, you will look at using load testing to test the network server that you wrote in the previous sections. You will be using an open source load testing tool called fortio. which can be downloaded from https:// github.com/fortio/fortio; for this book, use version v1.21.1.

Using the load testing tool, you will see the timing difference between code that is designed to handle requests without using goroutines vs. code that is designed to handle requests using goroutines. For this exercise, you will use the UDP server that is inside the chapter9/udp/loadtesting directory. You will compare between the UDP server that uses goroutines inside the chapter9/udp/loadtesting/concurrent directory and the UDP server that does not use goroutines inside chapter9/udp/ loadtesting/server.

The only difference between the code that you use for load testing with the code discussed in the previous section is the addition of the time. Sleep(..) function. This is added to simulate or mock a process that is doing something to the request before sending a response back. Here is the code:

```
func listen(i int, connection *net.UDPConn, quit chan
struct{}) {
  ...
  for {
    ...
    //pretend the code is doing some request processing for
    10milliseconds
    time.Sleep(10 * time.Millisecond)
    ...
  }
  ...
}

func main() {
  ...
  for {
    ...
    //pretend the code is doing some request processing for
    10milliseconds
    time.Sleep(10 * time.Millisecond)
    ...
  }
}
```

Let's run the code inside the chapter9/udp/loadtesting/concurrent directory first. Once the UDP server starts up, run the fortio tool as follows:

```
./fortio load -n 200 udp://0.0.0.0:3333/
```

The tool makes 200 calls to a server running locally on port 3000. You will see results something like the following:

```
...
00:00:44 I udprunner.go:223> Starting udp test for
udp://0.0.0.0:3333/ with 4 threads at 8.0 qps
Starting at 8 qps with 4 thread(s) [gomax 12] : exactly 200, 50
calls each (total 200 + 0)
...
Aggregated Function Time : count 200 avg 0.011425742 +/-
0.005649 min 0.010250676 max 0.054895756 sum 2.2851485
# range, mid point, percentile, count
>= 0.0102507 <= 0.011 , 0.0106253 , 94.50, 189
> 0.011 <= 0.012 , 0.0115 , 98.00, 7
> 0.045 <= 0.05 , 0.0475 , 99.00, 2
> 0.05 <= 0.0548958 , 0.0524479 , 100.00, 2
# target 50% 0.0106453
# target 75% 0.0108446
# target 90% 0.0109641
# target 99% 0.05
# target 99.9% 0.0544062
Sockets used: 200 (for perfect no error run, would be 4)
Total Bytes sent: 4800, received: 200
udp short read : 200 (100.0 %)
All done 200 calls (plus 0 warmup) 11.426 ms avg, 8.0 qps
```

The final result is that the average time it takes to process is 11.426 ms. Now let's compare this with the server code that does not use goroutines, which is inside the chapter9/udp/loadtesting/server directory. Once you run the UDP server, use the same command to run forti. You will see results that looks like the following:

```
...
00:00:07 I udprunner.go:223> Starting udp test for
udp://0.0.0.0:3000/ with 4 threads at 8.0 qps
Starting at 8 qps with 4 thread(s) [gomax 12] : exactly 200, 50
calls each (total 200 + 0)
...
Aggregated Function Time : count 200 avg 0.026354093 +/-
0.01187 min 0.010296825 max 0.054235708 sum 5.27081864
# range, mid point, percentile, count
>= 0.0102968 <= 0.011 , 0.0106484 , 24.50, 49
> 0.011 <= 0.012 , 0.0115 , 25.00, 1
> 0.02 <= 0.025 , 0.0225 , 50.00, 50
> 0.03 <= 0.035 , 0.0325 , 73.50, 47
> 0.035 <= 0.04 , 0.0375 , 74.00, 1
> 0.04 <= 0.045 , 0.0425 , 98.50, 49
> 0.045 <= 0.05 , 0.0475 , 99.00, 1
> 0.05 <= 0.0542357 , 0.0521179 , 100.00, 2
# target 50% 0.025
# target 75% 0.0402041
# target 90% 0.0432653
# target 99% 0.05
# target 99.9% 0.0538121
Sockets used: 200 (for perfect no error run, would be 4)
Total Bytes sent: 4800, received: 200
udp short read : 200 (100.0 %)
All done 200 calls (plus 0 warmup) 26.354 ms avg, 8.0 qps
```

The average time recorded this time is 26.354ms, which is more
than the previous result of 11.426. With this, you can conclude that it is
important to remember to use goroutines when writing a network server
application to ensure concurrent request processing.

Summary

In this chapter, you learned how to create network applications using TCP and UDP. You learned how to write client and server for both protocols. You learned how to write an application that can process multiple requests concurrently using goroutines.

This is an important step to understand because it is the foundation of how to write network applications that can process huge amounts of traffic. This chapter is a stepping-stone for the upcoming chapter where you will look at different styles of writing network applications in Linux.

CHAPTER 10

System Networking

In the previous chapter, you wrote TCP and UDP applications using the standard library. In this chapter, you will use this knowledge to build system network tools. The objective of writing these tools is to gain a better understanding of how easy it is to so using the capability of the Go standard library. This surfaces the fact that the standard library provides a lot of capabilities, enabling developers to build all kinds of network-related applications.

In this chapter, you will get a good understanding of the following:

- Using the standard library to write network tools
- The net/dns package
- How DNS packs and unpacks messages

Source Code

The source code for this chapter is available from the https://github.com/Apress/Software-Development-Go repository.

Ping Utility

In this section, you will write an application that provides ping-like functionality. The code can be found inside the chapter10/ping folder.

© Nanik Tolaram 2023
N. Tolaram, *Software Development with Go*,
https://doi.org/10.1007/978-1-4842-8731-6_10

The application uses the icmp package provided by the Go standard library, and the documentation can be found at https://pkg.go.dev/golang.org/x/net/icmp. As outlined in the documentation, this package provides functions to manipulate the ICMPv4/6, which is based on RFC 792 and RFC 4443.

Compile the app as follows:

```
go build -o pinggoogle .
```

Run the app with root, as shown:

```
sudo ./pinggoogle
```

You will see the following output:

```
2022/01/21 00:07:09 Ping golang.org (142.250.66.241):
21.30063ms
```

To provide ping-like functionality, the code uses the Internet Control Message Protocol (IMCP), which is part of the IP stack that all networking stacks use, which means that any computer that uses an IP stack can respond to ICMP requests unless it is disabled. The IP network stack has the capability to respond to an ICMP request regardless of where it is running. The ICMP is part of the IP stack, which is normally used for error reporting and network diagnostics.

Code Walkthrough

You are going to dive into the sample code to understand how the whole thing works. The application starts off by calling the Ping() function to ping a single domain. In this example, it will ping for the golang.org domain.

```
func main() {
  addr := "golang.org"
  dst, dur, err := Ping(addr)
```

```go
if err != nil {
    panic(err)
}
log.Printf("Ping %s (%s): %s\n", addr, dst, dur)
}
```

The function performs a number of operations. Let's take a look at the code section by section. The following code snippet calls icmp. ListenPacket(), which is part of the golang.org/x/net standard library package. This opens a local socket that will be used for ICMP communication with the remote host.

```go
func Ping(addr string) (*net.IPAddr, time.Duration, error) {
    // Listen for ICMP reply
    c, err := icmp.ListenPacket("ip4:icmp", ListenAddr)
    if err != nil {
        return nil, 0, err
    }
    defer c.Close()
    ...
}
```

The opened socket is used only for ICMP communication, which means the socket can only understand ICMP network packets. When the local socket has been successfully opened, the code must resolve the IP address of the domain that the application wants to ping. The following code uses the net.ResolveIPAddr() function call to resolve the domain to its respective IP address:

```go
dst, err := net.ResolveIPAddr("ip4", addr)
if err != nil {
    panic(err)
    return nil, 0, err
}
```

Now that you have opened a local socket connection for ICMP and resolved the IP address of the destination domain, the next step is to initialize the ICMP packet and send it off to the destination, as shown in the following code snippets:

```
// Prepare new ICMP message
m := icmp.Message{
    Type: ipv4.ICMPTypeEcho,
    Code: 0,
    Body: &icmp.Echo{
        ID:   os.Getpid() & 0xffff,
        Seq:  1,
        Data: []byte(""),
    },
}
```

The icmp.Message struct defines the information that will be sent as an ICMP packet to the destination, which is defined inside the golang.org/x/net package and looks like the following:

```
// A Message represents an ICMP message.
type Message struct {
    Type     Type         // type, either ipv4.ICMPType or ipv6.
                          // ICMPType
    Code     int          // code
    Checksum int          // checksum
    Body     MessageBody  // body
}
```

The ICMP packet can contain different kinds of ICMP parameters, and this can be specified using the Type field. Here, you use the ipv4. ICMPTypeEcho type. The following are the available types provided in Go:

```
const (
    ICMPTypeEchoReply               ICMPType = 0  // Echo Reply
    ICMPTypeDestinationUnreachable ICMPType = 3  // Destination
                                                    Unreachable
    ICMPTypeRedirect                ICMPType = 5  // Redirect
    ICMPTypeEcho                    ICMPType = 8  // Echo
    ICMPTypeRouterAdvertisement     ICMPType = 9  // Router
                                                    Advertisement
    ICMPTypeRouterSolicitation      ICMPType = 10 // Router
                                                    Solicitation
    ICMPTypeTimeExceeded            ICMPType = 11 // Time Exceeded
    ICMPTypeParameterProblem        ICMPType = 12 // Parameter
                                                    Problem
    ICMPTypeTimestamp               ICMPType = 13 // Timestamp
    ICMPTypeTimestampReply          ICMPType = 14 // Timestamp
                                                    Reply
    ICMPTypePhoturis                ICMPType = 40 // Photuris
    ICMPTypeExtendedEchoRequest     ICMPType = 42 // Extended
                                                    Echo Request
    ICMPTypeExtendedEchoReply       ICMPType = 43 // Extended
                                                    Echo Reply
)
```

Once the type has been defined, the next field that needs to contain information is the Body field. Here you use icmp.Echo, which will contain echo requests:

```
type Echo struct {
```

```
ID    int     // identifier
Seq   int     // sequence number
Data []byte // data
}
```

Data is converted to the byte format using the Marshal(..) function and is then sent out to a destination by using the WriteTo(b,dst) function.

```
...
// Marshal the data
b, err := m.Marshal(nil)
if err != nil {
    return dst, 0, err
}

...

// Send ICMP packet now
n, err := c.WriteTo(b, dst)
```

The last step is to read and parse the response message obtained from the server, as shown here:

```
// Allocate 1500 byte for reading response
reply := make([]byte, 1500)

// Set deadline of 1 minute
err = c.SetReadDeadline(time.Now().Add(1 * time.Minute))
...

// Read from the connection
n, peer, err := c.ReadFrom(reply)
...

// Use ParseMessage to parsed the bytes received
```

```
rm, err := icmp.ParseMessage(ICMPv4, reply[:n])
if err != nil {
    return dst, 0, err
}

// Check for the type of ICMP result
switch rm.Type {
case ipv4.ICMPTypeEchoReply:
    return dst, duration, nil
...
}
```

Reading the packet is performed when calling the ReadFrom(..) function with the result stored inside the reply variable. The reply variable contains a sequence of bytes, which is the ICMP response. To make it easy to read and manipulate the data, you use the ParseMessage(..) function specifying the ICMP format type of ICMPv4. The return value will be of type Message struct.

Once you have parsed the code, you check the response type that is received, as shown in the following snippet:

```
switch rm.Type {
case ipv4.ICMPTypeEchoReply:
  return dst, duration, nil
default:
  return dst, 0, fmt.Errorf("got %+v from %v; want echo reply",
  rm, peer)
}
```

In this section, you learned to open and use local socket connections to send and receive data when using ICMP provided in the standard library. You also learned how to parse and print the response like how a ping utility normally does.

DNS Server

Using the knowledge from the previous chapter on writing a UDP server, you will write a DNS server. The aim of this section is not to write a full-blown DNS server, but rather to show how to use UDP to write it. The DNS server is a DNS forwarder that uses other publicly available DNS servers to perform the DNS lookup functionality, or you can think of it as a DNS server proxy.

Running a DNS Server

The code is located inside the chapter10/dnsserver folder. Compile the code as follows:

```
go build -o dns cmd/main.go
```

Run it by executing the dns executable:

```
./dns
```

You get the following message when the app starts up successfully:

```
2022/03/14 22:17:15 Starting up DNS server on port 8090
```

The DNS server is now ready to serve DNS requests on port 8090. To test the DNS server, use dig as follows:

```
dig @localhost  -p 8090 golang.org
```

You get DNS output from dig, something like the following:

```
; <<>> DiG 9.11.5-P4-5.1ubuntu2.1-Ubuntu <<>> @localhost -p
8090 golang.org
; (2 servers found)
;; global options: +cmd
;; Got answer:
```

```
;; ->>HEADER<<- opcode: QUERY, status: NOERROR, id: 26897
;; flags: qr rd ra; QUERY: 1, ANSWER: 1, AUTHORITY: 0,
ADDITIONAL: 1

;; OPT PSEUDOSECTION:
; EDNS: version: 0, flags:; udp: 512
;; QUESTION SECTION:
;golang.org.                    IN      A

;; ANSWER SECTION:
golang.org.              294    IN      A       142.250.71.81

;; Query time: 6 msec
;; SERVER: ::1#8090(::1)
;; WHEN: Mon Mar 14 22:20:31 AEDT 2022
;; MSG SIZE  rcvd: 55
```

You can also use nslookup, as follows:

```
nslookup -port=8090 golang.org localhost
```

Now that you have successfully run and used the DNS server, in the next section you will look at how to write the code.

DNS Forwarder

In this section, you will use a DNS forwarder that is based on UDP to forward the query to an external DNS server and use the response to report back to the client. In your code, you'll use Google's public DNS server 8.8.8.8 to perform the query.

The first thing the code will do is to create a local UDP server that listens on port 8090, as shown here:

```
func main() {
  dnsConfig := DNSConfig{
```

```
  ...
  port:             8090,
}

conn, err := net.ListenUDP("udp", &net.UDPAddr{Port:
dnsConfig.port})
  ...
}
```

Once it successfully opens port 8090, the next thing it will do is to open a connection to the external DNS server and start the server.

```
func main() {
  dnsConfig := DNSConfig{
    dnsForwarder: "8.8.8.8:53",
    ...
  }

  ...
  dnsFwdConn, err := net.Dial("udp", dnsConfig.dnsForwarder)
  ...
  dnsServer := dns.NewServer(conn, dns.
  NewUDPResolver(dnsFwdConn))
  ...
  dnsServer.Start()
}
```

The local UDP server waits for incoming DNS requests. Once it receives an incoming UDP request, it is processed by handleRequest(). You saw in the previous section that the way to read a UDP request is to call the ReadFromUDP(..) function, as shown here:

```
func (s *Server) handleRequest() error {
  msg, clientAddr, err := s.readRequest()
```

```
  ...
}

func (s *Server) readRequest() (dnsmessage.Message, *net.
UDPAddr, error) {
  buf := make([]byte, 1024)
  _, addr, err := s.conn.ReadFromUDP(buf)
  ...
}
```

The readRequest() function, on receiving the incoming request, proceeds to unpack the data using the built-in golang.org/x/n/dns package, as shown here:

```
func (s *Server) readRequest() (dnsmessage.Message, *net.
UDPAddr, error) {
  ...
  var msg dnsmessage.Message
  err = msg.Unpack(buf)
  ...
}
```

The unpacked data is now stored in a dnsmessage.Message struct that has the following declaration:

```
type Message struct {
  Header
  Questions   []Question
  Answers     []Resource
  Authorities []Resource
  Additionals []Resource
}
```

The code successfully unpacks the data from the incoming request. The next step is to send the same request to the DNS forwarder and process the response to be forwarded back to the client. The ResolveDNS(..) function sends the newly created dnsmessage.Message struct to the DNS forwarder and processes the received response.

```go
func (r *DNSResolver) ResolveDNS(msg dnsmessage.Message)
(dnsmessage.Message, error) {
  packedMsg, err := msg.Pack()
  ...
  _, err = r.fwdConn.Write(packedMsg)
  ...

  resBuf := make([]byte, 1024)
  _, err = r.fwdConn.Read(resBuf)
  ...

  var resMsg dnsmessage.Message
  err = resMsg.Unpack(resBuf)
  ...
}
```

On receiving a response from the DNS forwarder, the handleRequest(..) function sends either a DNS normal response or an error message, depending on the returned value from ResolveDNS(..).

```go
func (s *Server) handleRequest() error {
  ...
  rMsg, err := s.resolver.ResolveDNS(msg)
  if err != nil {
    s.sendResponseWithError(clientAddr, msg, err)
    ...
  }
  ...
```

```go
    return s.sendResponse(clientAddr, rMsg)
}
```

The sendResponse(..) function just packs the received message from the DNS forwarder and sends it back to the client.

```go
func (s *Server) sendResponseWithError(clientAddr *net.UDPAddr,
msg dnsmessage.Message, err error) {
  ...
  err = s.sendResponse(clientAddr, msg)
  ...
}

func (s *Server) sendResponse(addr *net.UDPAddr, message
dnsmessage.Message) error {
  packed, err := message.Pack()
  ...

  _, err = s.conn.WriteToUDP(packed, addr)

}
```

Pack and Unpack

In the previous section, you looked at how requests are processed by unpacking the response and then packing and sending it back as a DNS response to a client. In this section, you will look at the structure of the DNS data.

An incoming request comes in a byte, which is unpacked or converted to a Message struct.

```go
type Message struct {
  Header
  Questions    []Question
```

```
  Answers       []Resource
  Authorities []Resource
  Additionals []Resource
}
```

The Header field contains the following structure, which corresponds to the header to the DNS protocol:

```
type Header struct {
    ID                    uint16
    Response              bool
    OpCode                OpCode
    Authoritative         bool
    Truncated             bool
    RecursionDesired      bool
    RecursionAvailable    bool
    RCode                 RCode
}
```

The Resource struct is used in the Answers, Authorities, and Additionals fields as follows:

```
type Resource struct {
  Header ResourceHeader
  Body   ResourceBody
}
```

The Questions field contains information about the DNS information that the client is requesting, while the Answers field contains the response to the questions. Figure 10-1 shows what the dnsmessage.Message struct contains when it unpacks data from an incoming request to query google. com using dig with the following command:

```
dig @localhost  -p 8090 google.com
```

```
∨  ≡ msg = {dnsmessage.Message}
   ∨ ⓕ Header = {dnsmessage.Header}
        ⓕ ID = {uint16} 18991
        ⓕ Response = {bool} false
        ⓕ OpCode = {dnsmessage.OpCode} 0
        ⓕ Authoritative = {bool} false
        ⓕ Truncated = {bool} false
        ⓕ RecursionDesired = {bool} true
        ⓕ RecursionAvailable = {bool} false
        ⓕ RCode = {dnsmessage.RCode} RCodeSuccess (0)
   ∨ ⓕ Questions = {[]dnsmessage.Question} len:1, cap:1
     ∨ ≡ 0 = {dnsmessage.Question}
        > ⓕ Name = {dnsmessage.Name}
          ⓕ Type = {dnsmessage.Type} TypeA (1)
          ⓕ Class = {dnsmessage.Class} ClassINET (1)
     ⓕ Answers = {[]dnsmessage.Resource} len:0, cap:0
     ⓕ Authorities = {[]dnsmessage.Resource} len:0, cap:0
   ∨ ⓕ Additionals = {[]dnsmessage.Resource} len:1, cap:1
     ∨ ≡ 0 = {dnsmessage.Resource}
        > ⓕ Header = {dnsmessage.ResourceHeader}
        > ⓕ Body = {dnsmessage.ResourceBody | *dnsmessage.OPTResource}
```

Figure 10-1. *dnsmessage.Message with DNS query data*

Figure 10-2 shows the response received from the DNS forwarder when the bytes are unpacked. As you can see, the Answers field is populated with the answer to the query.

```
∨ ≡ rMsg = {dnsmessage.Message}
  ∨ ⓕ Header = {dnsmessage.Header}
      ⓕ ID = {uint16} 18991
      ⓕ Response = {bool} true
      ⓕ OpCode = {dnsmessage.OpCode} 0
      ⓕ Authoritative = {bool} false
      ⓕ Truncated = {bool} false
      ⓕ RecursionDesired = {bool} true
      ⓕ RecursionAvailable = {bool} true
      ⓕ RCode = {dnsmessage.RCode} RCodeSuccess (0)
  ∨ ⓕ Questions = {[]dnsmessage.Question} len:1, cap:1
    ∨ ≡ 0 = {dnsmessage.Question}
      >  ⓕ Name = {dnsmessage.Name}
         ⓕ Type = {dnsmessage.Type} TypeA (1)
         ⓕ Class = {dnsmessage.Class} ClassINET (1)
  ∨ ⓕ Answers = {[]dnsmessage.Resource} len:1, cap:1
    ∨ ≡ 0 = {dnsmessage.Resource}
      ∨ ⓕ Header = {dnsmessage.ResourceHeader}
        >  ⓕ Name = {dnsmessage.Name}
           ⓕ Type = {dnsmessage.Type} TypeA (1)
           ⓕ Class = {dnsmessage.Class} ClassINET (1)
           ⓕ TTL = {uint32} 135
           ⓕ Length = {uint16} 4
      ∨ ⓕ Body = {dnsmessage.ResourceBody | *dnsmessage.AResource}
         >  ⓘ A = {[4]uint8} len:4 ... View
         ⓕ Authorities = {[]dnsmessage.Resource} len:0, cap:0
      >  ⓕ Additionals = {[]dnsmessage.Resource} len:1, cap:1
```

Figure 10-2.   dnsmessage.Message with DNS response data

Summary

In this chapter, you learn more details about using UDP. One of the features of the IP stack is to check the availability of a server using the ICMP protocol. You also learned about using UDP to write a DNS forwarder server that uses the net/dns package standard library to process DNS requests and responses. You now have a better understanding of the features of the standard library than the capability that is provided; at the same time, it shows how versatile the libraries are in allowing us to develop useful network tools.

CHAPTER 11

Google gopacket

In the previous chapter, you learned about building networking tools using the Go standard library. In this chapter, you will go further and investigate an open source library network library from Google called gopacket. The library source code can be found at `https://github.com/google/gopacket` and the library documentation can be found at `https://pkg.go.dev/github.com/google/gopacket`. The source branch that you will be looking at in this chapter is the *master* branch.

gopacket provides low-level network packet manipulation that cannot be found inside the standard library. It provides developers with a simple API to manipulate different network layers' information obtained from the network interface. In this chapter, you will learn

- How gopacket works

- How to use gopacket to write a network traffic sniffer

- About network capture files

Source Code

The source code for this chapter is available from the `https://github.com/Apress/Software-Development-Go` repository.

© Nanik Tolaram 2023
N. Tolaram, *Software Development with Go*,
https://doi.org/10.1007/978-1-4842-8731-6_11

gopacket

In this section, you will explore gopacket and learn about the main part of the library to understand how it works. This library provides the capability to write applications that need to capture and analyze network traffic. The library does the heavy lifting of communicating with the kernel to obtain all the network data and parse it and make it available to applications. gopacket uses a packet capture Linux library that has been part of the Linux toolbox for a long time called libpcap. More information can be found at www.tcpdump.org/index.html.

The libpcap library provides functionality to grab network packets from the network cards, which in turn are parsed and converted to the relevant protocols that are easily used by applications. gopacket provides two major types of data structures that applications can work with, namely Packet and Layer, which will be explored more in detail next.

Layer

In this section, you will look at the Layer interface. This interface is the main interface in the library that holds data in regard to the raw network data. The interface looks like the following:

```
type Layer interface {
  // LayerType is the gopacket type for this layer.
  LayerType() LayerType
  // LayerContents returns the set of bytes that make up
  this layer.
  LayerContents() []byte
  // LayerPayload returns the set of bytes contained within
  this layer, not
  // including the layer itself.
  LayerPayload() []byte
}
```

LayerContents contains the bytes representing a particular layer. For example, if this is an Ethernet layer, then it will contain bytes that make up the Ethernet frame, while LayerPayload will contain the bytes representing the Ethernet protocol.

The LayerType is defined as follows, which contains the type of layer it represents (for example: Ethernet, ARP, TCP, etc.):

```
type LayerType int64
```

The layertypes.go source contains the different network layers that are supported in the library, as shown in the code snippet here:

```
import (
   ...
)

var (
  LayerTypeARP                           = gopacket.
RegisterLayerType(10, gopacket.LayerTypeMetadata{Name: "ARP",
Decoder: gopacket.DecodeFunc(decodeARP)})
  LayerTypeCiscoDiscovery               = gopacket.
RegisterLayerType(11, gopacket.LayerTypeMetadata{Name:
"CiscoDiscovery", Decoder: gopacket.DecodeFunc(decodeCiscoDi
scovery)})
  LayerTypeEthernetCTP                   = gopacket.
RegisterLayerType(12, gopacket.LayerTypeMetadata{Name:
"EthernetCTP", Decoder: gopacket.DecodeFunc(decodeEthe
rnetCTP)})

   ...

  LayerTypeIPv4                          = gopacket.
RegisterLayerType(20, gopacket.LayerTypeMetadata{Name: "IPv4",
Decoder:
   ...
)
```

Different protocols using the Layer interface can be found inside the layers directory, shown in Figure 11-1.

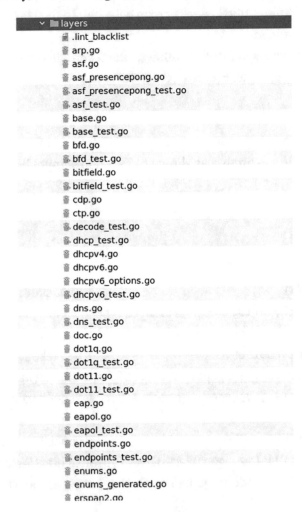

Figure 11-1. *Layer struct implementation*

The source code inside the layers directory contains implementations of each protocol and how to read them from the raw bytes obtained from the kernel.

TCP Layer

Let's take a look at an example of a TCP protocol implementation that can be found inside the layers/tcp.go file. The TCP struct declaration that contains the TCP protocol information is shown here:

```
type TCP struct {
  BaseLayer
  SrcPort, DstPort                               TCPPort
  Seq                                            uint32
  Ack                                            uint32
  DataOffset                                     uint8
  FIN, SYN, RST, PSH, ACK, URG, ECE, CWR, NS bool
  Window                                         uint16
  Checksum                                       uint16
  Urgent                                         uint16
  sPort, dPort                                   []byte
  Options                                        []TCPOption
  Padding                                        []byte
  opts                                           [4]TCPOption
  tcpipchecksum
}
```

The following code shows the function DecodeFromBytes that reads the raw bytes and converts them into a TCP struct:

```
func (tcp *TCP) DecodeFromBytes(data []byte, df gopacket.
DecodeFeedback) error {
  ...
  tcp.SrcPort = TCPPort(binary.BigEndian.Uint16(data[0:2]))
  tcp.sPort = data[0:2]
  tcp.DstPort = TCPPort(binary.BigEndian.Uint16(data[2:4]))
  tcp.dPort = data[2:4]
```

```
tcp.Seq = binary.BigEndian.Uint32(data[4:8])
tcp.Ack = binary.BigEndian.Uint32(data[8:12])
...
...
}
```

Going through each of the protocol source files, you will see the implementation of the different protocols that are supported by the library.

Packet

Packet is the primary type that your application will be working with. The data that has been read from the low-level libpcap library will end up here in a form that is easier to understand by the developer. Let's take a look at the Packet struct, which is defined inside the packet.go file:

```
type Packet interface {
  String() string
  Dump() string
  Layers() []Layer
  Layer(LayerType) Layer
  LayerClass(LayerClass) Layer
  LinkLayer() LinkLayer
  NetworkLayer() NetworkLayer
  TransportLayer() TransportLayer
  ApplicationLayer() ApplicationLayer
  ErrorLayer() ErrorLayer
  Data() []byte
  Metadata() *PacketMetadata
}
```

The struct holds different functions that return the different types of Layer that you looked at in the previous section. To understand a bit better, let's take a peek at the ApplicationLayer type that is returned by the ApplicationLayer() function, which is defined inside the same file, packet.go.

```
type ApplicationLayer interface {
  Layer
  Payload() []byte
}
```

The ApplicationLayer is an interface that holds the Layer type and the Payload() function that will return the original bytes relevant from the network capture for this particular layer. You will look at an example in the next section on how to use the different functions inside the Packet.

Using gopacket

In this section, you will look at examples of how to use gopacket. They will give you ideas of how to use the library and also show the library capabilities in reading network protocols.

pcap

Let's take a moment to understand pcap. It stands for packet capture. Linux has tools that allow a developer or sysadmin to perform network troubleshooting, and one of those tools is a packet capture tool. The packet capture tools allow Linux root users to capture network traffic in the machine.

The traffic data can be saved into a file and later read to be analyzed. This kind of capability is super useful for performing auditing plus security and network troubleshooting in a cloud or local environment. In this chapter, you will capture and analyze the pcap file.

Installing libpcap

The code relies on a Linux library called libpcap (www.tcpdump.org/manpages/pcap.3pcap.html). This library is the main library that helps in performing network captures. Make sure you have the library installed on your local Linux machine. Use the following command to install the library:

```
sudo apt-get install libpcap-dev
```

You will need to reboot your machine once it is successfully installed.

Networking Sniffer

For this section example, you will look at an example of a network sniffer application using the library. The sample application can be found inside the chapter11/gopacket/sniffer folder. The sample code will sniff out your local network and print out the following:

- IPv4 information

- DNS information

- TCP information

- UDP information

- Application layer protocol information

Before running the application, make sure you change the following line of code to use the correct network interface that exists in your machine:

```
const (
  iface = "enp7s0"
  ...
)
```

In my case, it's called enp7s0, which can be found by running the ifconfig tool. The following is the output of running ifconfig on my machine:

```
enp7s0: flags=4099<UP,BROADCAST,MULTICAST>  mtu 1500
        ether ...... txqueuelen 1000  (Ethernet)
        RX packets 0  bytes 0 (0.0 B)
        RX errors 0  dropped 0  overruns 0  frame 0
        TX packets 0  bytes 0 (0.0 B)
        TX errors 0  dropped 0 overruns 0  carrier
        0  collisions 0

lo: flags=73<UP,LOOPBACK,RUNNING>  mtu 65536
        inet 127.0.0.1  netmask 255.0.0.0
        ......
        TX errors 0  dropped 0 overruns 0  carrier
        0  collisions 0

wlp6s0: flags=4163<UP,BROADCAST,RUNNING,MULTICAST>  mtu 1500
        inet 192.168.1.17  netmask 255.255.255.0  broadcast
        192.168.1.255
        ......
        TX errors 239484  dropped 0 overruns 0  carrier
        0  collisions 0
        device interrupt 18
```

Change your directory to the chapter11/gopacket/sniffer folder and compile the app.

```
go build -o sniffer
```

Run the app with the root account.

```
sudo ./sniffer
```

Once the app runs, you will see output like the following:

```
2022/03/12 21:11:19 (TCP) Source address : 100.24.164.135,
Destination address : 192.168.1.6
2022/03/12 21:11:19 (TCP) From port 443 to 35232
2022/03/12 21:11:19 (TCP) Source address : 192.168.1.6,
Destination address : x.x.x.x
2022/03/12 21:11:19 (TCP) From port 35232 to 443
2022/03/12 21:11:20 (TCP) Source address : 192.168.1.6,
Destination address : x.x.x.x
2022/03/12 21:11:20 (TCP) From port 45988 to 443
2022/03/12 21:11:20 (TCP) Source address : x.x.x.x, Destination
address : x.x.x.x
...
2022/03/12 21:24:03 ---------------------
2022/03/12 21:24:03 (TCP) Source address : x.x.x.x, Destination
address : 192.168.1.6
2022/03/12 21:24:03 (TCP) From port 80 to 36910
2022/03/12 21:24:03 HTTP Application layer
2022/03/12 21:24:03 ---------------------
2022/03/12 21:24:03 HTTP/1.1 404 Not Found
Date: Sat, 12 Mar 2022 10:24:03 GMT
Server: Apache/2.4.29 (Ubuntu)
Content-Length: 283
Content-Type: text/html; charset=iso-8859-1
...
2022/03/12 21:24:03 ---------------------
2022/03/12 21:24:03 (TCP) Source address : 192.168.1.6,
Destination address : x.x.x.x
2022/03/12 21:24:03 (TCP) From port 36364 to 443
...
```

Code Walkthrough

Let's take a look step by step at the different parts of the app to understand how it uses gopacket . The following code shows the process of initializing the library to sniff the network traffic using the network interface specified:

```go
func main() {
    f, _ := os.Create(fName)
    ...
    handle, err := pcap.OpenLive(iface, sLen, true, -1)
    if err != nil {
        log.Fatal(err)
    }
    ...
}
```

The pcap.OpenLive function calls gopacket to open the network device and the true parameter sent indicates to the library that you want to open it in promiscuous mode.

Once the function returns without an error, it starts listening for incoming packets and processes them as follows:

```go
func main() {
    f, _ := os.Create(fName)
    ...
    pSource := gopacket.NewPacketSource(handle, handle.
    LinkType())
    for packet := range pSource.Packets() {
        printPacketInfo(packet)
        ...
    }
}
```

As mentioned in the "Packet" section, the application interacts with the network data via the Packet type. In the sample code case, you create a new PacketSource that the app can use in a for .. range to extract all the incoming packets and process them inside the printPacketInfo(..) function. So far, you have successfully initialized and received the packet; now let's dig further into how to use the information made available inside the Packet struct.

The following is the snippet of the printPacketInfo(..) function that shows how to use the Packet struct to check whether the network capture contains an HTTP protocol:

```
func printPacketInfo(packet gopacket.Packet) {
  ...
  applicationLayer := packet.ApplicationLayer()
  if applicationLayer != nil {
    // Search for a string inside the payload
    if strings.Contains(string(applicationLayer.Payload()),
    "HTTP") {
      //log.Println("HTTP found!")
      log.Println("HTTP Application layer")
      log.Println("----------------------")
      log.Println(fmt.Sprintf("%s", string(applicationLayer.
      Payload())))
      log.Println("---------------------")
    }
  }
  ...
}
```

The code uses the ApplicationLayer() function that instructs gopacket to return a layer that corresponds to the application layer, which corresponds to Layer 7 of the OSI network model. Once obtained, it will check whether the layer data is an HTTP request by checking for an HTTP string.

This shows the powerful functionality the library can provide when accessing the different network layers that are made available via the Packet struct.

Analyzing pcap Manually

The sample code not only prints out the capture network layers; it also stores them inside a file called test.pcap. The file is generated in the directory where you run the sample code; in this example, it is stored inside the gopacket/sniffer directory.

This file contains the raw network capture that can be viewed by other tools. In this section, you will look at one of the ways to view the captured file using another open source project, which can be found at https://github.com/mynameiscfed/go-cp-analyzer. Download and compile the file and run it as follows:

```
./go-cp-analyzer -r <directory_to_test.pcap>/filename.pcap
```

After a successful run, it will output something like the following:

```
+-----------------------------------+--------------------+
|       Packet Distribution         |                    |
+-----------------------------------+--------------------+
|    <= 66                          | 6474               |
|    <= 128                         | 5831               |
|    <= 256                         | 858                |
|    <= 384                         | 698                |
|    <= 512                         | 739                |
|    <= 768                         | 538                |
```

```
|    <= 1024                      | 77                 |
|    <= 1518                      | 3830               |
|    <= 9000                      | 489                |
+--------------------------------+--------------------+

+--------------------------------+--------------------+
|          Packet Metrics        |                    |
+--------------------------------+--------------------+
| Total pkts                     | 19534              |
| Avg pkt size                   | 446                |
| Avg pkts/second                | 99                 |
| Avg thoughput (Mbps)           | 0.36               |
+--------------------------------+--------------------+

+--------------------------------+--------------------+
|          Protocol Metrics      |                    |
+--------------------------------+--------------------+
| Ethernet                       | 19534              |
| TCP                            | 13019              |
| UDP                            | 6390               |
| !Ethernet                      | 0                  |
| ARP                            | 11                 |
| IPv4                           | 19419              |
| IPv6                           | 6                  |
| LLC                            | 98                 |
+--------------------------------+--------------------+

+--------------------------------+--------------------+
|        Connections Metrics     |                    |
+--------------------------------+--------------------+
| TCP connections                | 359                |
| TCP conns/sec (avg)            | 1                  |
| TCP peak conns/sec             | 12                 |
| UDP connections                | 138                |
```

```
| UDP conns/sec (avg)            | 0                    |
| UDP peak conns/sec             | 6                    |
+-------------------------------+----------------------+
```

This shows that the raw captured files are compatible with other raw network analyzers that are available.

Analyzing pcap Using WireShark

In this section, you will use Wireshark to see if you can read the file you created using the sample app to prove that it is compatible. You will use Docker to run Wireshark and use browsers to load the UI. Use the following command to run Wireshark using Docker:

```
docker run --name=wireshark --cap-add=NET_ADMIN --security-opt
seccomp=unconfined -e PUID=1000 -e PGID=1000 -p 3000:3000 -e
TZ=Europe/London -v <your_directory_that_contains_pcap_file>:
/config --restart unless-stopped lscr.io/linuxserver/
wireshark:latest
```

Replace <your_directory_that_contains_pcap_file> with your local directory that contains the test.pcap file. Once Wireshark is up and running, you will see output that looks like the following:

```
WARNING: Published ports are discarded when using host
network mode
...
-------------------------------------
         _           ()
   | |      __     _     _
   | | / _| | |  / \
   | | \_ \ | | | () |
   |_| |__/ |_|  \_/
```

```
Brought to you by linuxserver.io
---------------------------------------

To support LSIO projects visit:
https://www.linuxserver.io/donate/
---------------------------------------

GID/UID
---------------------------------------

User uid:    1000
User gid:    1000
---------------------------------------

....
[cont-init.d] done.
[services.d] starting services
[services.d] done.
[guac-init] Auto start not set, application start on login
guacd[429]: INFO:      Guacamole proxy daemon (guacd) version
1.1.0 started
guacd[429]: INFO:      Listening on host 0.0.0.0, port 4822
Starting guacamole-lite websocket server
listening on *:3000

...
```

Wireshark is ready and is listening on port 3000. Open your browser and type in http://localhost:3000 and you will see a screen like Figure 11-2.

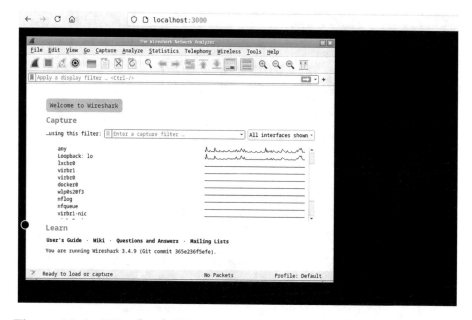

Figure 11-2. *Wireshark UI*

Open the test.pcap file by selecting File ➤ Open and you will see
a screen like Figure 11-3. Select the test.pcap file from the selection of
available files.

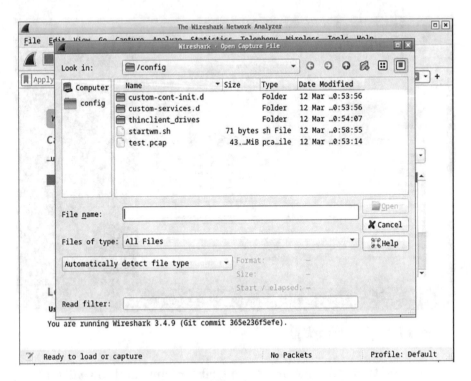

Figure 11-3. *Wireshark open file selection*

Wireshark will successfully read the test.pcap file and will open it, as shown in Figure 11-4.

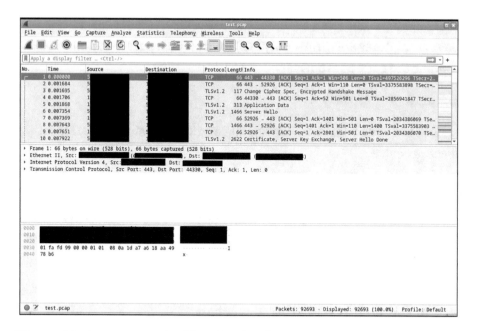

Figure 11-4. *test.pcap inside Wireshark*

In this section, you proved that the network capture performed by
gopacket can be successfully read using two different tools. In the next
section, you will look at how to use BPF (Berkeley Packet Filter) to filter the
network traffic that you are interested in.

Capturing With BPF

gopacket provides the ability to filter network traffic that applications are
interested in, and this is possible by using BPF. BPF stands for Berkeley
Packet Filter and it allows an application to attach a filter to allow or
disallow certain types of data through a socket. More detail information
can be found at www.kernel.org/doc/html/latest/networking/
filter.html.

The sample code can be found inside the chapter11/gopacket/http folder. It captures and prints only TCP traffic with a port destination of 80. Compile the code as follows:

```
go build -o httponly .
```

Run the code with root. Replace <network_device> with your local network device.

```
sudo ./httponly -i <network_device>
```

After a successful run, you will see output that looks like the following. You can see that it only prints TCP traffic connecting to an external server on port 80.

```
2022/03/14 17:10:39 Starting capture on interface "enp0s31f6"
2022/03/14 17:10:39 reading in packets
2022/03/14 17:10:39 -- Extracted Http Data --
2022/03/14 17:10:39 Accept text/*
2022/03/14 17:10:39 If-Modified-Since Thu, 20 May 2021
01:37:53 GMT
2022/03/14 17:10:39 User-Agent Debian APT-HTTP/1.3 (1.9.4)
2022/03/14 17:10:39 Cache-Control max-age=0
2022/03/14 17:10:39 Proto : HTTP/1.1, Host : ppa.launchpad.net,
Method : GET, URI : ...
2022/03/14 17:10:39 ------------------------
2022/03/14 17:10:39 Received request from stream
192.168.1.6->x.x.x.x 59494->80 : &{GET ...} with 0 bytes in
request body
2022/03/14 17:10:40 -- Extracted Http Data --
2022/03/14 17:10:40 Cache-Control max-age=0
2022/03/14 17:10:40 Accept text/*
2022/03/14 17:10:40 If-Modified-Since Tue, 24 Mar 2020
13:38:15 GMT
```

```
2022/03/14 17:10:40 User-Agent Debian APT-HTTP/1.3 (1.9.4)
2022/03/14 17:10:40 Proto : HTTP/1.1, Host : ppa.launchpad.net,
Method : GET, URI : ...
2022/03/14 17:10:40 ------------------------
...
```

Let's take a look at how the code uses BPF to filter the network capture. The following snippet shows what you learned in the previous section: how to perform packet capture using the gopacket `OpenLive` function:

```
if *fname != "" {
  ...
} else {
  log.Printf("Starting capture on interface %q", *iface)
  handle, err = pcap.OpenLive(*iface, int32(*snaplen), true,
  pcap.BlockForever)
}
...
```

Next, the code calls the `SetBPFFilter` function to specify the network filter that you want to apply.

```
var filter = flag.String("f", "tcp and dst port 80", "BPF
filter for pcap")
...

func main() {
  ...
  if err := handle.SetBPFFilter(*filter); err != nil {
    log.Fatal(err)
  }
  ...
}
```

The `filter` variable contains a simple English-like filter rule, `tcp` and `dst port 80`, which means it is only interested in TCP traffic that is accessing port 80. Here is a link to more information about the different filters you can write: `www.ibm.com/docs/en/qsip/7.4?topic=queries-berkeley-packet-filters`.

The code specifies the filter that it wants. The next thing it needs to do is specify the parser that gopacket will use to parse the TCP raw data, and this is done by the `httpStreamFactory` struct type, which defines the `New(..)` and `run()` function. These two functions are called internally by gopacket every time there is data available for the application to consume.

```go
type httpStreamFactory struct{}

func (h *httpStreamFactory) New(net, transport gopacket.Flow)
tcpassembly.Stream {
  hstream := &httpStream{
    net:       net,
    transport: transport,
    r:         tcpreader.NewReaderStream(),
  }
  ...
}

func (h *httpStream) run() {
  buf := bufio.NewReader(&h.r)
  for {
    ...
  }
}
```

The main job of the run() function is to assemble and parsed the raw bytes into a more readable format to print out, as shown:

```go
func (h *httpStream) run() {
  buf := bufio.NewReader(&h.r)
  for {
    req, err := http.ReadRequest(buf)
    if err == io.EOF {
      ...
    }
      ...
    else {
      log.Println("-- Extracted Http Data --")
      for k, v := range req.Header {
        log.Println(k, v[0])
      }

      log.Println(fmt.Sprintf("Proto : %s, Host : %s, Method
      : %s, URI : %s ", req.Proto, req.Host, req.Method, req.
      RequestURI))
      log.Println("------------------------")
      ...
    }
  }
}
```

Summary

In this chapter, you learned about capturing raw networks using the open source gopacket project. The library provides a lot of functionality made available through its simple public API. You learned how to write applications using the library and use the information provided in the different structures.

You looked at BPF (Berkeley Packet Filter) and learned to use it inside your code to filter network captures using gopacket. Using BPF allows an application to process only the network capture that it is interested in rather than spending time processing all incoming traffic. This makes it easier to develop apps targeted for specific traffic.

CHAPTER 12

Epoll Library

Building an application that processes a huge amount of network processing requires a special way of handling connections in a distributed or cloud environment. Applications running on Linux are able to do this thanks to the scalable I/O event notification mechanism that was introduced in version 2.5.44. In this chapter, you will look at epoll. According to the documentation at `https://linux.die.net/man/7/epoll,`

The epoll API performs a similar task to poll: monitoring multiple file descriptors to see if I/O is possible on any of them.

You will start by looking at what `epoll` is and then move on to writing a simple application and finish off looking at the Go `epoll` library and how it works and also how to use it in an application.

On completion of this chapter, you will understand the following:

- How `epoll` works in Linux

- How to write a Go application to use the `epoll` API

- How the `epoll` library works

- How to write a Go application using the `epoll` library

© Nanik Tolaram 2023
N. Tolaram, *Software Development with Go*,
https://doi.org/10.1007/978-1-4842-8731-6_12

Source Code

The source code for this chapter is available from the `https://github.com/Apress/Software-Development-Go` repository.

Understanding epoll

In this section, you will start by looking at what epoll is all about from a system perspective. When you open a socket in Linux, you are given a file descriptor (or FD for short), which is a non-negative value. When the user application wants to perform an I/O operation to the socket, it passes the FD to the kernel. The epoll mechanism is event-driven, so the user application is notified when an I/O operation happens.

As shown in Figure 12-1, epoll is actually a data structure inside Linux that is provided to multiplex I/O operations on multiple file descriptors. Linux provides system calls for user applications to register, modify, or delete FDs from the data structure. Another thing to note is that epoll has Linux-specific features, which means applications can only be run on Linux kernel-based operating systems.

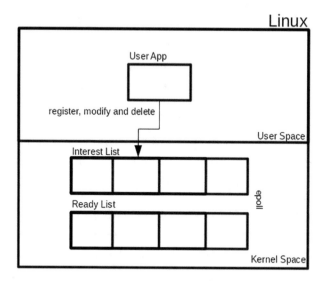

Figure 12-1. *epoll data structure*

The data structure contains two sets of lists:

- **Interest List**: This list/set contains FDs that applications are interested in. The kernel will only send events related to a particular FD that applications are interested in.

- **Ready List**: This list/set contains a subset of reference FDs from the Interest List FDs. The FDs in this list are in the *ready* state that the user application will be notified of.

The following are the system calls used by applications to work with the data structure. In the later sections, you will look closely at how you are going to use them in application and also inside an epoll library.

- epoll_create: A system call to create a new epoll instance and return a file descriptor.

- epoll_ctl: A system call to register, modify, and delete a FD from the Interest List.

- epoll_wait: A system call to wait for I/O events or another way the system call is called to fetch items that are ready from the Ready List.

To use epoll effectively in application, you need to understand how event distribution is performed. Simply put, there are two different ways events are distributed to applications:

- **Edge triggered**: A monitored FD configured with edge will be guaranteed to get one notification if the readiness state changed since the last time it called epoll_wait. The application will receive one event and, if it requires more events, it must perform an operation via a system call to inform epoll that it is waiting for more events.

- **Level triggered**: A monitored FD configured with level will be batch together as a single notification and an application can process them all at once.

From the above, it is obvious that *edge triggered* requires an application to do more work compared to *level triggered*. By default, epoll operates using a level triggered mechanism.

epoll in Golang

In this section, you will write a simple application that uses epoll. The app is an echo server that receives connections and sends responses to the value that is sent to it.

Run the code inside the chapter12/epolling/epollecho folder. Open your terminal to run the following command:

```
go run main.go
```

Once the app runs, open another terminal and use the nc (network connect) tool to connect to the application. Type in something in the console and press Enter. This will be sent to the server.

```
nc 127.0.0.1 9999
```

The sample app will respond by sending the string that was sent by the client. Before diving into the code, let's take a look at how epoll is used in an application.

Epoll Registration

As you can see in Figure 12-2, the application creates a listener on port 9999 to listen for incoming connections. When a client connects to this port, the application spins off a goroutine to handle the client connection.

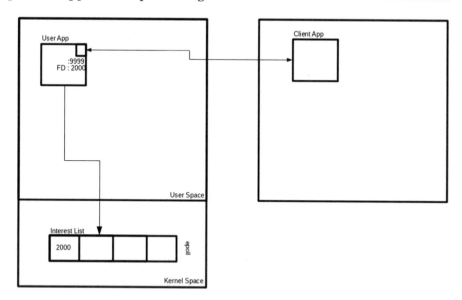

Figure 12-2. *Listener epoll registration*

Now, let's take a more detailed look at how the whole thing works inside the app. The following snippet shows the application creating a socket listener using the syscall.Socket system call and binding it to port 9999 using syscall.Bind:

```
...
fd, err := syscall.Socket(syscall.AF_INET, syscall.O_
NONBLOCK|syscall.SOCK_STREAM, 0)
if err != nil {
    fmt.Println("Socket err : ", err)
    os.Exit(1)
}
defer syscall.Close(fd)

if err = syscall.SetNonblock(fd, true); err != nil {
    ...
}

// prepare listener
addr := syscall.SockaddrInet4{Port: 9999}
copy(addr.Addr[:], net.ParseIP("127.0.0.1").To4())

err = syscall.Bind(fd, &addr)
...

// listener
err = syscall.Listen(fd, 10)
...
...
```

On successfully listening on the port, the app creates a new epoll by calling syscall.EpollCreate1. This instructs the kernel to prepare a data structure that the application will use to listen for I/O events for file descriptors that it is interested in.

```
...
epfd, e := syscall.EpollCreate1(0)
if e != nil {
    ...
}
...
```

Once the data structure successfully creates the application, it proceeds by registering the socket listener file descriptor, as seen in the following code snippet. The code uses syscall.EPOLL_CTL_ADD to specify to the system call that it is interested in doing a new registration.

The registration is done based on the information provided in the event struct, which contains the file descriptor and the event that it is interested in monitoring.

The application uses the EPOLLIN flag to indicate that it is only interested in reading the event. The epoll documentation at https://man7.org/linux/man-pages/man2/epoll_ctl.2.html provides details on the different flags that can be set for the event.Events field.

```
// register listener fd to Interest List
event.Events = syscall.EPOLLIN
event.Fd = int32(fd)
if e = syscall.EpollCtl(epfd, syscall.EPOLL_CTL_ADD, fd,
&event); e != nil {
    ...
}
```

Epoll Wait

The last step after registering is to call syscall.EpollWait to wait for an incoming event from the kernel, which is wrapped inside a for {} loop as shown in the following snippet. The -1 parameter passed as the timeout

parameter to the system indicates the application will wait indefinitely
until an event is ready to be delivered by the kernel.

```
for {
    n, err := syscall.EpollWait(epfd, events[:], -1)
    ...
}
```

When the application receives events, it start processing by looping
through the number of events it receives, as shown here:

```
for {
    n, err := syscall.EpollWait(epfd, events[:], -1)
    ...
    // go through the events
    for ev := 0; ev < n; ev++ {
        ...
    }
}
```

The event received contains the event type generated by the system
and the file descriptor that it is for. This information is used by the code
to check for a new client connection. This is done by checking whether
the file descriptor it received is the same as the listener; if it is, then it will
accept the connection by calling syscall.Accept using the listener FD.

Once it gets a new FD for the client connection, it will also be
registered by the code into epoll using EpollCtl with EPOLL_CTL_ADD flag.
Once completed, both listener FD and client connection FD are registered
inside epoll and the application can multiplex I/O operations for both.

```
for {
    n, err := syscall.EpollWait(epfd, events[:], -1)
    ...
    // go through the events
```

```
for ev := 0; ev < n; ev++ {
    // if it is the same as the listener then accept
    connection
    if int(events[ev].Fd) == fd {
        connFd, _, err := syscall.Accept(fd)
        ...

        // new connection should be non blocking
        syscall.SetNonblock(fd, true)
        event.Events = syscall.EPOLLIN
        event.Fd = int32(connFd)

        // register new client connection fd to
        Interest List
        if err := syscall.EpollCtl(epfd, syscall.EPOLL_
        CTL_ADD, connFd, &event); err != nil {
            log.Print("EpollCtl err : ", connFd, err)
            os.Exit(1)
        }
    } else {
        ...
    }
}
}
```

As a final step, when the code detects that the FD received from the event is not the same as the listener FD, it will spin off a goroutine to handle the connection, which will echo back data received from the client.

Epoll Library

You looked at what epoll is all about and created an app that uses it. Writing an app that uses epoll requires writing a lot of repetitive code that takes care of accepting connections, reading requests, registering file descriptors, and more.

Using an open source library can help in writing better applications because the library takes care of the heavy lifting required for epoll. In this section, you will look at netpoll (http://github.com/cloudwego/netpoll). You will create an application using the library and see how the library takes care of epoll internally.

The code can be found inside the chapter12/epolling/netpoll folder. It is an echo server that sends requests received as a response to the user.

```
import (
    ...

    "github.com/cloudwego/netpoll"
)

func main() {
    listener, err := netpoll.CreateListener("tcp",
    "127.0.0.1:8000")
    if err != nil {
        panic("Failure to create listener")
    }

    var opts = []netpoll.Option{
        netpoll.WithIdleTimeout(1 * time.Second),
        netpoll.WithIdleTimeout(10 * time.Minute),
    }
    eventLoop, err := netpoll.NewEventLoop(echoHandler, opts...)
    if err != nil {
```

```
        panic("Failure to create netpoll")
    }
    err = eventLoop.Serve(listener)
    if err != nil {
        panic("Failure to run netpoll")
    }
}
    ...
```

This code snippet shows the creation of a socket listener using CreateListener from the library to listen on port 8000. After successfully opening the listener, the code proceeds to configure the netpoll by specifying the timeout and specifying the echoHandler function to handle the incoming request. The code starts listening to incoming requests by calling the Serve function of netpoll.

The echoHandler function handles reading and writing from the client socket connection using the passed-in parameter netpoll.Connection. The function reads using the connection.Reader() and writes using connection.Write().

```
func echoHandler(ctx context.Context, connection netpoll.
Connection) error {
    reader := connection.Reader()
    bts, err := reader.Next(reader.Len())
    if err != nil {
        log.Println("error reading data")
        return err
    }
    log.Println(fmt.Sprintf("Data: %s", string(bts)))

    connection.Write([]byte("-> " + string(bts)))
    return connection.Writer().Flush()
}
```

You can see that the code written using the netpoll library is easier to read than the code that you looked at in the previous section. A lot of the heavy lifting is performed by the library; it also provides more features and stability when writing high-performance networking code. Let's take a look at how netpoll works behind the scenes. Figure 12-3 shows at a high level the different components of netpoll.

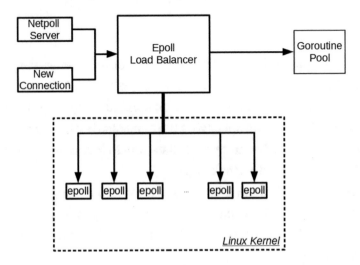

Figure 12-3. *netpoll high-level architecture*

The library creates more than one epoll and it uses the number of CPUs as the total number of epolls it will create. Internally, it uses a load balancing strategy to decide which epoll a file descriptor will be registered to.

The library will register to the epoll when it receives a new connection or when the netpoll server runs for the first time, and it decides which epoll to use by using either a random or round-robin load balance mechanism, as shown in Figure 12-4. The load balancer type can be modified in an app using the following function call:

```
netpoll.SetLoadBalance(netpoll.Random)
netpoll.SetLoadBalance(netpoll.RoundRobin)
```

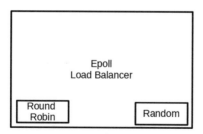

Figure 12-4. *netpoll load balancer*

The library takes care of a high volume of traffic by using goroutines. This is performed internally by utilizing a pool of goroutine pooling mechanisms. Developers just need to focus to ensure that their application and infrastructure can scale properly.

Summary

In this chapter, you looked at different ways of writing applications using epoll. Using your previous learning from Chapter 2 about system calls, you build an epoll-based application using the standard library. You learned that designing and writing epoll network applications is different from normal networking applications. You dove into an epoll library and learned how to use it to write a network application. Also, you looked at how the library works internally.

PART V

Securing Linux

CHAPTER 13

Vulnerability Scanner

The proliferation of cloud providers enables organizations to deploy applications that are affordable at scale. Deploying applications at scale is one thing, but securing applications and resources is another thing and this has become a headache for organizations everywhere. Security is a big topic, and it covers a lot of different aspects. In this chapter, you will look at one of the tools that helped in identifying vulnerabilities in the infrastructure.

You are going to look at a tool for detecting vulnerabilities inside Linux. The primary focus of the chapter is to understand how and where to use this tool and also to take a closer look at the source code to understand better how the tool works. In this chapter, you will learn

- How a vulnerability scanner works

- How the tool uses a different technology to achieve its objectives

- About port scans, command line executions, and databases using SQLite in Go

Source Code

The source code for this chapter is available from the `https://github.com/Apress/Software-Development-Go` repository.

© Nanik Tolaram 2023
N. Tolaram, *Software Development with Go*,
https://doi.org/10.1007/978-1-4842-8731-6_13

Vulnerability Scanners

Vulnerability scanners are tools that are used to search and report for known vulnerabilities that exist in your IT infrastructure. Every organization has an IT infrastructure that it manages in-house or in the cloud. In this infrastructure is a variety of applications, networks, and other things running, which requires constant supervision when it comes to security. Every day we read news of new vulnerabilities uncovered or exploited that can cause damage to organizations and sometimes to an extended community.

Tools like vulnerability scanners use a lot of interesting technology stacks that are useful to learn from, and this is the intention of this chapter. You will look at an open source project named Vuls (`https://github.com/future-architect/vuls`), which is written in Go, and look at how it implements some of the functionality it provides in Go. The objective is to apply this knowledge in your own project or use it as a knowledge base to understand how this kind of tool works. Please remember that this chapter is by no means a go-to chapter for installing or using Vuls or for vulnerability scanners.

The reason for choosing Vuls for this chapter is the fact that the project is heavily maintained and updated by the community and it has a high star rating. The project uses a database of information from different sources rather than relying on its own source, making it up to date in terms of detecting vulnerabilities.

Some of the key features that Vuls provides are

- Support for scanning vulnerabilities for major Linux/ FreeBSD operating systems

- Can be used to scan cloud infrastructures like Amazon, Google, and more

- Uses multiple vulnerability databases. One of the databases it uses is the National Vulnerability Database from NIST (U.S. National Institute of Standards and Technology).

- Ability to do quick, deep, or other kinds of scanning depending on the need

- Notifications via email or slack channel

In the next section, you will download the source code, compile it, and use it to understand how it works.

Using Vuls

In this section, you will explore Vuls and do the following:

- Check out the code

- Run a scan on a local machine

Checking Out the Code

Vuls requires Go 1.8, so make sure you have it installed before proceeding further. The easiest way to check out code is to use the go get command as in the following:

```
GO111MODULE=off go get github.com/future-architect/vuls
```

Make sure you have your GOPATH directory set up to the correct folder where you want to store your Go modules (in my case, my GOPATH points to /home/nanik/Gopath). Once the command has successfully run, it downloads the source code inside the src/github.com/future-architect/vuls directory inside GOPATH, like so:

```
...
drwxrwxr-x  2 nanik nanik   4096 Jun 26 15:48 detector
-rw-rw-r--  1 nanik nanik    596 Jun 26 15:48 Dockerfile
-rw-rw-r--  1 nanik nanik     55 Jun 26 15:48 .dockerignore
...
```

```
drwxrwxr-x  2 nanik nanik  4096 Jun 26 15:48 saas
drwxrwxr-x  2 nanik nanik  4096 Jun 26 15:48 scanner
-rw-rw-r--  1 nanik nanik   137 Jun 26 15:48 SECURITY.md
drwxrwxr-x  2 nanik nanik  4096 Jun 26 15:48 server
drwxrwxr-x  3 nanik nanik  4096 Jun 26 15:48 setup
drwxrwxr-x  2 nanik nanik  4096 Jun 26 15:48 subcmds
drwxrwxr-x  2 nanik nanik  4096 Jun 26 15:48 tui
drwxrwxr-x  2 nanik nanik  4096 Jun 26 15:48 util
```

The discussion in this chapter focuses on the v0.19.7 version, so you need to switch to a different branch. Change to the GOPATH directory to the src/github.com/future-architect/vuls directory and change the branch as follows:

```
git checkout v0.19.7
```

The code is all set and ready to be built. Use the make command to build it.

```
make build
```

The compilation process starts and all the related modules are downloaded. Once compilation completes, you get an executable file called Vuls. Run the application as follows:

```
./vuls
```

You will get output like the following:

```
Usage: vuls <flags> <subcommand> <subcommand args>

Subcommands:
        commands        list all command names
        flags           describe all known top-level flags
        help            describe subcommands and their syntax
```

```
Subcommands for configtest:
    configtest         Test configuration

Subcommands for discover:
    discover           Host discovery in the CIDR

Subcommands for history:
    history            List history of scanning.

Subcommands for report:
    report             Reporting

Subcommands for scan:
    scan               Scan vulnerabilities

Subcommands for server:
    server             Server

Subcommands for tui:
    tui                Run Tui view to analyze vulnerabilities

Use "vuls flags" for a list of top-level flags
```

Running Scan

Vuls require a configuration file in the `.toml` format. For this section, you can use the configuration file found inside the `chapter13` directory called `config.toml`, which is as follows:

```
[servers.localhost]
host = "localhost"
port = "local"
```

The configuration specifies the machine to be scanned. In your example, it's the localhost on your local machine. It performs the standard local mode scanning operation, which does not include port scanning as the one excluded service.

Run Vuls as follows:

```
./vuls scan --config <directory>/config.toml --debug --results-
dir <report_directory>
```

Vuls runs with the configuration specified with the –config parameter
and stores the report inside the directory specified by the –results-dir
parameter. You get verbose output that looks like the following:

```
[Jun 26 18:33:45]  INFO [localhost] vuls-v0.19.7-
build-20220626_181254_91ed318
[Jun 26 18:33:45]  INFO [localhost] Start scanning
[Jun 26 18:33:45]  INFO [localhost] config: /home/nanik/
Downloads/config.toml
[Jun 26 18:33:45] DEBUG [localhost] map[string]config.
ServerInfo{
  "localhost": config.ServerInfo{
    ServerName:         "localhost",
    User:               "",
...
    SSHConfigPath:      "",
    KeyPath:            "",
...
}
[Jun 26 18:33:45]  INFO [localhost] Validating config...
...
[Jun 26 18:33:45] DEBUG [localhost] execResult: servername:
  cmd: ls /etc/debian_version
  exitstatus: 0
  stdout: /etc/debian_version
...
[Jun 26 18:33:45] DEBUG [localhost] Executing... cat /etc/issue
[Jun 26 18:33:45] DEBUG [localhost] execResult: servername:
```

```
  cmd: cat /etc/issue
...
[Jun 26 18:33:45] DEBUG [localhost] Executing... lsb_
release -ir
...
  cmd: lsb_release -ir
  exitstatus: 0
...
[Jun 26 18:33:45] DEBUG [localhost] Executing... type curl
[Jun 26 18:33:45] DEBUG [localhost] execResult: servername:
  cmd: type curl
  exitstatus: 0
  stdout: curl is /usr/bin/curl
...
Scan Summary
================
localhost    pop22.04    2378 installed, 0 updatable
```

The scan reports generated by Vuls contain comprehensive information about the things that have been scanned or found. The report looks like the following:

```
{
    "jsonVersion": 4,
    "lang": "",
    "serverUUID": "",
    "serverName": "192-168-1-3",
    "family": "pop",
    "release": "22.04",
    ...
    "ipv4Addrs": [
        "192.168.1.3"
    ],
```

```
"ipv6Addrs": [
    ...
],
"scannedAt": "2022-06-26T18:40:16.045650086+10:00",
"scanMode": "fast mode",
"...
"scannedVia": "remote",
"scannedIpv4Addrs": [
    ...
],
"scannedIpv6Addrs": [
    ...
],
"reportedAt": "0001-01-01T00:00:00Z",
"reportedVersion": "",
"reportedRevision": "",
"reportedBy": "",
"errors": [],
...
    "release": "5.17.5-76051705-generic",
    "version": "",
    "rebootRequired": false
},
"packages": {
    ...
    }
},
"config": {
    "scan": {
        "debug": true,
        "logDir": "/var/log/vuls",
```

```
    "logJSON": false,
    "resultsDir": "/home/nanik/go/src/github.com/
    future-architect/vuls/result",
    "default": {},
    "servers": {
        "192-168-1-3": {

            ...

        }
    },
    "cveDict": {

        ...

    },
    "ovalDict": {

        ...

    },
    ...
},
"report": {
    "logJSON": false,

    ...

}
    }
}
```

In the next section, you will explore some of the features provided by Vuls.

Learning From Vuls

There are many features in Vuls that are useful to learn and can be applied when developing systems or security applications. You will look at three main features that Vuls uses: port scanning, using a SQLite database, and executing on the command line from the Go application. These features will be discussed in depth in the following sections

Port Scan

A port scan is a way to perform an operation to determine which ports are open in a network. A ports is like a number that is picked by an application to listen to. For example, HTTP servers listen to port 80 while FTP servers listen to port 21. A list of standard port numbers that are followed in different operating system can be seen at www.iana.org/assignments/service-names-port-numbers/service-names-port-numbers.xhtml.

Looking at Vuls source code (scanner/base.go), you can see the following function that performs a network scan:

```
package scanner

import (
  ...
  nmap "github.com/Ullaakut/nmap/v2"
)

func (l *base) execExternalPortScan(scanDestIPPorts map[string]
[]string) ([]string, error) {
  ...
  baseCmd := formatNmapOptionsToString(portScanConf)

  listenIPPorts := []string{}

  for ip, ports := range scanDestIPPorts {
```

```
    ...
    scanner, err := nmap.NewScanner(nmap.
    WithBinaryPath(portScanConf.ScannerBinPath))
    ...
  return listenIPPorts, nil
}
```

The code uses the open source nmap library from github.com/ Ullaakut/nmap to perform the scanning operation. Before getting into the details on how nmap is performed in the library, let's get an understanding of what nmap is first. The tool nmap is a command-line tool that is used for network exploration and security auditing. It is used for gathering real-time information about the network, detecting which ports are open in a network environment, checking which IP addresses are activated in the network, and more.

Make sure you have the nmap tool install on your local machine. If you are using a Debian-based Linux distro, use the following command to install it:

```
sudo apt install nmap
```

Run nmap to check if you can run it successfully.

```
nmap
```

You get output that looks like the following:

```
Nmap 7.80 ( https://nmap.org )
Usage: nmap [Scan Type(s)] [Options] {target specification}
TARGET SPECIFICATION:
  ...
HOST DISCOVERY:
  ...
SCAN TECHNIQUES:
```

...

```
EXAMPLES:
  nmap -v -A scanme.nmap.org
  nmap -v -sn 192.168.0.0/16 10.0.0.0/8
  nmap -v -iR 10000 -Pn -p 80
```

Let's take a look at the sample code that is provided inside the chapter13/nmap directory and run it as follows:

```
go run main.go
```

The application runs and scans your local machine for an open port. In my machine, the output looks like the following:

```
Host "127.0.0.1":
        Port 22/tcp open ssh
        Port 631/tcp open ipp
        Port 5432/tcp open postgresql
Nmap done: 1 hosts up scanned in 0.020000 seconds
```

The code detects three open ports, which are related to the ssh, ipp, and postgresql applications. You will get different results depending on what ports are open on your local machine.

The code snippet that uses the nmap library is as follows:

```
package main

import (
  ...

  "github.com/Ullaakut/nmap/v2"
)

func main() {
  ...
```

```
scanner, err := nmap.NewScanner(
    nmap.WithTargets("localhost"),
    nmap.WithContext(ctx),
)
...
}
```

The sample code initializes the library by calling nmap.NewScanner(..).
Inside the function, the initialization code checks to ensure that the nmap
tool is installed, as shown in the following code snippet:

```
func NewScanner(options ...Option) (*Scanner, error) {
    ...

    if scanner.binaryPath == "" {
        var err error
        scanner.binaryPath, err = exec.LookPath("nmap")
        if err != nil {
            return nil, ErrNmapNotInstalled
        }
    }

    ...

    return scanner, nil
}
```

The function uses the Go os/exec package to check for the existence
of the nmap tool. Once the library has been initialized successfully, it calls
the Run() function to perform the scan operation.

```
package main

import (
    ...
    "github.com/Ullaakut/nmap/v2"
```

```
)

func main() {
    ...

  result, warnings, err := scanner.Run()

    ...
  }

  ...
}
```

The library Run() function performs the following tasks:

- Executes the nmap tool with the provided parameters

- Executes the go routine to wait for the result from the nmap tool that will be parsed and converted into a struct that will be returned to the caller

The variable result is of type Run struct and is declared as follows in the library:

```
type Run struct {
  XMLName xml.Name `xml:"nmaprun"`

  Args          string        `xml:"args,attr" json:"args"`
  ProfileName   string        `xml:"profile_name,attr"
                               json:"profile_name"`
  Scanner       string        `xml:"scanner,attr"
                               json:"scanner"`
  StartStr      string        `xml:"startstr,attr"
                               json:"start_str"`
  Version       string        `xml:"version,attr"
                               json:"version"`
```

```
XMLOutputVersion string          `xml:"xmloutputversion,attr"
                                  json:"xml_output_version"`
Debugging        Debugging       `xml:"debugging" json:"debugging"`
Stats            Stats           `xml:"runstats" json:"run_stats"`
ScanInfo         ScanInfo        `xml:"scaninfo" json:"scan_info"`
Start            Timestamp       `xml:"start,attr" json:"start"`
Verbose          Verbose         `xml:"verbose" json:"verbose"`
Hosts            []Host           `xml:"host" json:"hosts"`
PostScripts      []Script         `xml:"postscript>script"
                                  json:"post_scripts"`
PreScripts       []Script         `xml:"prescript>script"
                                  json:"pre_scripts"`
Targets          []Target         `xml:"target" json:"targets"`
TaskBegin        []Task           `xml:"taskbegin"
                                  json:"task_begin"`
TaskProgress     []TaskProgress `xml:"taskprogress"
                                  json:"task_progress"`
TaskEnd          []Task           `xml:"taskend"
                                  json:"task_end"`

NmapErrors []string
rawXML     []byte
}
```

The raw output from nmap, the library in the XML format, looks like the following:

```
<?xml version="1.0" encoding="UTF-8"?>
<!DOCTYPE nmaprun>
<?xml-stylesheet href="file:///usr/bin/../share/nmap/nmap.xsl"
type="text/xsl"?>
<!-- Nmap 7.80 scan initiated Sun Jun 26 20:39:01 2022 as: /
usr/bin/nmap -oX - localhost -->
```

```
<nmaprun scanner="nmap" args="/usr/bin/nmap -oX - localhost"
start="1656239941" startstr="Sun Jun 26 20:39:01 2022"
version="7.80" xmloutputversion="1.04">
  <scaninfo type="syn" protocol="tcp" numservices="1000"
services="...,61532,61900,62078,63331,64623,64680,
65000,65129,65389"/>
  <verbose level="0"/>
  <debugging level="0"/>
  <host starttime="1656239941" endtime="1656239941">
    <status state="up" reason="localhost-response" reason_
    ttl="0"/>
    <address addr="127.0.0.1" addrtype="ipv4"/>
    <hostnames>
      <hostname name="localhost" type="user"/>
      <hostname name="localhost" type="PTR"/>
    </hostnames>
    <ports>
      ...
    </ports>
    <times srtt="3" rttvar="0" to="100000"/>
  </host>
  <runstats>
    <finished time="1656239941" timestr="Sun Jun 26 20:39:01
    2022" elapsed="0.12"
    summary="Nmap done at Sun Jun 26 20:39:01 2022;
    1 IP address (1 host up) scanned in 0.12 seconds"
    exit="success"/>
    <hosts up="1" down="0" total="1"/>
  </runstats>
</nmaprun>
```

Exec

The next feature that is used quite often inside Vuls is executing an external tool to perform some operation as part of the scanning process. The following are some of the commands that Vuls uses for getting network IP information, getting kernel information, updating the index of package manager, and many others.

apk update	Downloads the updated package index from repositories
/sbin/ip -o addr	Lists network devices, routing, and other network-related information
uname -r	Prints out system information
stat /proc/1/exe	Gets information about PID 1
systemctl status	Lists information that is registered with system

The commands used are different for different operating systems, but the way it is run is the same using the os/exec package.

Take a look at the sample app that is inside the chapter13/exec folder and run the sample in your terminal as follows:

```
go run main.go
```

You get output that looks like the following:

```
2022/06/26 21:18:28 --------------
2022/06/26 21:18:28 Running ip link
2022/06/26 21:18:28 -------------
2022/06/26 21:18:28 1: lo: <LOOPBACK,UP,LOWER_UP> mtu 65536
qdisc noqueue state UNKNOWN mode DEFAULT group default
qlen 1000
    link/loopback 00:00:00:00:00:00 brd 00:00:00:00:00:00
...
2022/06/26 21:18:28
```

```
2022/06/26 21:18:28 ----------------
2022/06/26 21:18:28 Running noexist
2022/06/26 21:18:28 ----------------
2022/06/26 21:18:28 %v exit status 127
2022/06/26 21:18:28 Running uname -r
2022/06/26 21:18:28 ----------------
2022/06/26 21:18:28 5.17.5-76051705-generic
```

The sample app uses the os/exec package to execute commands and print the output to the console. The following code snippet shows the function that uses the os/exec package:

```go
package main

import (
  ..
  ex "os/exec"
)

func main() {
  ...
  Run("ip link")
  ...
  Run("noexist")
  ...
  Run("uname -r")
}

func Run(arg string) {
  var cmd *ex.Cmd
  cmd = ex.Command("/bin/sh", "-c", arg)
  ...
}
```

The Run(..) function is called with a string parameter, which is added to the parameter when calling the Command(..) function. The sample runs the argument passed into the Run(..) function as part of the /bin/sh command tool. For example, when the Run("ip link") is called, it runs it as follows:

```
/bin/sh -c ip link
```

The app specifies that the output is stored into the variable because it will be printed out into the console:

```
func Run(arg string) {
    ...
    cmd.Stdout = &stdoutBuf
    cmd.Stderr = &stderrBuf
    log.Println(stdoutBuf.String())
    log.Println(stderrBuf.String())
}
```

SQLite

In this section, you will learn how to use SQLite databases. In particular, you will learn how to use the sqlite3 library to read and write databases.

SQLite is a lightweight and self-contained SQL database that allows applications to read and store information. Applications use normal SQL syntax to perform different kinds of data manipulation such as inserting, updating, and deleting data. The lightweight and portable nature of SQLite makes it an attractive proposition to use in a project that doesn't require a centralized database. Mobile phones such as Android use SQLite databases that applications can use for their mobile apps.

Internally, Vuls uses SQLite extensively for storing data that it downloads from different sources. You will look at sample applications using SQLite. Sample code for this section can be found inside the chapter13/sqlite directory. Let's run the sample application as follows from your terminal:

```
go run main.go
```

You get output that looks like the following:

```
2022/06/27 19:40:04 Initialize database -  local.db
2022/06/27 19:40:04 Creating table in -   local.db
2022/06/27 19:40:04 Inserting data into -  local.db
Reading Table:
2022/06/27 19:40:04 Total rows read -  [{0 CAD} {1 AUD} {2
AUD} {3 GBP} {4 CAD} {5 EUR} {6 USD} {7 USD} {8 CAD} {9 USD}
{10 GBP} {11 CAD} {12 AUD} {13 GBP} {14 EUR} {15 GBP} {16 CAD}
{17 USD} {18 AUD} {19 CAD} {20 USD} {21 CAD} {22 EUR} {23 EUR}
{24 AUD}]
```

The sample code creates a new database called local.db and creates a new table called currencies. It also inserts a little data into it and prints out the newly inserted data into the console.

The following snippet shows the code that initialize the database:

```
package main

import (
  ...
  _ "github.com/mattn/go-sqlite3"
  ...
)

...

func main() {
  ...
  dbHandle = InitDB(dbname)
  ...
}
```

```go
// InitDB initialize database
func InitDB(filepath string) *sql.DB {
  db, err := sql.Open("sqlite3", filepath)
  if err != nil {
    panic(err)
  }
  return db
}
```

The InitDB function creates the new database using sql.Open, passing in sqlite3 as the parameter. The sqlite3 parameter is used as a reference by the database/sql module to look up the appropriate driver for this. If successful, it will return the sql.DB struct stored inside the db variable

The sql.DB struct is declared in the database/sql module as follows:

```go
type DB struct {
  ...
  connector driver.Connector
  ...
  closed            bool
  ...
  stop func()
}
```

Once the database has been created successfully, the code creates a table called currencies, which is performed by the following InitTable(..) function:

```go
...

func InitTable(db *sql.DB) {
  q := `
```

```
  CREATE TABLE IF NOT EXISTS currencies(
      Id TEXT NOT NULL PRIMARY KEY,
      Name TEXT,
      InsertedDatetime DATETIME
  );`

  _, err := db.Exec(q)
  if err != nil {
      log.Fatal(err)
  }
}
```

The function executes the CREATE TABLE.. SQL command using the db.Exec(..) function. The function db.Exec(..) is used to execute the query against a database without returning any rows. The returned value is of type Result, which is not used in the InitTable(..) function. The Result struct is declared as follows in the database/sql module:

```
type Result interface {
  LastInsertId() (int64, error)
  RowsAffected() (int64, error)
}
```

After successfully creating the table, the code then proceeds to inserting data. There are two parts to this operation. The first part is to prepare the data to be inserted, which is shown in the following code snippet:

```
func main() {
  ...
  records := []Record{}

  for i := 0; i < 25; i++ {
      r := (rand.Intn(len(curNames)-0) + 0)
```

```
    d := strconv.Itoa(i)
    rec := Record{Id: d, Name: curNames[r]}
    records = append(records, rec)
  }
  ...
}
```

The code creates an array of the Record struct and populates it, where the populated array is passed in as a parameter to the InsertData(..) function as follows:

```
func InsertData(db *sql.DB, records []Record) {
  q := `
  INSERT OR REPLACE INTO currencies(
      Id,
      Name,
      InsertedDatetime
  ) values(?, ?,  CURRENT_TIMESTAMP)`

  stmt, err := db.Prepare(q)
  ...
  defer stmt.Close()

  for _, r := range records {
      _, err := stmt.Exec(r.Id, r.Name)
      ...
  }
}
```

The function uses the INSERT INTO statement, which is used inside
the Prepare(..) function. This function is used to create prepared
statements that can be executed in isolation later. The SQL statement uses
a parameter placeholder for the values (the placeholder is marked by the
? symbol), which are included as part of the parameter when executing
using the Exec(..) function. The value is obtained from the Id and Name of
the Record struct.

Now that the data has been inserted into the table, the code completes
the execution by reading the data from the table and printing it out to the
console as follows:

```
func ReadData(db *sql.DB) []Record {
  q := `
  SELECT Id, Name  FROM currencies
  ORDER BY datetime(InsertedDatetime) DESC`

  rows, err := db.Query(q)
  ...

  var records []Record
  for rows.Next() {
     item := Record{}
     err := rows.Scan(&item.Id, &item.Name)
     ...
     records = append(records, item)
  }
  return records
}
```

The function ReadData(..) uses the SELECT SQL statement to read
the fields from the table with the result sorted by the InsertedDateTime
field in ascending order. The code uses the Query(..) function, returning
the Rows struct and looping through it. Inside the loop, the code uses the

Scan(..) function to copy fields from each row and read into the values passed in the parameter. In the code example, the fields are read into item.Id and item.Name.

The number of parameters passed to Scan(..) must match with the number of fields read from the table. The Rows struct that is returned when using the Query(..) function is defined inside the database/sql module.

```
type Rows struct {
    dc          *driverConn
    releaseConn func(error)
    ...
    closemu sync.RWMutex
    closed  bool
    lasterr error
    ...
}
```

Summary

In this chapter, you looked at an open source security project called Vuls, which provides vulnerability scanning capability. You learned about Vuls by checking out the code and performing a scan operation on your local machine.

Vuls provides a lot of functionality. In learning how Vuls works, you learned about port scanning, executing external command-line applications from Go, and writing code that performs database operations using SQLite.

CHAPTER 14

CrowdSec

In this chapter, you will look at an open source security tool called CrowdSec (`https://github.com/crowdsecurity/crowdsec`). There are few reasons why this tool is interesting to study:

- It uses crowd-sourced data to collect IP information across the globe, which is shared with the community.

- It offers code designs that are useful to look at and learn from

- The GeoIP database is interesting on its own.

The chapter is broken down into the installation part and the learning part. In the installation part, you will look at installing CrowdSec to understand how it works. In the learning section, you will look deeply into how CrowdSec implements something that you can learn from by looking at sample code.

Source Code

The source code for this chapter is available from the `https://github.com/Apress/Software-Development-Go` repository.

© Nanik Tolaram 2023
N. Tolaram, *Software Development with Go*,
https://doi.org/10.1007/978-1-4842-8731-6_14

CrowdSec Project

The documentation at `https://doc.crowdsec.net/docs/intro` explain it nicely:

CrowdSec is an open-source and lightweight software that allows you to detect peers with malevolent behaviors and block them from accessing your systems at various levels (infrastructural, system, applicative).

CrowdSec, as an open source security tool, provides quite a number of features that sit nicely in a cloud environment. The thing that is intriguing about the tool is the data that is collected by the community. This crowd-sourced data allows CrowdSec to determine whether a certain IP address has to be banned or should be allowed into your infrastructure.

There are many architectures and code designs that you are going to learn from the project, which you will explore more in the "Learning From CrowdSec" section.

Using CrowdSec

I will not go through the complete installation process of CrowdSec. Rather, I will cover the steps of a bare minimum installation that will allow you to understand what you need for the section "Learning From CrowdSec." The objective of this installation is to get to a point to see the community data that is collected by a central server replicated to a local database.

Create an empty directory to do the following steps. In my local installation, I created a new directory under `/home/nanik/GolandPojects/crowdsec`. Follow these steps:

- Download the release from GitHub. For this section, use v1.4.1 for Linux, downloading it using the following command:

```
wget https://github.com/crowdsecurity/crowdsec/
releases/download/v1.4.1/crowdsec-release.tgz
```

- Once downloaded, use `gunzip` and `tar` to unzip as follows:

```
gunzip ./crowdsec-release.tgz && tar -xvf crowdsec-
release.tar
```

- A new directory named `crowdsec-v1.4.1` will be created, as shown:

```
└── crowdsec-v1.4.1
    ├── cmd
    ├── config
    ├── plugins
    ├── test_env.ps1
    ├── test_env.sh
    └── wizard.sh
```

- Change your directory to `crowdsec-v1.4.1` and run the `test_env.sh` command.

```
./test_env.sh
```

Let the script run. It will take a bit of time because it's downloading a few things. You will see output that looks like the following:

```
[07/27/2022:03:50:14 PM][INFO] Creating test arboresence in
/home/nanik/GolandProjects/crowdsec/crowdsec-v1.4.1/tests
[07/27/2022:03:50:14 PM][INFO] Arboresence created
```

```
[07/27/2022:03:50:14 PM][INFO] Copying needed files for tests
environment
[07/27/2022:03:50:15 PM][INFO] Files copied
...
INFO[27-07-2022 03:50:15 PM] Machine 'test' successfully added
to the local API
INFO[27-07-2022 03:50:15 PM] API credentials dumped to '/home/
nanik/GolandProjects/crowdsec/crowdsec-v1.4.1/tests/config/
local_api_credentials.yaml'
INFO[27-07-2022 03:50:15 PM] Wrote new 438269 bytes index to
/home/nanik/GolandProjects/crowdsec/crowdsec-v1.4.1/tests/
config/hub/.index.json
INFO[27-07-2022 03:50:16 PM] crowdsecurity/syslog-logs : OK
INFO[27-07-2022 03:50:16 PM] Enabled parsers : crowdsecurity/
syslog-logs
INFO[27-07-2022 03:50:16 PM] crowdsecurity/geoip-enrich : OK
INFO[27-07-2022 03:50:16 PM] downloading data 'https://
crowdsec-statics-assets.s3-eu-west-1.amazonaws.com/
GeoLite2-City.mmdb' in '/home/nanik/GolandProjects/crowdsec/
crowdsec-v1.4.1/tests/data/GeoLite2-City.mmdb'
INFO[27-07-2022 03:51:25 PM] downloading data 'https://
crowdsec-statics-assets.s3-eu-west-1.amazonaws.com/
GeoLite2-ASN.mmdb' in '/home/nanik/GolandProjects/crowdsec/
crowdsec-v1.4.1/tests/data/GeoLite2-ASN.mmdb'
INFO[27-07-2022 03:51:41 PM] Enabled parsers : crowdsecurity/
geoip-enrich
INFO[27-07-2022 03:51:41 PM] crowdsecurity/dateparse-
enrich : OK
INFO[27-07-2022 03:51:41 PM] Enabled parsers : crowdsecurity/
dateparse-enrich
...
```

The script creates a new directory called tests containing a complete test environment for CrowdSec. The directory will look like the following:

```
nanik@nanik:~/GolandProjects/crowdsec/crowdsec-v1.4.1$ tree -L
2 ./tests/
./tests/
├── config
│   ├── acquis.yaml
│   ├── collections
│   ├── crowdsec-cli
│   ├── hub
...
│   ├── scenarios
│   └── simulation.yaml
├── crowdsec
├── cscli
├── data
│   ├── crowdsec.db
│   ├── GeoLite2-ASN.mmdb
│   └── GeoLite2-City.mmdb
├── dev.yaml
├── logs
└── plugins
    ├── notification-email
...
    └── notification-splunk
```

The directory contains a variety of files including the CrowdSec command line tools crowdsec and cscli along with a folder called data that you will look at in the next section in more detail. The database with extension .mmdb is the database that you will look at in detail in the "GeoIP Database" section.

crowdsec.db

CrowdSec stores data inside a SQLite database called crowdsec.db. The database contains a number of tables, shown in Figure 14-1.

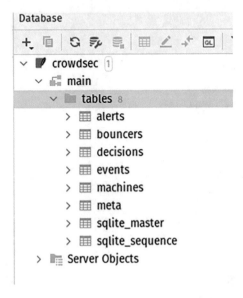

Figure 14-1. *CrowdSec database*

The test environment does not populate any data when the database is created, so you need to set up your environment so that it will sync from a central server. To do this, you need to register first with the CrowdSec server using the cscli tool, as outlined in the doc at https://docs. crowdsec.net/docs/cscli/cscli_capi_register/. Open terminal and change to the tests directory, and execute the following command:

```
./cscli capi register -c ./dev.yaml
```

You will get output like the following:

```
WARN[27-07-2022 04:10:11 PM] can't load CAPI credentials from
'./config/online_api_credentials.yaml' (missing field)
```

```
INFO[27-07-2022 04:10:11 PM] push and pull to Central API
disabled
INFO[27-07-2022 04:10:13 PM] Successfully registered to Central
API (CAPI)
INFO[27-07-2022 04:10:13 PM] Central API credentials dumped to
'./config/online_api_credentials.yaml'
...
```

Using the cscli command tool, you must register to a central server. online_api_credentials.yaml is populated with the registration details, which look like the following:

```
url: https://api.crowdsec.net/
login: <login_details>
password: <password>
```

You are now ready to populate your database with the central server. Use the following command:

```
./crowdsec -c ./dev.yaml
```

You will see output that looks like the following:

```
...
INFO[27-07-2022 16:16:45] Crowdsec v1.4.1-linux-e1954adc325ba
a9e3420c324caabd50b7074dd77
WARN[27-07-2022 16:16:45] prometheus is enabled, but the listen
address is empty, using '127.0.0.1'
WARN[27-07-2022 16:16:45] prometheus is enabled, but the listen
port is empty, using '6060'
INFO[27-07-2022 16:16:45] Loading prometheus collectors
INFO[27-07-2022 16:16:45] Loading CAPI pusher
INFO[27-07-2022 16:16:45] CrowdSec Local API listening on
127.0.0.1:8081
```

```
INFO[27-07-2022 16:16:45] Start push to CrowdSec Central API
(interval: 30s)
INFO[27-07-2022 16:16:45] Start pull from CrowdSec Central API
(interval: 2h0m0s)
INFO[27-07-2022 16:16:45] Loading grok library /home/nanik/
GolandProjects/crowdsec/crowdsec-v1.4.1/tests/config/patterns
INFO[27-07-2022 16:16:46] Loading enrich plugins
INFO[27-07-2022 16:16:46] Successfully registered enricher
'GeoIpCity'
...
INFO[27-07-2022 16:16:46] Loading parsers from 4 files
...
INFO[27-07-2022 16:16:47] capi metrics: metrics sent
successfully
INFO[27-07-2022 16:16:47] Start send metrics to CrowdSec
Central API (interval: 30m0s)
INFO[27-07-2022 16:16:54] capi/community-blocklist : 0 explicit
deletions
INFO[27-07-2022 16:17:15] crowdsecurity/community-blocklist :
added 8761 entries, deleted 0 entries (alert:1)
```

Notice the last log message that says **added 8761 entries**, which means that it has added 8761 entries into your database. If you are not getting this message, rerun the crowdsec command.

Looking into the decisions table, you will the populated data, as shown in Figure 14-2

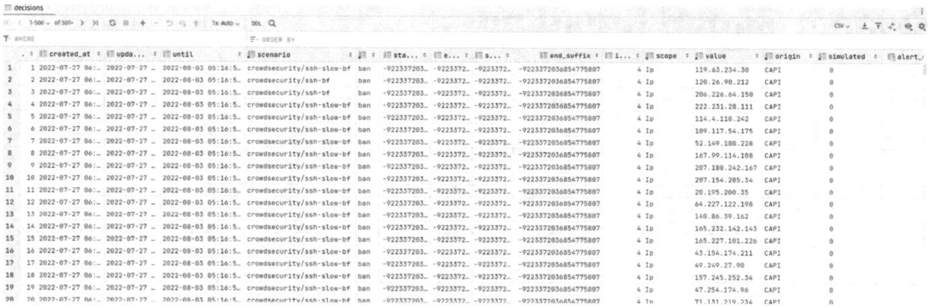

Figure 14-2. Data inside the decisions table

The table contains interesting information:

- IP addresses that are banned

- Date until when a particular IP is banned

- Scenarios when an IP address is detected

You have learned briefly how to set up CrowdSec and you have seen the data it uses. In the next section, you will look at parts of CrowdSec that are interesting. You will look at how certain things are implemented inside CrowdSec and then look at a simpler code sample of how to do it.

Learning From CrowdSec

CrowdSec as a project is quite complex and it contains a lot of different things that are very interesting to learn from. In this section, you will pick up a few topics that are used inside CrowdSec that are useful to learn. These topics can also be applied when designing your own software with Go.

System Signal Handling

As a system, CrowdSec provides an extensive list of features that are broken down into several different modules. The reason for features to be broken down into modules is to make it easy for development, maintenance, and testing. When building a system, one of the key things to remember is to make sure all the different modules can be gracefully terminated and all resources such as memory, network connections, and disk space are released. To make sure that different parts of the system shut down properly, you need some sort of coordinated communication to understand when modules need to prepare for the shutdown process.

Imagine a scenario where you are designing an application and it is terminated by the operating system because of some resource constraint. The application must be aware of this and have the capability to shut down all the different modules independently before shutting itself down permanently. You will look at an example on how this is done using the code sample in the chapter14/signalhandler folder.

Open your terminal and run the sample as follows:

```
go run main.go
```

The application will keep on running, printing out loop messages on the terminal until you stop it by hitting Ctrl+C to stop. Then it will print out the following:

```
2022/07/24 22:31:32 loop1000Times -  0
2022/07/24 22:31:32 loop100Times -  0
2022/07/24 22:31:32 loop100Times -  1
...
2022/07/24 22:31:32 loop1000Times -  14
2022/07/24 22:31:33 loop1000Times -  15
2022/07/24 22:31:33 loop100Times -  15
^C2022/07/24 22:31:33 SIGTERM received
```

```
2022/07/24 22:31:33 loop1000Times - quit
2022/07/24 22:31:33 loop100Times - quit
2022/07/24 22:31:33 Complete!
```

The application successfully shuts down gracefully because the Ctrl+C key combo is detected. Before going through the code, Figure 14-3 shows the app design. Use Figure 14-3 as guidance when you walk through the sample code.

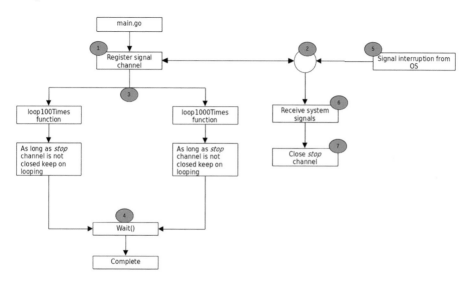

Figure 14-3. *CrowdSec system signal handling*

The following code snippet shows the registration of system interruption events using Go's built-in os/signal package (step 1). The function signal.Notify(..) is called, passing in the signals that will be registered to listen to. In the sample code, you register SIGHUP, SIGTERM, and SIGINT.

```
func main() {
  signalChan := make(chan os.Signal, 1)
  signal.Notify(signalChan,
    syscall.SIGHUP,
```

```
    syscall.SIGTERM,
    syscall.SIGINT)
  ...
  go func() {
    for {
        s := <-signalChan
        switch s {
        case syscall.SIGHUP, syscall.SIGINT, syscall.SIGTERM:
  ...
        }
    }
  }()
  ...
}
```

The following explains the meaning of the signals:

- SIGHUP: The operating system sends this signal when the terminal used to execute the application is disconnected, closed, or broken.

- SIGTERM: This is a generic signal that is used by the operating system to signal terminating a process or application.

- SIGINT: This is also referred to as a program interrupt and this signal occurs when the Ctrl+C combination is detected.

The code listens to all these signals to ensure that if any of them are detected, it will do its job to shut itself down properly.

The signalChan variable is a channel that accepts os.Signal and it is passed as parameter when calling signal.Notify(). The goroutine takes care of handling the signal received from the library in a for{} loop (step 2). Receiving a signal (step 6) means that there is an interruption, so the code must take the necessary steps to start the shutdown process (step 7).

Now that the code is ready to receive the system event and it knows what it is supposed to when it receives it, let's take a look at how other modules/goroutines are informed about this. The sample code spawns two goroutines, as shown here:

```
func main() {
    ...

    wg.Add(2)
    go loop100Times(stop, &wg)
    go loop1000Times(stop, &wg)

    wg.Wait()
    log.Println("Complete!")
}
```

loop100Times and loop1000Times are called as goroutines (step 3) and are passed two parameters, stop and wg. The stop variable is a channel variable that is used by the goroutine function to know when it needs to stop processing. The following code snippet shows the code that closes the stop channel:

```
func main() {
    ...
    go func() {
        for {
            ...
            switch s {
            case syscall.SIGHUP, syscall.SIGINT, syscall.SIGTERM:
                ...
                close(stop)
                ...
```

```
        }
     }
  }()

  ...
}
```

The close(stop) function closes the channel, and any part of the application that is checking for this channel will detect there is activity happening on the channel and will act on it. The checking of the stop channel can be seen in the following code snippet:

```
func loop100Times(stop <-chan string, wg *sync.WaitGroup) {
  ...
  for {
     select {
     case <-stop:
        log.Println("loop100Times - quit")
        return
     default:
        ...
     }
  }
}
```

The loop100Times function runs inside a for{} loop where it checks the channel condition inside the select{} statement. To make it easy to understand, basically the for{ select {} } block of code translate to the following:

Keep on doing the for loop, and on every loop check do the following:

- Is there any value to read from the `stop` channel? if there is something, processes must stop.

- Otherwise, just print to the console and increment the counter.

The same logic is used inside the `loop1000Times` function, so it works exactly the same. Both functions will stop processing and will print the counter value to the terminal once the `stop` channel is closed. The application has achieved the state of shutting down itself gracefully by informing the different parts of the code that it is shutting down.

The last thing you are going to look at is the wait state (step 4). Now the different goroutines know when to shut down, but the application can only completely shut itself down *after* all the goroutines complete their processes. This is made possible by the use of `sync.WaitGroup`. The following code snippet shows the usage of `WaitGroup`:

```
package main

import (
  ...
)

func main() {
  ...
  var wg sync.WaitGroup
  ...
  wg.Add(2)
  go loop100Times(stop, &wg)
  go loop1000Times(stop, &wg)

  wg.Wait()
```

```go
  log.Println("Complete!")
}

func loop100Times(stop <-chan string, wg *sync.WaitGroup) {
  ...
  defer wg.Done()
  for {
    ...
  }
}

func loop1000Times(stop <-chan string, wg *sync.WaitGroup) {
  ...
  defer wg.Done()
  for {
    ...
  }
}
```

Handling Service Dependencies

Complex applications like CrowdSec have multiple services that run at
the same time or at scheduled times. In order for services to run properly,
there needs to be service coordination that takes care of the dependencies
between services.

Figure 14-4 shows how the service coordination is done inside
CrowdSec using the channel.

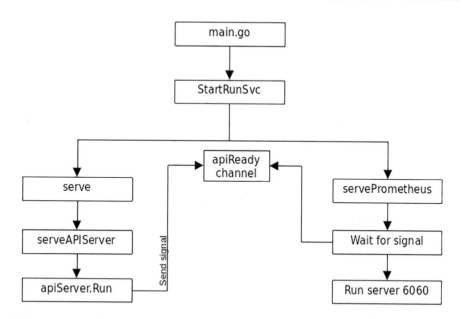

Figure 14-4. *Service coordination*

In Figure 14-4, the apiReady channel is the central part of the service coordination when CrowdSec starts up. The diagram shows that the apiServer.Run function sends a signal to the apiReady channel, which allows the other service, servePrometheus, to run the server listening on port 6060.

The following code snippet shows the StartRunSvc function running servePrometheus as a goroutine and passing in the apiReady channel, and it also pass the same channel when the Serve function is called:

```
package main

import (
    "os"

    ...
)
```

```go
func StartRunSvc() error {
  ...

  apiReady := make(chan bool, 1)
  agentReady := make(chan bool, 1)

  // Enable profiling early
  if cConfig.Prometheus != nil {
    ...
    go servePrometheus(cConfig.Prometheus, dbClient, apiReady,
    agentReady)
  }
  return Serve(cConfig, apiReady, agentReady)
}
```

The servePrometheus function starts running the server to listen on port 6060 only when it is able to read the value from the apiReady channel (<- apiReady), as shown in the following snippet:

```go
func servePrometheus(config *csconfig.PrometheusCfg, dbClient
*database.Client, apiReady chan bool, agentReady chan bool) {
  ...
  <-apiReady
  ...
  if err := http.ListenAndServe(fmt.Sprintf("%s:%d", config.
  ListenAddr, config.ListenPort), nil); err != nil {
    log.Warningf("prometheus: %s", err)
  }
}
```

The apiReady channel is set only when the CrowdSec API server has been run successfully, as shown in the following code snippet. The serveAPIServer function spawns off another goroutine when calling

the apiServer.Run(..) function, where it sends a value to the apiReady
channel where the API server starts up.

```
func serveAPIServer(apiServer *apiserver.APIServer, apiReady
chan bool) {
  apiTomb.Go(func() error {
    ...
    go func() {
      ...
      if err := apiServer.Run(apiReady); err != nil {
        log.Fatalf(err.Error())
      }
    }()

    ...
  })
}

func (s *APIServer) Run(apiReady chan bool) error {
  ...
  s.httpServerTomb.Go(func() error {
    go func() {
      apiReady <- true
      ...
    }()
    ...
  })

  return nil
}
```

Let's take a look at a simpler version of the service coordination, which
is in the chapter14/services folder. The sample code demonstrates
how to use service coordination between two different services, serviceA

and serviceB. Open up terminal and make sure you are in the correct chapter14/services directory and run the code as follows:

```
go run main.go
```

You will get output like the following:

```
2022/07/26 20:40:20 ....Starting serviceB
2022/07/26 20:40:21 ....Done with serviceB
2022/07/26 20:40:21 ..Starting serviceA
2022/07/26 20:40:23 ..Done with serviceA
```

Since the code is running inside a goroutine, the output sequence printed on your console will vary; however, the service will be run correctly. The following code shows the code that runs the service as a goroutine:

```
func main() {
  serviceBDone := make(chan bool, 1)
  alldone := make(chan bool, 1)

  go serviceB(serviceBDone)
  go serviceA(serviceBDone, alldone)

  <-alldone
}
```

There are two channels created by the sample app. Let's take a look the function of each channel:

- serviceBDone: This channel is used to inform that serviceB has done its job.

- alldone: This channel is used to inform that serviceA has done its job so the application can exit.

The following code snippet shows the `serviceA` and `serviceB` functions:

```go
func serviceB(serviceBDone chan bool) {
  ...
  serviceBDone <- true
  log.Println("....Done with serviceB")
}

//2nd service
func serviceA(serviceBDone chan bool, finish chan bool) {
  <-serviceBDone
  ...
  log.Println("..Done with serviceA")
  finish <- true
}
```

GeoIP Database

CrowdSec uses a GeoIP database that contains geographical information of an IP address. This database is downloaded as part of setting up the test environment discussed in the "Using CrowdSec" section.

In this section, you will look into this database and learn how to read the data from the database. One of the use cases for this database is the ability to build a security tool for your infrastructure to label each incoming IP, which is useful to monitor and understand the incoming traffic to your infrastructure. The GeoIP database comes from the following website: https://dev.maxmind.com/geoip/geolite2-free-geolocation-data?lang=en#databases. Have a read through the website to get an understanding of the licensing

The sample code is inside the `chapter14/geoip/city` folder, but before running it, you need to specify the location of the GeoIP database that the code will use. If you followed the "Using CrowdSec" section, you will have a database file called GeoLite2-City.mmdb database inside the data folder. Copy the location of the file to use it inside the snippet, as shown below. My file location is shown in the code snippet.

```
package main

...

func main() {
  db, err := maxminddb.Open("/home/nanik/GolandProjects/
  cloudprogramminggo/chapter14/geoip/city/GeoLite2-City.mmdb")
  ...
}
```

Once the file location has been specified, open terminal and run the sample as follows:

```
go run main.go
```

You will see output like the following:

```
IP : 2.0.0.0/17, Long : 2.338700, Lat : 48.858200, Country :
FR, Continent: EU
IP : 2.0.128.0/19, Long : -0.947200, Lat : 47.171600, Country :
FR, Continent: EU
...
IP : 2.0.192.0/18, Long : 2.338700, Lat : 48.858200, Country :
FR, Continent: EU
IP : 2.1.0.0/19, Long : 2.338700, Lat : 48.858200, Country :
FR, Continent: EU
IP : 2.1.32.0/19, Long : 2.302200, Lat : 44.858601, Country :
FR, Continent: EU
...
```

The code reads the database to get all IP addresses in the 2.0.0.0 IP range and prints all the IP addresses found in that range along with other country- and continent-related information. Let's go through the code and understand how it uses the database.

The data is stored in a single file, which is efficiently packed together, so in order to read the database, you must to use another library. Use the github.com/oschwald/maxminddb-golang library. The documentation of the library can be found at https://pkg.go.dev/github.com/oschwald/maxminddb-golang.

The library provides a function to convert the data into a struct. In the sample code, you create your own struct to represent the data that will be read.

```go
package main

...

type GeoCityRecord struct {
  Continent struct {
    Code       string                 `json:"code"`
    GeonameId  int                    `json:"geoname_id"`
    Names      map[string]interface{} `json:"names"`
  } `json:"continent"`
  Country struct {
    GeonameId  int                    `json:"geoname_id"`
    IsoCode    string                 `json:"iso_code"`
    Names      map[string]interface{} `json:"names"`
  } `json:"country"`
  Location struct {
    AccuracyRadius int     `json:"accuracy_radius"`
    Latitude       float32 `json:"latitude"`
    Longitude      float32 `json:"longitude"`
```

```
    TimeZone         string  `json:"time_zone"`
  } `json:"location"`
  RegisteredCountry struct {
    GeoNameID int                      `json:"geoname_id"`
    IsoCode   string                   `json:"iso_code"`
    Names     map[string]interface{} `json:"names"`
  } `json:"registered_country"`
}

func main() {
  ...
}
```

The GeoCityRecord struct will be populated when calling the library to read the data, as shown here:

```
package main

import (
  ...
)

...

func main() {
  ...
  _, network, err := net.ParseCIDR("2.0.0.0/8")
  ...
  for networks.Next() {
    var rec interface{}
    r := GeoCityRecord{}
    ip, err := networks.Network(&rec)
    ...
}
```

networks.Next() loops through the records found and reads all geographical information from the database by calling the networks. Network(..) function, which populates the rec variable.

The rec variable is an interface, so the code uses json.Marshal(..) to marshal the content into a proper struct, defined by the r variable, as shown here:

```go
package main
...

func main() {
    ...
    for networks.Next() {
        var rec interface{}
        r := GeoCityRecord{}
        ip, err := networks.Network(&rec)

        ...
        j, _ := json.Marshal(rec)

        err = json.Unmarshal([]byte(j), &r)
        ...
        fmt.Printf("IP : %s, Long : %f, Lat : %f, Country : %s,
        Continent: %s\n", ip.String(), r.Location.Longitude,
        r.Location.Latitude,
            r.Country.IsoCode, r.Continent.Code)
    }
}
```

Once the JSON has been unmarshalled back to the r variable, the code prints out the information into the console.

Summary

In this chapter, you not only looked at the crowd source nature of data collection used by CrowdSec and how the community benefits from it, you also learned how to use it in your application.

You learned how to use channels to inform applications when system signals are sent by the operating system. You also looked at using channels to handle service dependencies during startup. Lastly, you looked at how to read a GeoIP database, which is useful to know when you want to use the information in your infrastructure for logging or monitoring IP traffic purposes.

PART VI

Terminal User Interface

CHAPTER 15

ANSI and UI

In this chapter, you will learn about writing command-line applications that have a user interface (UI). You will look at adding text styling, such as italic or bold text, text of a different color, a UI that uses a spinner, and more. This kind of user interface is possible by using ANSI escape codes, which contain code to do certain things in the terminal.

You will also look at an open source library that makes it easy to write a user interface that takes care of all the heavy lifting of writing the different ANSI escape codes to do fancy UI tricks. In this chapter, you will learn about the following:

- ANSI escape codes for UI

- An open source library to write different kinds of UIs

- Styling text, such as italic and bold

Source Code

The source code for this chapter is available from the `https://github.com/Apress/Software-Development-Go` repository.

© Nanik Tolaram 2023
N. Tolaram, *Software Development with Go*,
https://doi.org/10.1007/978-1-4842-8731-6_15

ANSI Escape Code

Terminal-based applications that provide a user interface are normally built using ANSI escape codes. The Wikipedia page at `https://en.wikipedia.org/wiki/ANSI_escape_code` provides a comprehensive explanation of the ANSI code:

ANSI escape sequences are a standard for in-band signaling to control cursor location, color, font styling, and other options on video text terminals and terminal emulators.

With the help of ANSI code, there are a proliferation of terminal-based applications that provide a rich terminal-based user interface.

Let's experiment with a simple Bash script to print different background and foreground colors with text using ANSI code, as shown in the following example script:

```
for x in {0..8}; do for i in {30..37}; do
    for a in {40..47}; do echo -ne "\e[$i;$a""m\\\e[$i;$a""m\
    e[37;40m "; done
    echo
done; done
echo ""
```

Figure 15-1 shows the output that you will see on your screen.

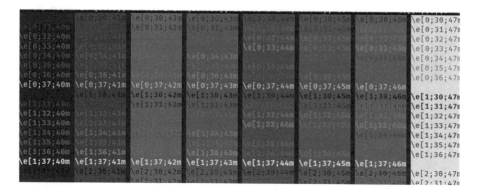

Figure 15-1. *Bash output*

The following script prints out numbers in 256 different foreground colors using ANSI code. Figure 15-2 shows the output.

```
for i in {0..255}; do printf '\e[38;5;%dm%3d ' $i $i; (((i+3)
% 18)) || printf '\e[0m\n'; done
```

Figure 15-2. *256 color output*

Both Bash scripts use ANSI code to select color. For Figure 15-2, the ANSI code is the following:

```
\e[38;5;228m
```

Table 15-1 explains what the code means.

Table 15-1. *Code Description*

Code	Description
\e	Escape character
38;5	ANSI code specifying foreground color
228	Color code for bright yellow

In this section, you learned about ANSI codes and how to use them to print text with different colors by writing Bash scripts. This lays the foundation for the next section where you are going to use ANSI code to write different kinds of terminal-based user interfaces inside Go.

ANSI-Based UI

In the previous section, you looked at ANSI codes and how to use them in Bash. In this section, you are going to use the ANSI codes inside a Go application. You will use ANSI code to set text color, style the text such as italic, and more.

Color Table

Open your terminal and run the code inside the chapter15/ansi folder.

```
go run main.go
```

Figure 15-3 shows the output.

		40	41	42	43	44	45	46	47	100	101	102	103	104	105	106	107
			Aa	Aa	Aa	Aa	Aa	Aa	Aa	Aa	Aa	Aa	Aa	Aa	Aa	Aa	Aa
30	Aa		Aa	Aa	Aa	Aa	Aa	Aa	Aa	Aa	Aa	Aa	Aa	Aa	Aa	Aa	Aa
31	Aa	Aa	Aa	Aa	Aa	Aa	Aa	Aa	Aa	Aa	Aa	Aa	Aa	Aa	Aa	Aa	Aa
32	Aa	Aa	Aa	Aa	Aa	Aa	Aa	Aa	Aa	Aa	Aa	Aa	Aa	Aa	Aa	Aa	Aa
33	Aa	Aa	Aa	Aa	Aa	Aa	Aa	Aa	Aa	Aa	Aa	Aa	Aa	Aa	Aa	Aa	Aa
34	Aa	Aa	Aa	Aa	Aa	Aa	Aa	Aa	Aa	Aa	Aa	Aa	Aa	Aa	Aa	Aa	Aa
35	Aa	Aa	Aa	Aa	Aa	Aa	Aa	Aa	Aa	Aa	Aa	Aa	Aa	Aa	Aa	Aa	Aa
36	Aa	Aa	Aa	Aa	Aa	Aa	Aa	Aa	Aa	Aa	Aa	Aa	Aa	Aa	Aa	Aa	Aa
37	Aa	Aa	Aa	Aa	Aa	Aa	Aa	Aa	Aa	Aa	Aa	Aa	Aa	Aa	Aa	Aa	Aa
90	Aa	Aa	Aa	Aa	Aa	Aa	Aa	Aa	Aa	Aa	Aa	Aa	Aa	Aa	Aa	Aa	Aa
91	Aa	Aa	Aa	Aa	Aa	Aa	Aa	Aa	Aa	Aa	Aa	Aa	Aa	Aa	Aa	Aa	Aa
92	Aa	Aa	Aa	Aa	Aa	Aa	Aa	Aa	Aa	Aa	Aa	Aa	Aa	Aa	Aa	Aa	Aa
93	Aa	Aa	Aa	Aa	Aa	Aa	Aa	Aa	Aa	Aa	Aa	Aa	Aa	Aa	Aa	Aa	Aa
94	Aa	Aa	Aa	Aa	Aa	Aa	Aa	Aa	Aa	Aa	Aa	Aa	Aa	Aa	Aa	Aa	Aa
95	Aa	Aa	Aa	Aa	Aa	Aa	Aa	Aa	Aa	Aa	Aa	Aa	Aa	Aa	Aa	Aa	Aa
96	Aa	Aa	Aa	Aa	Aa	Aa	Aa	Aa	Aa	Aa	Aa	Aa	Aa	Aa	Aa	Aa	Aa
97		Aa	Aa	Aa	Aa	Aa	Aa	Aa	Aa	Aa	Aa	Aa	Aa	Aa	Aa	Aa	Aa

Figure 15-3. *Different color text output*

The code prints the text *Aa* combined with the foreground and background color. The color values are set using escape code, which is obtained from the fg and bg variables, as shown in the following snippet:

```
...
for _, fg := range fgColors {
  fmt.Printf("%2s ", fg)
...
    if len(fg) > 0 {
...
      fmt.Printf("\x1b[%sm Aa \x1b[0m", bg)
    }
  }
}
```

Then different foreground and background numbers are specified in the fgColors and bgColors arrays, as follows:

```
var fgColors = []string{
  "", "30", "31", "32", "33", "34", "35", "36", "37",
  "90", "91", "92", "93", "94", "95", "96", "97",
}

var bgColors = []string{
  "", "40", "41", "42", "43", "44", "45", "46", "47",
  "100", "101", "102", "103", "104", "105", "106", "107",
}
```

The string printed to the screen looks like the following:

```
[31;40m Aa [0m
```

Here is the breakdown of what the code means:

- [31;40m: ANSI escape code for black background with red color text

- Aa: The *Aa* text

- [0m: Reset

Figure 15-4 shows a table extracted from https://en.wikipedia.org/wiki/ANSI_escape_code showing the different foreground and background value combinations and the color each represents.

FG	BG	Name	VGA[b]	Windows XP Console[c]	Windows PowerShell[d]	Visual Studio Code[e]	Windows 10 Console[f]	Terminal.app	PuTTY	mIRC	xterm	Ubuntu[g]	Eclipse Terminal
30	40	Black	0, 0, 0				12, 12, 12	0, 0, 0				1, 1, 1	0, 0, 0
31	41	Red	170, 0, 0	128, 0, 0		205, 49, 49	197, 15, 31	194, 54, 33	187, 0, 0	127, 0, 0	205, 0, 0	222, 56, 43	205, 0, 0
32	42	Green	0, 170, 0	0, 128, 0		13, 188, 121	19, 161, 14	37, 188, 36	0, 187, 0	0, 147, 0	0, 205, 0	57, 181, 74	0, 205, 0
33	43	Yellow	170, 85, 0	128, 128, 0	238, 237, 240	229, 229, 16	193, 156, 0	173, 173, 39	187, 187, 0	252, 127, 0	205, 205, 0	255, 199, 6	205, 205, 0
34	44	Blue	0, 0, 170	0, 0, 128		36, 114, 200	0, 55, 218	73, 46, 225	0, 0, 187	0, 0, 127	0, 0, 238	0, 111, 184	0, 0, 238
35	45	Magenta	170, 0, 170	128, 0, 128	1, 36, 86	188, 63, 188	136, 23, 152	211, 56, 211	187, 0, 187	156, 0, 156	205, 0, 205	118, 38, 113	205, 0, 205
36	46	Cyan	0, 170, 170	0, 128, 128		17, 168, 205	58, 150, 221	51, 187, 200	0, 187, 187	0, 147, 147	0, 205, 205	44, 181, 233	205, 0, 205
37	47	White	170, 170, 170	192, 192, 192		229, 229, 229	204, 204, 204	203, 204, 205	187, 187, 187	210, 210, 210	229, 229, 229	204, 204, 204	229, 229, 229
90	100	Bright Black (Gray)	85, 85, 85	128, 128, 128		102, 102, 102	118, 118, 118	129, 131, 131	85, 85, 85	127, 127, 127	127, 127, 127	128, 128, 128	0, 0, 0
91	101	Bright Red	255, 85, 85	255, 0, 0		241, 76, 76	231, 72, 86	252, 57, 31	255, 85, 85	255, 0, 0	255, 0, 0	255, 0, 0	255, 0, 0
92	102	Bright Green	85, 255, 85	0, 255, 0		35, 209, 139	22, 198, 12	49, 231, 34	85, 255, 85	0, 252, 0	0, 255, 0	0, 255, 0	0, 255, 0
93	103	Bright Yellow	255, 255, 85	255, 255, 0		245, 245, 67	249, 241, 165	234, 236, 35	255, 255, 85	255, 255, 0	255, 255, 0	255, 255, 0	255, 255, 0
94	104	Bright Blue	85, 85, 255	0, 0, 255		59, 142, 234	59, 120, 255	88, 51, 255	85, 85, 255	0, 0, 252	92, 92, 255	0, 0, 255	92, 92, 255
95	105	Bright Magenta	255, 85, 255	255, 0, 255		214, 112, 214	180, 0, 158	249, 53, 248	255, 85, 255	255, 0, 255	255, 0, 255	255, 0, 255	255, 0, 255
96	106	Bright Cyan	85, 255, 255	0, 255, 255		41, 184, 219	97, 214, 214	20, 240, 240	85, 255, 255	0, 255, 255	0, 255, 255	0, 255, 255	0, 255, 255
97	107	Bright White	255, 255, 255	255, 255, 255		229, 229, 229	242, 242, 242	233, 235, 235	255, 255, 255	255, 255, 255	255, 255, 255	255, 255, 255	255, 255, 255

Figure 15-4. *Foreground and background mapping*

In the next section, you will look at examples of how to use ANSI code to format text on a screen.

Styling Text

ANSI code is also available to style text such as italic, superscript, and more. Let's take a look at the sample code inside the chapter15/textstyle folder, which will print output like Figure 15-5.

```
Italics text

Underline text
```

Figure 15-5. *Text styling using ANSI*

The following code declares different constants containing ANSI code to format text with different styles:

```
package main

import "fmt"

const (
```

```
Underline     = "\x1b[4m"
UnderlineOff  = "\x1b[24m"
Italics       = "\x1b[3m"
ItalicsOff    = "\x1b[23m"
)
...
```

In this section, you used different ANSI codes to format text in the console with different colors and formats. Going through the sample code, it is obvious that writing a command-line application that uses ANSI codes is quite laborious because you need to specify the different ANSI codes that are required in the application.

In the next section, you will look at some open source projects that take care of the different aspects of command-line user interface development to make writing code easier.

Open Source Library

In this section, you will look at two different open source libraries that are useful when writing command-line user interfaces. You will look at examples of how to use the libraries and look at how the internals of the libraries work.

Gookit

This library provides a simple API for applications to print text in different foreground and background colors. It also provides text styling such as italics, superscript, etc. The following is the link to the library project: https://github.com/gookit/color.

Run the sample code inside the chapter15/gookit folder as shown:

```
go run main.go
```

Figure 15-6 shows the output.

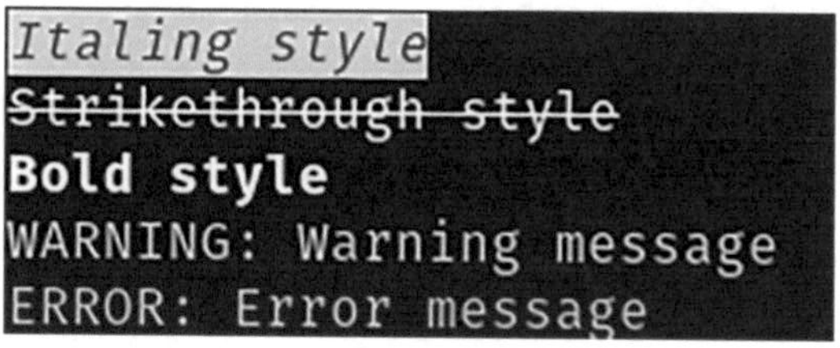

Figure 15-6. *Gookit sample output*

The following code snippet shows the simple API call:

```
...
func main() {
  color.Warn = &color.Theme{"warning", color.Style{color.
  BgDefault, color.FgWhite}}
  ...
  color.Style{color.FgDefault, color.BgDefault, color.
  OpStrikethrough}.Println("Strikethrough style")
  color.Style{color.FgDefault, color.BgDefault, color.OpBold}.
  Println("Bold style")
  ...
}
```

Calling color.Style.Println prints the text that you want using the foreground and background colors specified. For example,

```
color.Style{color.FgDefault, color.BgDefault, color.
OpStrikethrough}.Println("Strikethrough style")
```

prints the words *Strikethrough style* in the default foreground and background colors with the strikethrough text format.

The library uses a constant value to define the different colors it provides, as shown in the following code snippets, which can be found in the library under the file color_16.go:

```
const (
  FgBlack Color = iota + 30
  FgRed
  FgGreen
  FgYellow
  ...
)

const (
  FgDarkGray Color = iota + 90
  FgLightRed
  FgLightGreen
  ...
)

const (
  BgBlack Color = iota + 40
  BgRed
  ...
)

const (
  BgDarkGray Color = iota + 100
  BgLightRed
  ...
)

const (
  OpReset          Color = iota
  OpBold
  OpFuzzy
  OpItalic
  ...
)
```

The library uses the same ANSI codes to format the color and text styling as you saw in the previous section. The following code snippet is from the file color.go:

```
const (
  SettingTpl   = "\x1b[%sm"
  FullColorTpl = "\x1b[%sm%s\x1b[0m"
)
```

Spinner

This library provides progress indicators for command-line applications. Progress indicators are mostly found in mobile applications or in graphical user interfaces like browsers. Progress indicators are used to indicate to the user that the application is processing the user's request. The library project's home is https://github.com/briandowns/spinner. Open your terminal and run the code inside the chapter15/spinner folder as follows:

```
go run main.go
```

Figure 15-7 shows the output you will see when running the sample code. It prints the words *Processing request* with a red bar moving back and forth as the spinner.

Processing request : ▐█████░░░░

Figure 15-7. *Spinner sample output*

The library is straightforward to use, as shown in the following code snippet:

```
func main() {
  s := spinner.New(spinner.CharSets[35], 100*time.Millisecond)
  s.Color("red")
```

```
    s.Prefix = "Processing request : "
    s.Start()
    ...
    s.Stop()
}
```

Calling spinner.New initializes a new spinner with the type specified, in this case spinner.CharSets[35], and the time delay rendering the spinner, which is 100 milliseconds.

You can specify the different spinners, which can be found inside the library in the file character_sets.go.

```
var CharSets = map[int][]string{
    0:  {"←", "↖", "↑", "↗", "→", "↘", "↓", "↙"},
    1:  {"▁", "▂", "▃", "▄", "▅", "▆", "▇", "█", "▆", "▅", "▄", "▃", "▁"},
    2:  {"▉", "▊", "▋", "▌"},
    3:  {"┤", "┘", "┴", "└", "├", "┌", "┬", "┐"},
    ...
    90: {"←", "↑", "→", "↓"},
}
```

The library renders the spinner to the screen by printing through each character byte in the array specified after a certain amount of delay. By doing this, it gives the illusion of animation when seeing it printed on the screen.

In Figure 15-8, you can see in the debugging window how the different characters that will form the spinner are stored inside the Spinner struct, allowing the library to render them individually. This way, when the library renders the different characters, it looks like an animation.

Figure 15-8. *Spinner struct containing spinner characters*

The spinner.Start() function is the central piece of the logic inside the library that renders the spinner's animation.

```go
func (s *Spinner) Start() {
  ...

  go func() {
    for {
      for i := 0; i < len(s.chars); i++ {
        select {
        ...
        default:
          ...
          if runtime.GOOS == "windows" {
            ...
          } else {
            outColor = fmt.Sprintf("\r%s%s%s", s.Prefix,
            s.color(s.chars[i]), s.Suffix)
          }
          ...
          fmt.Fprint(s.Writer, outColor)
          ...
          time.Sleep(delay)
        }
      }
    }
  }()
}
```

The function fires off a goroutine and endlessly loops the animation on the screen until the stop() function is called by the application.

The outColor variable contains the text to be printed. In this example, it's *Processing request*, along with the ANSI code of the color specified in the sample code, so the content of the variable looks like Figure 15-9.

```
>  ≡ s = {*spinner.Spinner | 0xc0000d00b0}
   01 i = {int} 0
   01 outColor = {string} "\rProcessing request : [31m←[0m"
```

Figure 15-9. *outColor final output*

Summary

In this chapter, you learn about ANSI codes and how they are useful for creating user interfaces in terminals. The available ANSI codes allow you to write text in color and apply different formatting to the text printed on the screen. You learned that the ANSI codes can be used inside a Bash script and inside Go code.

You explored deeper into the usage of ANSI codes by looking at different open source libraries that provide richer user interface functionality for terminal-based applications. The libraries you looked at provide text-based formatting such as color and styles and progress indicators.

CHAPTER 16

TUI Framework

You saw in Chapter 15 that ANSI codes contain a different variety of code that can be used to develop text-based user interfaces. You also saw examples of using ANSI codes and learned what the different codes mean. There are a number of user interface libraries for Go that take care of user interface operations, thereby making development easier and faster. In this chapter, you will look at these libraries and explore in detail how they work internally.

In this chapter, you will look at two libraries. The first library is a simple library called `uiprogress` that allows an application to create a text-based progress bar. The other is called `bubbletea` and it is a more comprehensive library that allows an application to create different kinds of text-based UIs such as text input, boxes, spinners, and more.

By the end of this chapter, you will learn the following:

- How to use the libraries
- How the libraries work internally

uiprogress

In this section, you will look at the `uiprogress` library, which is hosted at `https://github.com/gosuri/uiprogress`. The library provides a progress bar user interface, as shown in Figure 16-1. The application uses the library to create a progress bar as a feedback mechanism to show that an operation is currently in progress.

© Nanik Tolaram 2023
N. Tolaram, *Software Development with Go*,
https://doi.org/10.1007/978-1-4842-8731-6_16

```
apps: deployment started: app1, app2
app2: deploying        4s [=====================================>-------]  86%
app1: staring servers  4s [============================================] 100%
```

Figure 16-1. *uiprogress progress bar*

Check the project out from GitHub to your local environment and run the sample application that is provided inside the example/simple directory.

```
go run main.go
```

The output is shown in Figure 16-2.

```
1s [=============================================================>-----------]  84%
```

Figure 16-2. *Progress bar output from simple.go*

The sample code is quite simple.

```go
func main() {
  uiprogress.Start()              // start rendering
  bar := uiprogress.AddBar(100) // Add a new bar

  // optionally, append and prepend completion and elapsed time
  bar.AppendCompleted()
  bar.PrependElapsed()

  for bar.Incr() {
    time.Sleep(time.Millisecond * 20)
  }
}
```

Code Flow

You will use this sample application as the basis to do a walk-through of the library. Figure 16-3 shows how the application interacts with the library and shows what is actually happening behind the scenes inside the library.

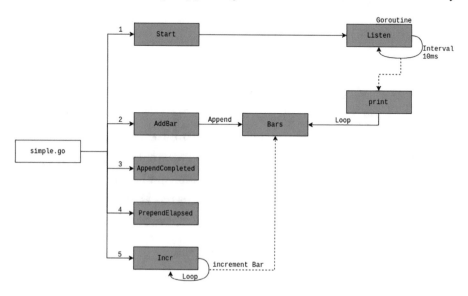

***Figure 16-3.** Code flow from simple.go to the library*

Let's walk through the diagram to understand what's happening. The first thing the app does is call the Start() function. This is to initialize the internals of the library. The function spins off a goroutine and calls the Listen() function, which reside inside the progress.go file shown here:

```go
func (p *Progress) Listen() {
  for {

    p.mtx.Lock()
    interval := p.RefreshInterval
    p.mtx.Unlock()

    select {
```

```
    case <-time.After(interval):
        p.print()
    case <-p.tdone:
        p.print()
        close(p.tdone)
        return
    }
  }
}
```

The function is in a for{} loop and calls the print() function at an interval that has been set at the default of 10 milliseconds.

Upon completing the Start() function, the sample app calls the AddBar() function to create a new progress bar that will be shown to the user. The library can process multiple progress bar at the same time, so any new bar created will be stored in the Bars slice, as shown:

```
func (p *Progress) AddBar(total int) *Bar {
  ...
  bar := NewBar(total)
  bar.Width = p.Width
  p.Bars = append(p.Bars, bar)
  ...
}
```

Updating Progress

Upon expiry of the 10 milliseconds interval, the library updates each of the registered progress bars using the print() function running in the background. The code snippet of running the print() function is as follows:

```go
func (p *Progress) print() {
  ...
  for _, bar := range p.Bars {
    fmt.Fprintln(p.lw, bar.String())
  }
  ...
}
```

The print() function loops through the Bars slice and calls the String() function, which in turn calls the Bytes() function. The Bytes() function performs calculations to get the correct value for the progress bar and prints this with a suffix and prefix.

```go
func (b *Bar) Bytes() []byte {
  completedWidth := int(float64(b.Width) *
  (b.CompletedPercent() / 100.00))

  for i := 0; i < completedWidth; i++ {
    ...
  }
  ...

  pb := buf.Bytes()
  if completedWidth > 0 && completedWidth < b.Width {
    pb[completedWidth-1] = b.Head
  }
  ...
  return pb
}
```

The function calls AppendCompleted() and PrependElapsed() are used to define the following:

AppendCompleted() adds a function that will print out the percentage completed when the progress bar has completed its operation.

```go
func (b *Bar) AppendCompleted() *Bar {
  b.AppendFunc(func(b *Bar) string {
    return b.CompletedPercentString()
  })
  return b
}
```

PrependElapsed() prefixes the progress bar with the time it has taken to complete so far.

```go
func (b *Bar) PrependElapsed() *Bar {
  b.PrependFunc(func(b *Bar) string {
    return strutil.PadLeft(b.TimeElapsedString(), 5, ' ')
  })
  return b
}
```

Lastly, the application needs to specify the increment or decrement of the progress bar value. In the sample code case, it increments as follows:

```go
func main() {
  ...
  for bar.Incr() {
    time.Sleep(time.Millisecond * 20)
  }
}
```

The code will look as long as the bar.Incr() returns true and will sleep for 20 milliseconds before incrementing again.

From your code perspective, the library takes care of updating and managing the progress bar, allowing your application to focus on its main task. All the application needs to do is just inform the library about the new value of the bar by calling the Incr() or Decr() function.

In the next section, you will look at a more comprehensive library that provides a better user interface for an application.

Bubbletea

In the previous section, you saw the uiprogress progress bar library and looked at how it works internally. In this section, you will take a look at another user interface framework called bubbletea. The code can be checked out from https://github.com/charmbracelet/bubbletea.

Run the sample application inside the examples/tui-daemon-combo folder as follows:

```
go run main.go
```

You will get output that looks like Figure 16-4.

Figure 16-4. *tui-daemon-combo sample output*

The interesting thing about this TUI framework is it provides a variety of user interfaces: progress bars, spinners, lists, and more. Figure 16-5 shows the different functions the application must provide in order to use the library.

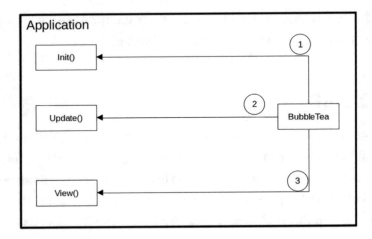

Figure 16-5. *Application functions for bubbletea interaction*

In the next few sections, you will use the tui-daemon-combo sample code to work out how the code flows inside the library.

Using bubbletea is quite straightforward, as shown here:

```
func main() {
  ...
  p := tea.NewProgram(newModel(), opts...)
  if err := p.Start(); err != nil {
    fmt.Println("Error starting Bubble Tea program:", err)
    os.Exit(1)
  }
}
```

The code calls tea.NewProgram(), passing in the Model interface and options that need to be set. The Model interface defined by the library is as follows:

```
type Model interface {
  Init() Cmd
  Update(Msg) (Model, Cmd)
  View() string
}
```

The newModel() function returns the implementation of the Model interface, which is defined as follows:

```
func (m model) Init() tea.Cmd {
  ...
}

func (m model) Update(msg tea.Msg) (tea.Model, tea.Cmd) {
  ...
}

func (m model) View() string {
  ...
}
```

Now you have defined the different functions that will be called by the library when constructing and updating the UI. Next, you will look at how each of these functions are used by the library.

Init

The Init() function is the first function called by bubbletea after calling the Start() function. You saw that Init() must return a Cmd type, which is declared as the function type shown here:

```
type Cmd func() Msg
```

The Init() functions use batches to return different kinds of function types: spinner.Tick and runPretendProcess. This is done by using the tea.Batch() function, as shown here:

```
func (m model) Init() tea.Cmd {
  ...
  return tea.Batch(
    spinner.Tick,
    runPretendProcess,
  )
}
```

Internally, tea.Batch() returns an anonymous function that wraps the different Cmd function types into an array of Cmd, as shown in this snippet:

```
type batchMsg []Cmd

func Batch(cmds ...Cmd) Cmd {
  ...
  return func() Msg {
    return batchMsg(validCmds)
  }
}
```

After bubbletea completes calling the application Init() function, it kickstarts the process. Internally, it uses channels to read different incoming messages to perform different user interface operations, so in your sample code case, it processes the batchMsg array and starts calling the Cmd function types.

The Cmd function type implementation returns Msg, which is an interface as defined in the library.

```
type Msg interface{}
```

In the sample code, you uses `spinner.Tick` and `runPretendProcess`, which are defined as follows:

```
type processFinishedMsg time.Duration

func Tick() tea.Msg {
  return TickMsg{Time: time.Now()}
}

func runPretendProcess() tea.Msg {
  ...
  return processFinishedMsg(pause)
}
```

Figure 16-6 shows that the library uses a number of goroutines to do several things in the background including processing the `Msg` that are returned by the function types that will be used in the `Update()` function, which you will look at in the next section.

317

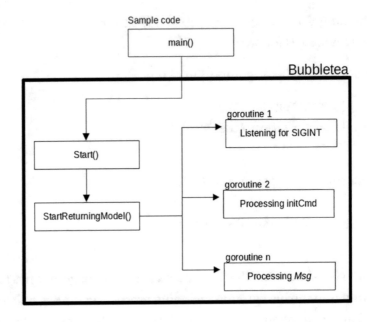

Figure 16-6. *Initialization of the internal execution flow*

Update

The Update function is called to update the state of the user interface. In the sample app, it is defined as follows:

```
func (m model) Update(msg tea.Msg) (tea.Model, tea.Cmd) {
  switch msg := msg.(type) {
  case tea.KeyMsg:

    ...

    return m, tea.Quit
  case spinner.TickMsg:
```

```
    ...
    m.spinner, cmd = m.spinner.Update(msg)
    ...
  case processFinishedMsg:
    ...
    m.results = append(m.results[1:], res)
    ...
  default:
    return m, nil
  }
}
```

The Update function receives different kinds of tea.Msg because it is defined as an interface, so the code needs to do type checking and handle the type it wants to handle. For example, when the function receives spinner.TickMsg, it updates the spinner by calling the spinner.Update() function, and when it receives tea.KeyMsg, it quits the application.

The function only needs to process messages that it is interested in and process any user interface state management that it needs to do. Other heavy operations must be avoided in the function.

View

The last function, View(), is called by the library to update the user interface. The application is given the freedom to update the user interface as it sees fit. This flexibility allows the application to render a user interface that suits its needs.

This does not mean that the application needs to know how to draw the user interface. This is taken care of by the functions available for each user interface. Here is the View() function:

```go
func (m model) View() string {
  s := "\n" +
    m.spinner.View() + " Doing some work...\n\n"

  for _, res := range m.results {
    ...
  }

  ...

  if m.quitting {
    s += "\n"
  }

  return indent.String(s, 1)
}
```

The app combines all the user interfaces that it needs to display to the user by extracting the different values from the different variables. For example, it extract the results array values to show it to the user. The results array is populated in the Update function when it receives the processFinishedMsg message type.

The function returns a string containing the user interface that will be rendered by the library to the terminal.

Figure 16-7 shows at a high level the different goroutines that are spun off by the library and that take care of the different parts of the user interfaces such as user input using the keyboard, mouse, terminal resizing, and more.

The architecture is like a pub/sub model where the central goroutine process all the different messages and calls the relevant functions internally to perform the operations.

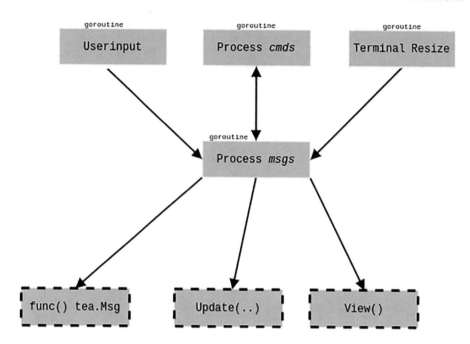

Figure 16-7. Centralized processing of messages

Summary

In this chapter, you look at two different terminal-based user interface frameworks that provide APIs for developers to build command-line user interfaces. You looked at sample applications of how to use the frameworks to build simple command-line user interfaces.

You looked at the internals of the frameworks to understand how they work. Knowing this gives you better insight into how to troubleshoot issues when using these kinds of frameworks. And understanding the complexity of these frameworks helps you build your own asynchronous applications.

PART VII

Linux System

CHAPTER 17

systemd

In this chapter, you will look at systemd, what it is, and how to write Go applications to interact with it. systemd is an important piece of software inside the Linux system, and it is too big to be covered entirely in this chapter.

You will look at an open source systemd Go library that is available and how to use it to access systemd. In this chapter, you will do the following:

- Learn what systemd provides

- Interact with systemd using systemctl and journalctl

- Use the go-systemd library to write code

- Write log messages to a systemd journal

- Query systemd to get a list of registered services

Source Code

The source code for this chapter is available from the https://github.com/Apress/Software-Development-Go repository.

systemd

systemd is a suite of applications that are used in Linux systems to get them up and running. It provides more than just starting the core Linux systems run; it also starts a number of programs such as network stack, user logins,

© Nanik Tolaram 2023
N. Tolaram, *Software Development with Go*,
https://doi.org/10.1007/978-1-4842-8731-6_17

325

the logging server, and more. It uses socket and D-Bus activation to start up services, on-demand starting of background applications, and more.

D-Bus stands for Desktop Bus. It is a specification that is used for an inter-process communication mechanism, allowing different processes to communicate with one another on the same machine. Implementation of D-Bus consists of server components and a client library. For systemd, the implementation is known as sd-bus, and in a later section, you will look at using the D-Bus client library to communicate with the server component.

Socket activation is a mechanism in systemd to listen to a network port or Unix socket. When connected from an external source, it will trigger the running of a server application. This is useful in situations when a resource-hungry application needs to run only when it is needed and not during the time when the Linux system is started up.

systemd Units

Files that are used for systemd are called units. It is a standard way to represent resources managed by systemd. System-related systemd unit files can be found inside /lib/systemd/system, which looks this:

```
...
-rw-r--r--  1 root root   389 Nov 18  2021  apt-daily-
upgrade.service
-rw-r--r--  1 root root   184 Nov 18  2021  apt-daily-
upgrade.timer
lrwxrwxrwx  1 root root    14 Apr 25 23:23  autovt@.service ->
getty@.service
-rw-r--r--  1 root root  1044 Jul  7  2021  avahi-
daemon.service
-rw-r--r--  1 root root   870 Jul  7  2021  avahi-daemon.socket
-rw-r--r--  1 root root   927 Apr 25 23:23  basic.target
-rw-r--r--  1 root root  1159 Apr 18  2020  binfmt-
support.service
```

```
-rw-r--r-- 1 root root   380 Oct  6  2021  blk-
availability.service
-rw-r--r-- 1 root root   449 Apr 25 23:23  blockdev@.target
-rw-r--r-- 1 root root   419 Feb  1 11:49  bluetooth.service
...
-rw-r--r-- 1 root root   758 Apr 25 23:23  dev-hugepages.mount
-rw-r--r-- 1 root root   701 Apr 25 23:23  dev-mqueue.mount
...
-rw-r--r-- 1 root root   251 Aug 31  2021  e2scrub_all.timer
-rw-r--r-- 1 root root   245 Aug 31  2021  e2scrub_
fail@.service
-rw-r--r-- 1 root root   550 Aug 31  2021  e2scrub_
reap.service
...
-rw-r--r-- 1 root root   444 Apr 25 23:23  remote-fs-
pre.target
-rw-r--r-- 1 root root   530 Apr 25 23:23  remote-fs.target
```

The other location for unit files is inside the /etc/systemd/system
directory. Unit files in this directory take precedence over any other unit
files found on the filesystem, The following shows a snippet of the unit files
in a local machine inside the /etc/system/system directory:

```
...
lrwxrwxrwx 1 root root    40 Mar  4 04:53 dbus-org.
freedesktop.ModemManager1.service -> /lib/systemd/system/
ModemManager.service
lrwxrwxrwx 1 root root    53 Mar  4 04:51 dbus-org.freedesktop.
nm-dispatcher.service -> /lib/systemd/system/NetworkManager-
dispatcher.service
```

```
lrwxrwxrwx  1 root root   44 Aug  7  2021 dbus-org.
freedesktop.resolve1.service -> /lib/systemd/system/systemd-
resolved.service
lrwxrwxrwx  1 root root   36 Mar  4 04:53 dbus-org.freedesktop.
thermald.service -> /lib/systemd/system/thermald.service
lrwxrwxrwx  1 root root   45 Aug  7  2021 dbus-org.
freedesktop.timesync1.service -> /lib/systemd/system/systemd-
timesyncd.service
...
drwxr-xr-x  2 root root 4096 Mar  4 04:53 graphical.
target.wants/
drwxr-xr-x  2 root root 4096 Mar  4 04:51 mdmonitor.
service.wants/
drwxr-xr-x  2 root root 4096 May 27 10:10 multi-user.
target.wants/
...
lrwxrwxrwx  1 root root   31 Apr  6 17:55 sshd.service -> /lib/
systemd/system/ssh.service
...
```

The following is a non-exhaustive list of the different unit files:

- .service: Describe a service or application and how to start or stop the service

- .socket: Describes a network or Unix socket used for socket-based activation

- .device: Describes a device exposed in the sysfs/udev device tree

- .timer: Defines a timer that will be managed by systemd

You looked at systemd and what it is used for. In the next section, you will look at using the provided tools to look at the services provided by systemd using systemctl.

systemctl

systemctl is the main tool used to communicate with systemd that is running in your local machine. Type in the following command in your terminal:

systemctl

Without any parameter, it will list all the services that are currently registered with the system, as shown in Figure 17-1.

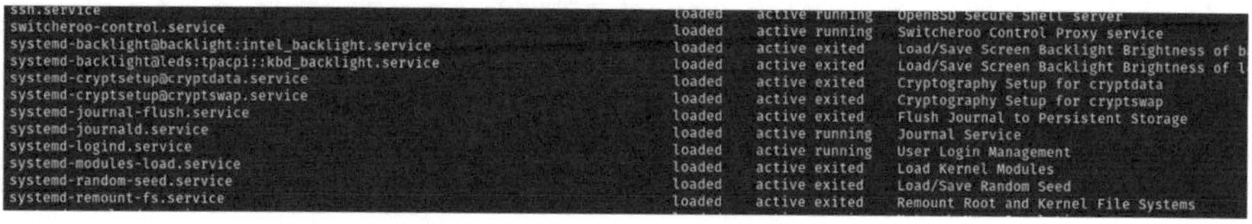

Figure 17-1. *Registered service in systemd*

Let's take a peek at the services that are currently running on local machines. You will look at the systemd-journal.service, which is running a systemd logging service. Open your terminal and use the following command:

systemctl status systemd-journald.service

You will see output that looks like the following:

- systemd-journald.service - Journal Service
  Loaded: loaded (/lib/systemd/system/systemd-journald.
  service; static)
  Active: active (running) since Thu 2022-06-16 23:21:09
  AEST; 1 week 0 days ago

```
TriggeredBy: • systemd-journald-dev-log.socket
             • systemd-journald-audit.socket
             • systemd-journald.socket
        Docs: man:systemd-journald.service(8)
              man:journald.conf(5)
    Main PID: 370 (systemd-journal)
      Status: "Processing requests..."
       Tasks: 1 (limit: 9294)
      Memory: 54.2M
         CPU: 3.263s
      CGroup: /system.slice/systemd-journald.service
              └─370 /lib/systemd/systemd-journald

Jun 16 23:21:09 nanik systemd-journald[370]: Journal started
...
Jun 16 23:21:09 nanik systemd-journald[370]: System Journal
```

The output shows information about the service such as the amount of memory the service is using, the process ID (PID), location of the `.service` file, and whether the service is active or not.

To stop a service, use the command `systemctl stop`. As an example, let's try to stop `cups.service` (a service used to provide printing services in Linux). Use the following command in your terminal to check the status:

```
systemctl status cups.service
```

You will see output like the following:

```
• cups.service - CUPS Scheduler
    Loaded: loaded (/lib/systemd/system/cups.service; enabled;
    vendor preset: enabled)
    Active: active (running) since Fri 2022-06-24 00:00:35
    AEST; 22h ago
```

```
TriggeredBy: • cups.socket
             • cups.path
       Docs: man:cupsd(8)
   Main PID: 39757 (cupsd)
     Status: "Scheduler is running..."
      Tasks: 1 (limit: 9294)
     Memory: 2.8M
        CPU: 51ms
     CGroup: /system.slice/cups.service
             └─39757 /usr/sbin/cupsd -l

Jun 24 00:00:35 nanik systemd[1]: Starting CUPS Scheduler...
Jun 24 00:00:35 nanik systemd[1]: Started CUPS Scheduler.
```

To stop the service, use the following command in your terminal:

```
sudo systemctl stop  cups.service
```

If you check the status again using the same systemctl status cups.
service command, you will see output that looks like the following:

```
○ cups.service - CUPS Scheduler
     Loaded: loaded (/lib/systemd/system/cups.service; enabled;
     vendor preset: enabled)
     Active: inactive (dead) since Fri 2022-06-24 22:47:52
     AEST; 1s ago
TriggeredBy: ○ cups.socket
             ○ cups.path
       Docs: man:cupsd(8)
    Process: 39757 ExecStart=/usr/sbin/cupsd -l (code=exited,
    status=0/SUCCESS)
   Main PID: 39757 (code=exited, status=0/SUCCESS)
     Status: "Scheduler is running..."
        CPU: 54ms
```

```
Jun 24 00:00:35 nanik systemd[1]: Starting CUPS Scheduler...
...
Jun 24 22:47:52 nanik systemd[1]: Stopped CUPS Scheduler.
```

Using systemctl allows you to take a look at the status of the registered service in systemd. In the next section, you will write a simple server application and control it using systemctl.

Hello Server systemd

In this section, you will look at the sample code that can be found inside the chapter17/httpservice directory. The application is a simple HTTP server listening on port 8111. Let's run the application normally first using the following command in your terminal:

```
go run main.go
```

You will see output like following:

```
2022/06/24 22:55:40 Server running - port 8111
```

Open your browser and access it using http://localhost:8111. You will see output that looks like the following:

```
Hello !!! you are getting response from app running via systemd
```

Figure 17-2. *HTTP server output*

The application is working now. Let's create the executable file that you will use to run it as a systemd service. Compile the application using the following command. Make sure you are in the chapter17/httpservice directory.

```
go build -o httpservice
```

Your application is now ready to be installed as a systemd service. Follow the steps below to do the installation.

1. Copy the httpservice executable file into the /usr/local/bin directory in your terminal, as shown:

   ```
   sudo cp ./httpservice /usr/local/bin
   ```

2. Copy the httpservice.service file into the /etc/systemd/system directory in your terminal, as shown:

   ```
   sudo cp ./httpservice.service /etc/systemd/system
   ```

3. Take a look at the status of your newly created service using the following command:

   ```
   sudo systemctl status  httpservice.service
   ```

   You will see output as follows:

   ```
   o httpservice.service - HTTP Server Application
        Loaded: loaded (/etc/systemd/system/httpservice.
        service; disabled; vendor preset: enabled)
        Active: inactive (dead)
   ```

   The service is recognized by systemd but it is not enabled or dead.

4. Start/enable the service using the following command:

   ```
   sudo systemctl start  httpservice.service
   ```

5. If you run the same status command (step 3), you will get the following output:

   ```
   ● httpservice.service - HTTP Server Application
   ```

```
      Loaded: loaded (/etc/systemd/system/httpservice.
      service; disabled; vendor preset: enabled)
      Active: active (running) since Fri 2022-06-24
      23:09:34 AEST; 39s ago
    Main PID: 44068 (httpservice)
       Tasks: 5 (limit: 9294)
      Memory: 1.0M
         CPU: 3ms
      CGroup: /system.slice/httpservice.service
              └─44068 /usr/local/bin/httpservice
```

```
Jun 24 23:09:34 nanik systemd[1]: Started HTTP Server
Application.
Jun 24 23:09:34 nanik httpservice[44068]: 2022/06/24 23:09:34
Server running - port 8111
```

6. To ensure that the service starts up when you reboot
   your machine, use the following command:

```
sudo systemctl enable  httpservice.service
```

Now you can access the application by pointing your browser to http://
localhost:8111.

You have successfully deployed your sample app. It is configured to
start up when you boot up your machine. In next section, you will look at
using a Go library to write a system application.

go-systemd Library

You learned early in this chapter that the D-Bus specification contains a
client library. The client library allows applications to interact with system.
The client library that you are going to take a look at is for a Go application
called go-systemd. The library can be found at http:/github.com/
coreos/go-systemd.

The library provides the following features:

- Using socket activation

- Notifying `systemd` of service status changes

- Starting, stopping, and inspecting services and units

- Registering machines or containers

- ...and many more

For this chapter, you will look at code samples using the library to write to journal logs, list services available on local machines, and query machines.

Querying Services

The sample code for this section can be found inside the `chapter17/listservices` directory. The sample code queryies from `systemd` all the services that are registered, similar to how `systemctl list-units` works.

Open your terminal and make sure you are inside the `chapter17/listservices` directory. Build the application as follows:

```
go build -o listservices
```

Once compiled, run the executable as root.

```
sudo ./listservices
```

You will see output of the services registered in `systemd`.

```
...
Name : sys-module-fuse.device, LoadState : loaded, ActiveState
: active, Substate : plugged
```

```
Name : gdm.service, LoadState : loaded, ActiveState : active,
Substate : running
Name : sysinit.target, LoadState : loaded, ActiveState :
active, Substate : active
Name : graphical.target, LoadState : loaded, ActiveState :
active, Substate : active
Name : veritysetup.target, LoadState : loaded, ActiveState :
active, Substate : active
...
Name : remote-fs-pre.target, LoadState : loaded, ActiveState :
inactive, Substate : dead
Name : apt-daily-upgrade.timer, LoadState : loaded, ActiveState
: active, Substate : waiting
Name : ssh.service, LoadState : loaded, ActiveState : active,
Substate : running
Name : system.slice, LoadState : loaded, ActiveState : active,
Substate : active
Name : systemd-ask-password-plymouth.path, LoadState : loaded,
ActiveState : active, Substate : waiting
Name : dev-ttyS15.device, LoadState : loaded, ActiveState :
active, Substate : plugged
...
```

Let's walk through the code to understand how the app
uses the library. The following snippet shows that it is using the
NewSystemdConnectionContext function to connect to the systemd server:

```
import (
...
)

func main() {
  ...
```

```go
  c, err := d.NewSystemdConnectionContext(ctx)
  ...
}
```

Once it successfully connects to systemd, it sends a request to get the list of units and print it out to the console.

```go
import (
...
)

func main() {
  ...

  js, err := c.ListUnitsContext(ctx)

  ...

  for _, j := range js {
    fmt.Println(fmt.Sprintf("Name : %s, LoadState : %s,
    ActiveState : %s, Substate : %s", j.Name, j.LoadState,
    j.ActiveState, j.SubState))
  }

  c.Close()
}
```

The library takes care of all the heavy lifting of connecting to systemd, sending requests, and converting requests to a format that it passes to the application.

Journal

Another example you will look at is using the library to write log messages
to the journal that provides a logging service. To access the logging service,
you can use the journalctl command line.

```
journalctl -r
```

The output looks like following on my local machine (it will look
different in your machine):

```
...
Jun 25 00:06:43 nanik sshd[2567]: pam_unix(sshd:session):
session opened for user nanik(uid=1000) by (uid=0)
...
Jun 25 00:00:32 nanik kernel: audit: type=1400
audit(1656079232.440:30): apparmor="DENIED" operation="capable"
profile="/usr/sbin/cups-browsed" pid=2527 comm="cups-browsed"
capability=23  c>
Jun 25 00:00:32 nanik audit[2527]: AVC apparmor="DENIED"
operation="capable" profile="/usr/sbin/cups-browsed" pid=2527
comm="cups-browsed" capability=23  capname="sys_nice"
Jun 25 00:00:32 nanik systemd[1]: Finished Rotate log files.
...
```

The parameter -r shows the latest log message on the top. Now you
know how to look at the journal logging service. Let's run your sample
application to write log messages into it.

Open terminal and make sure you are inside the chapter17/journal
directory. Run the sample using the following command:

```
go run main.go
```

Open another terminal and run the same `journalctl -r` command. You will see the log message from the sample application in the output, as shown:

```
Jun 25 00:06:48 nanik journal[2591]: This log message is from
Go application
Jun 25 00:06:44 nanik systemd[908]: Started Tracker metadata
extractor.
Jun 25 00:06:44 nanik systemd[908]: Starting Tracker metadata
extractor...
Jun 25 00:06:44 nanik systemd-logind[778]: Removed session 6.
Jun 25 00:06:44 nanik systemd[1]: session-6.scope: Deactivated
successfully.
...
```

The code to write to the journal is very simple.

```
package main

import (
  j "github.com/coreos/go-systemd/v22/journal"
)

func main() {
  j.Print(j.PriErr, "This log message is from Go application")
}
```

The `Print(..)` function prints the message *This log message is from Go application* with the error priority. This is normally printed in red when you view it using `journalctl`. The following is a list of the different priorities available from the library:

```
const (
  PriEmerg Priority = iota
  PriAlert
```

```
PriCrit
PriErr
PriWarning
PriNotice
PriInfo
PriDebug
)
```

The following priorities are assigned the red color: `PriErr`, `PriCrit`, `PriAlert`, and `PriEmerg`. `PriNotice` and `PriWarning` are highlighted, and `PriDebug` is in lighter grey. One of the interesting priorities is `PriEmerg`, which broadcasts the log message to all open terminals in the local machine.

In the next section, you will look at an advanced feature of `systemd`, which is registering and running a machine or container.

Machines

One advanced feature that `systemd` provides is the ability to run virtual machines or containers in local machines. This feature does not come by default; there is extra installation of services and steps performed in order to use this feature. This feature is made available by installing a package called `systemd-container`. Let's understand what this package is all about.

The `systemd-container` package contains a number of tools, particularly the tool called `systemd-nspawn`. This tool is similar to `chroot` (which I discussed in Chapter 4) but provides more advanced features such as virtualizing the file system hierarchy, process tree, and various IPC subsystems. Basically, it allows you to run a lightweight container with its own `rootfs`.

The following steps will walk you through in installing the package and configuring it.

1. Copy the file systemd-machined.service from the chapter17/machine directory to /usr/lib/systemd/user.

```
sudo cp systemd-machined.service /usr/lib/systemd/user
```

2. Install the systemd-container package using the following command:

```
sudo apt install systemd-container
```

3. Start the service using the following command:

```
sudo systemctl start systemd-machined.service
```

4. Check the status using the command:

```
sudo systemctl status  systemd-machined.service
```

   You will see output like the following:

- systemd-machined.service - Virtual Machine and
  Container Registration Service
      Loaded: loaded (/lib/systemd/system/systemd-
      machined.service; static)
      Active: active (running) since Sat 2022-06-25
      00:51:10 AEST; 21h ago
        Docs: man:systemd-machined.service(8)
              man:org.freedesktop.machine1(5)
    Main PID: 2744 (systemd-machine)
      Status: "Processing requests..."
       Tasks: 1 (limit: 9294)
      Memory: 1.2M
         CPU: 220ms
      CGroup: /system.slice/systemd-machined.service

```
└─2744 /lib/systemd/systemd-machined
```

```
Jun 25 00:51:10 nanik systemd[1]: Starting Virtual Machine and
Container Registration Service...
Jun 25 00:51:10 nanik systemd[1]: Started Virtual Machine and
Container Registration Service.
```

Use the `machinectl` command-line tool to interact with the new machine service that you just installed. Use the tool to download and run Ubuntu operating system images locally as a container.

Use the following command to download the Ubuntu image:

```
machinectl pull-tar https://cloud-images.ubuntu.com/trusty/
current/trusty-server-cloudimg-amd64-root.tar.gz trusty-server
```

If this way does not work for your Linux system, use the following command:

```
wget https://cloud-images.ubuntu.com/trusty/current/trusty-
server-cloudimg-amd64-root.tar.gz
```

```
machinectl import-tar trusty-server-cloudimg-amd64-root.tar.gz
```

Let's check to make sure that the image has been downloaded successfully by using the following command:

```
machinectl list-images
```

You will get output like following:

```
NAME                                      TYPE       RO   USAGE CREATED
MODIFIED
trusty-server-cloudimg-amd64-root   directory no   n/a   Sat
2022-06-25 23:16:16 AEST n/a

1 images listed.
```

The image download is stored inside the /var/lib/machines folder, as shown:

```
nanik@nanik:~/Downloads/alpine-container$ sudo ls -la  /var/
lib/machines
total 24
drwx------  6 root root 4096 Jun 25 23:16 .
drwxr-xr-x 69 root root 4096 May 25 16:19 ..
drwxr-xr-x 22 root root 4096 Jun 25 23:16 trusty-server-
cloudimg-amd64-root
```

Looking inside the trusty-server-cloudimg-amd64-root directory, you will see the rootfs directory structure.

```
drwx------  6 root root 4096 Jun 25 23:16 ..
drwxr-xr-x  2 root root 4096 Nov  8  2019 bin
drwxr-xr-x  3 root root 4096 Nov  8  2019 boot
drwxr-xr-x  4 root root 4096 Nov  8  2019 dev
...
drwxr-xr-x  2 root root 4096 Nov  8  2019 sbin
drwxr-xr-x  2 root root 4096 Nov  8  2019 srv
drwxr-xr-x  2 root root 4096 Mar 13  2014 sys
...
drwxr-xr-x 10 root root 4096 Nov  8  2019 usr
drwxr-xr-x 12 root root 4096 Nov  8  2019 var
```

Finally, now that you have the image downloaded and stored locally, you can run it using the following command:

```
sudo systemd-nspawn -M trusty-server-cloudimg-amd64-root
```

You will see output like the following:

```
nanik@nanik:~/Downloads/alpine-container$ sudo systemd-nspawn-M
trusty-server-cloudimg-amd64-root
```

```
Spawning container trusty-server-cloudimg-amd64-root on /var/
lib/machines/trusty-server-cloudimg-amd64-root.
Press ^] three times within 1s to kill container.
root@trusty-server-cloudimg-amd64-root:~#
```

Let's take a look at the sample application inside the chapter17/machine folder. The sample uses a go-systemd library to query for the images that are stored locally. Change the directory to chapter17/machine and run the sample as follows:

```
go run main.go
```

You will get output that look like the following:

```
2022/06/25 23:22:19 image - .host directory
2022/06/25 23:22:19 image - trusty-server-cloudimg-amd64-root
directory
```

The sample uses the machine1 package of the go-systemd library and it calls the New() function to establish a connection to the systemd system. Once connected, it uses the ListImages() function to retrieve the available images and print them out in the console.

```
package main

import (
  m "github.com/coreos/go-systemd/v22/machine1"

  ...
)

func main() {
  conn, err := m.New()

  ...

  s, err := conn.ListImages()

  ...
```

```
  for _, img := range s {
    log.Println("image - "+img.Name, img.ImageType)
  }
}
```

Summary

In this chapter, you learned about systemd and its functions in the Linux operating system. You explored the different tools that are available to allow you to interact with systemd. You looked at Go code samples that show how to interact with systemd using the go-systemd library.

go-systemd provides a different capability to interact with system. One of the advanced features you looked at was interacting with the systemd-machine service that provides virtual machine and container registration capability.

CHAPTER 18

cadvisor

In this chapter, you will look at an open source project called cAdvisor, which stands for Container Advisor. The complete source code can be found at `https://github.com/google/cadvisor`. This chapter uses version v0.39.3 of the project. The project is used to collect resource usage and performance data on running containers. cAdvisor supports Docker containers, and this is specifically what you are going to look at in this chapter.

The reason for choosing this project is to explore further the topics we discussed in previous chapters, such as

- Using system calls to monitor filesystem
- Using cgroups
- Collecting machine information using `/proc` and `/sys`

Source Code

The source code for this chapter is available from the `https://github.com/Apress/Software-Development-Go` repository.

Running cAdvisor

This section walks through how to check out cAdvisor source code to run it locally. Let's start by checking out the code using the following command:

```
GO111MODULE=off go get github.com/google/cadvisor
```

The command uses the go get command to download the source code from the given URL. The environment GO111MODULE=off tells the go tool to get the module (google/cadvisor) and store it in the GOPATH directory. Once the module has been downloaded, you can go to your GOPATH/src directory and you will see something like the following:

```
drwxrwxr-x 32 nanik nanik  4096 Jun 17 22:31 ./
drwxrwxr-x  9 nanik nanik  4096 Jun 15 22:19 ../
drwxrwxr-x  2 nanik nanik  4096 Jun 17 22:31 accelerators/
-rw-rw-r--  1 nanik nanik   256 Jun 15 22:19 AUTHORS
drwxrwxr-x  4 nanik nanik  4096 Jun 17 22:31 build/
drwxrwxr-x  3 nanik nanik  4096 Jun 15 22:19 cache/
-rw-rw-r--  1 nanik nanik 22048 Jun 15 22:19 CHANGELOG.md
drwxrwxr-x  4 nanik nanik  4096 Jun 17 22:31 client/
drwxrwxr-x  3 nanik nanik  4096 Jun 17 22:32 cmd/
drwxrwxr-x  3 nanik nanik  4096 Jun 17 22:31 collector/
...
```

Build the project by changing into the cmd directory and running the following command:

```
go build -o cadvisor
```

You will get an executable file called cadvisor. Let's run the project using the following command to print out the different parameters it can accept:

```
./cadvisor -help
```

You will get a printout that looks like the following:

```
-add_dir_header
```

If true, adds the file directory to the header of the
log messages

...

-boot_id_file string
   Comma-separated list of files to check for boot-id. Use
   the first one that exists. (default "/proc/sys/kernel/
   random/boot_id")

...

-v value
   number for the log level verbosity

...

I will not go through all the different parameters that cAdvisor has. You are just going to use whatever default value it assigns. cAdvisor requires root access to run it, so do so as follows:

```
sudo ./cadvisor -v 9
```

By default, it uses port 8080 to run the application, so if you have another application running that uses port 8080, it will fail to run. Use the -p flag to specify a different port number for cAdvisor.

```
sudo ./cadvisor -port <port_number>
```

When cAdvisor runs, it collects different information related to the machine and containers, which can only be done if it has root access.

Once cAdvisor is up and running, you will see a lot of log information printed out in the terminal.

```
I0617 23:06:13.122455 2311171 storagedriver.go:55] Caching
stats in memory for 2m0s
W0617 23:06:13.122498 2311171 manager.go:159] Cannot detect
current cgroup on cgroup v2
```

```
I0617 23:06:13.122591 2311171 plugin.go:40] CRI-O not
connected: Get "http://%2Fvar%2Frun%2Fcrio%2Fcrio.sock/info":
dial unix /var/run/crio/crio.sock: connect: no such file or
directory
...
I0617 23:06:13.139451 2311171 nvidia.go:61] NVIDIA setup
failed: no NVIDIA devices found
...
I0617 23:06:13.192306 2311171 manager.go:991] Added container:
"/" (aliases: [], namespace: "")
I0617 23:06:13.192340 2311171 handler.go:325] Added event &{/
2022-06-14 09:44:58.365378218 +1000 AEST containerCreation
{<nil>}}
I0617 23:06:13.192356 2311171 manager.go:301] Starting recovery
of all containers
I0617 23:06:13.192424 2311171 container.go:527] Start
housekeeping for container "/"
...
I0617 23:06:13.197502 2311171 handler.go:325] Added event
&{/user.slice/user-1000.slice/user@1000.service/app.slice/
dbus.socket 2022-06-14 09:43:53.204034932 +1000 AEST
containerCreation {<nil>}}
I0617 23:06:13.197513 2311171 factory.go:220] Factory "docker"
was unable to handle container "/user.slice/user-1000.slice/
user@1000.service/app.slice/app-org.gnome.Terminal.slice/vte-sp
awn-642db2f1-1648-487e-8c09-58ec92a50865.scope"
```

Open up your browser and type in http://localhost:8080 to access the user interface. You will something like Figure 18-1.

/

root

Docker Containers

Subcontainers

/cpu

/init.scope

/machine.slice

/memory

/pids

/system.slice

/user.slice

Isolation

Figure 18-1. *cAdvisor UI*

To see the containers that are running locally, click the *Docker Containers* link on the main page. You will see a different container UI, like the one shown in Figure 18-2. My local machine has a Postgres container running, so you are seeing a Postgres container. You will see all the different containers that are running on your local machine.

Docker Containers

Docker Containers

Subcontainers

postgres (/system.slice/docker-9530eda1479793f26685f281db584f053063a0edda11af5054edd63e50ca1271.scope)

Figure 18-2. *cAdvisor container UI*

In the next section, you will explore further the cAdvisor UI and concepts that are related to the project.

Web User Interface

Make sure you have your cAdvisor running locally and open your browser to access it via URL http://localhost:8080. Let's understand some of the data that is presented on the webpage.

Note   The information you see on your local machine might be different from what you read in this book. It depends on the operating system or Linux distribution you are using.

Figure 18-3 shows the subdirectory called subcontainers in cAdvisor. This directory provide important statistics and performance information that cAdvisor uses for reporting purposes.

Subcontainers

/blkio
/cpu
/cpuacct
/cpuset
/devices
/freezer
/hugetlb
/init.scope
/misc
/net_cls
/net_prio
/perf_event
/rdma
/system.slice
/user.slice

Figure 18-3. *Subcontainers view*

Click the `system.slice` link and you will see something like Figure 18-4, which shows the different services running on the local machine.

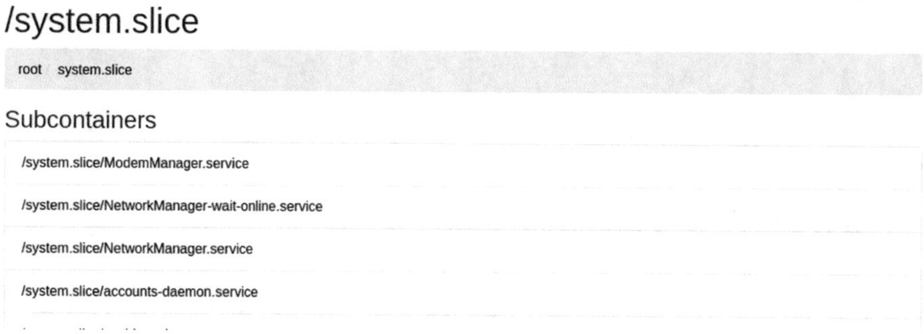

/system.slice

root	system.slice

Subcontainers

/system.slice/ModemManager.service

/system.slice/NetworkManager-wait-online.service

/system.slice/NetworkManager.service

/system.slice/accounts-daemon.service

Figure 18-4. */system.slice view*

Figure 18-5 shows gauges of the percentage of memory and disk usage.

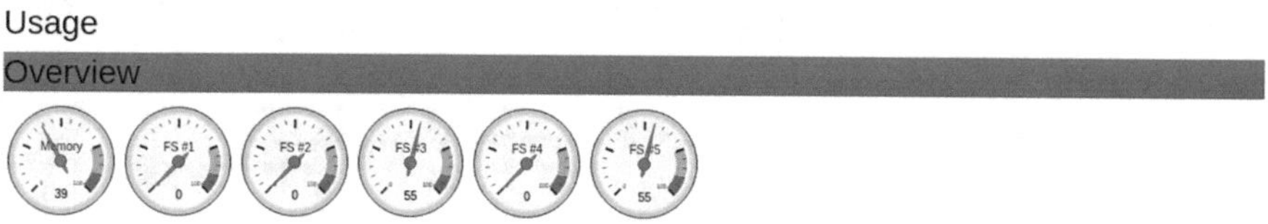

Usage

Overview

Figure 18-5. *Memory and disk usage*

cAdvisor also shows the different processes that are currently running in your system. Figure 18-6 shows information about the process name, CPU usage, memory usage, running time, and other information.

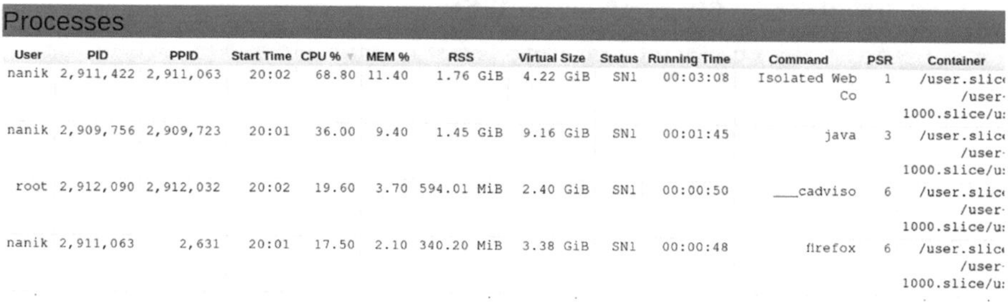

Processes

User	PID	PPID	Start Time	CPU %	MEM %	RSS	Virtual Size	Status	Running Time	Command	PSR	Container
nanik	2,911,422	2,911,063	20:02	68.80	11.40	1.76 GiB	4.22 GiB	SN1	00:03:08	Isolated Web Co	1	/user.slic /user 1000.slice/u:
nanik	2,909,756	2,909,723	20:01	36.00	9.40	1.45 GiB	9.16 GiB	SN1	00:01:45	java	3	/user.slic /user 1000.slice/u:
root	2,912,090	2,912,032	20:02	19.60	3.70	594.01 MiB	2.40 GiB	SN1	00:00:50	__cadviso	6	/user.slic /user 1000.slice/u:
nanik	2,911,063	2,631	20:01	17.50	2.10	340.20 MiB	3.38 GiB	SN1	00:00:48	firefox	6	/user.slic /user 1000.slice/u:

Figure 18-6. *Running process information*

Besides the processes that are running on your local machine, cAdvisor also reports information about the different Docker containers that are currently running on your machine. Click the *Docker Containers* link shown in Figure 18-7.

/

root

Docker Containers

Figure 18-7. *Docker Containers link*

After clicking the *Docker Containers* link, you will be shown the list of containers that you can look into. In my case, as shown in Figure 18-8, there is a Postgres container currently running on my local machine.

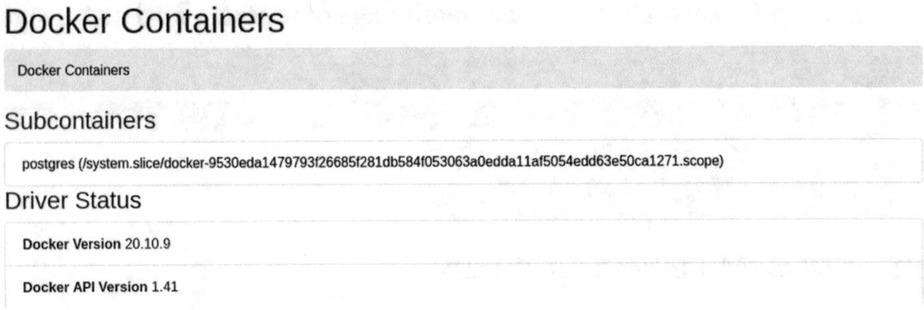

Docker Containers

Docker Containers

Subcontainers

postgres (/system.slice/docker-9530eda1479793f26685f281db584f053063a0edda11af5054edd63e50ca1271.scope)

Driver Status

Docker Version 20.10.9

Docker API Version 1.41

Figure 18-8. *Docker subcontainers view*

Clicking the Postgres container will show the different metrics related to the container, as shown in Figure 18-9.

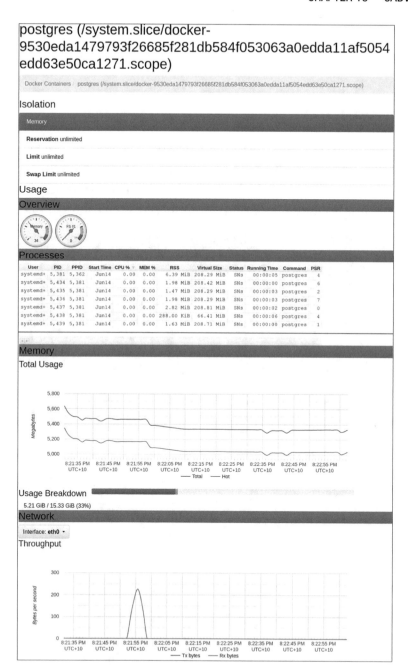

Figure 18-9. *Postgres metrics*

In the next section, you will dive into the internals of cAdvisor and learn how it is able to do all these things in the code.

Architecture

In this section and the next, you will look at the internals of cAdvisor and how the different components work. cAdvisor supports different containers, but for this chapter you will focus on the code that is relevant to Docker only. Let's take a look at the high-level component view of cAdvisor shown in Figure 18-10.

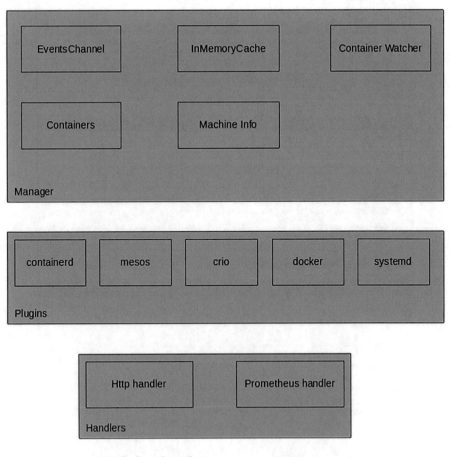

Figure 18-10. *High-level architecture*

Table 18-1 outlines the different components and usage inside cAdvisor.

Table 18-1. *Components*

Events Channel	Channel used to report creation or deletion of containers
InMemoryCache	Cache used to store metric information relevant to all containers being monitored
Container Watcher	Watcher that monitors container activities
Containers	Different containers monitored by cAdvisor
Machine Info	Information related to the local machine that cAdvisor is running on
Plugins	The different container that cAdvisor supports: Docker, Mesos, CRIO, Systemd, and ContainerD
Handlers	HTTP handlers that take care of requests for metrics and other relevant APIs exposed by cAdvisor

In the next few sections, you will look at different parts of cAdvisor and how they work.

Initialization

Like any other Go application, the entry point of cAdvisor is main.go.

```go
func main() {
  ...
  memoryStorage, err := NewMemoryStorage()
  if err != nil {
    klog.Fatalf("Failed to initialize storage driver:
    %s", err)
```

```
    }
    ...
    resourceManager, err := manager.New(memoryStorage, sysFs,
housekeepingConfig, includedMetrics, &collectorHttpClient,
strings.Split(*rawCgroupPrefixWhiteList, ","), *perfEvents)
    ...
    cadvisorhttp.RegisterPrometheusHandler(mux, resourceManager,
*prometheusEndpoint, containerLabelFunc, includedMetrics)
    ...
    rootMux := http.NewServeMux()
    ...
}
```

The main() function performs the following initialization process steps:

- Setting up cache for storing a container and its metrics

- Setting up Manager, which performs all the major processing to monitor containers

- Setting up HTTP handlers to allow the web user interface to get metric data for different containers

- Start collecting containers and metrics by starting up the Manager

The cache management is taken care by InMemoryCache, which can be found inside memory.go.

```
type InMemoryCache struct {
        lock              sync.RWMutex
        containerCacheMap map[string]*containerCache
        maxAge            time.Duration
        backend           []storage.StorageDriver
}
```

```
func (c *InMemoryCache) AddStats(cInfo *info.ContainerInfo,
stats *info.ContainerStats) error {
    ...
}

func (c *InMemoryCache) RecentStats(name string, start, end
time.Time, maxStats int) ([]*info.ContainerStats, error) {
    ...
}

func (c *InMemoryCache) Close() error {
    ...
}

func (c *InMemoryCache) RemoveContainer(containerName
string) error {
    ...
}
```

There are two different HTTP handlers that are initialized by cAdvisor:
API-based HTTP handlers that are used by the web user interface and
metric HTTP handlers that report metric information in raw format.
The following snippet shows the main handlers registration that register
the different paths that are made available (inside cmd/internal/http/
handlers.go):

```
func RegisterHandlers(mux httpmux.Mux, containerManager
manager.Manager, httpAuthFile, httpAuthRealm, httpDigestFile,
httpDigestRealm string, urlBasePrefix string) error {
    ...
    if err := api.RegisterHandlers(mux, containerManager); err
    != nil {
        return fmt.Errorf("failed to register API handlers:
        %s", err)
```

```
}

mux.Handle("/", http.RedirectHandler(urlBasePrefix+pages.
ContainersPage, http.StatusTemporaryRedirect))

...

return nil
}
```

The API-based handlers are found inside cmd/internal/api/handler.
go, as shown:

```
func RegisterHandlers(mux httpmux.Mux, m manager.
Manager) error {

...

mux.HandleFunc(apiResource, func(w http.ResponseWriter, r
*http.Request) {
    err := handleRequest(supportedApiVersions, m, w, r)
    if err != nil {
        http.Error(w, err.Error(), 500)
    }
})
return nil
}
```

The API handlers expose the /api path. To test this handler, make sure
you have cAdvisor running and open your browser and enter the URL
http://localhost:8080/api/v1.0/containers. You will see something
like Figure 18-11.

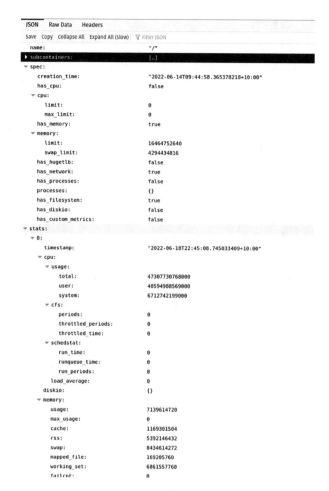

Figure 18-11. *Output of /api/v1.0/containers*

Manager

Manager is the main component of cAdvisor. It takes care of the initialization, maintenance, and reporting of different metrics for the containers it manages. The interfaces are declared as follows:

```
type Manager interface {
```

```
Start() error
Stop() error
GetContainerInfo(containerName string, query *info.
ContainerInfoRequest) (*info.ContainerInfo, error)
GetContainerInfoV2(containerName string, options
v2.RequestOptions) (map[string]v2.ContainerInfo, error)
SubcontainersInfo(containerName string, query *info.
ContainerInfoRequest) ([]*info.ContainerInfo, error)
AllDockerContainers(query *info.ContainerInfoRequest)
(map[string]info.ContainerInfo, error)
DockerContainer(dockerName string, query *info.
ContainerInfoRequest) (info.ContainerInfo, error)
GetContainerSpec(containerName string, options
v2.RequestOptions) (map[string]v2.ContainerSpec, error)
GetDerivedStats(containerName string, options
v2.RequestOptions) (map[string]v2.DerivedStats, error)
GetRequestedContainersInfo(containerName string,
options v2.RequestOptions) (map[string]*info.
ContainerInfo, error)
Exists(containerName string) bool
GetMachineInfo() (*info.MachineInfo, error)
GetVersionInfo() (*info.VersionInfo, error)
GetFsInfoByFsUUID(uuid string) (v2.FsInfo, error)
GetDirFsInfo(dir string) (v2.FsInfo, error)
GetFsInfo(label string) ([]v2.FsInfo, error)
GetProcessList(containerName string, options
v2.RequestOptions) ([]v2.ProcessInfo, error)
WatchForEvents(request *events.Request) (*events.
EventChannel, error)
GetPastEvents(request *events.Request) ([]*info.
Event, error)
CloseEventChannel(watchID int)
```

```
    DockerInfo() (info.DockerStatus, error)
    DockerImages() ([]info.DockerImage, error)
    DebugInfo() map[string][]string
}
```

The interfaces and implementation are found inside manager.go.

Manager uses plugins for different container technologies. For example, the Docker plugin is responsible for communicating with the Docker engine. The Docker plugin resides inside the container/docker/plugin.go file. The following is the Docker plugin code:

```
package docker

import (
    ...
)

const dockerClientTimeout = 10 * time.Second
    ...
func (p *plugin) InitializeFSContext(context *fs.
Context) error {
    SetTimeout(dockerClientTimeout)
    // Try to connect to docker indefinitely on startup.
    dockerStatus := retryDockerStatus()
    ...
}
    ...
func retryDockerStatus() info.DockerStatus {
    startupTimeout := dockerClientTimeout
    maxTimeout := 4 * startupTimeout
    for {
        ...
    }
}
```

The main job of Manager is to monitor containers, but before it is able to do that, it needs to find out what containers are available and how to monitor them. Let's take a look at the first step, which is finding out what containers will be monitored.

In the previous section, it was mentioned that conceptually cAdvisor refers to containers not only for Docker, but anything that it monitors is considered as containers. Let's take a look at how cAdvisor finds the containers that it monitors. The collection of containers that it will monitor are collected when the Start() function of Manager is called, as shown here:

```go
func (m *manager) Start() error {
  ...

  err := raw.Register(m, m.fsInfo, m.includedMetrics, m.rawCont
  ainerCgroupPathPrefixWhiteList)
  if err != nil {
     klog.Errorf("Registration of the raw container factory
     failed: %v", err)
  }

  rawWatcher, err := raw.NewRawContainerWatcher()
  if err != nil {
     return err
  }
  m.containerWatchers = append(m.containerWatchers, rawWatcher)
  ...

  // Create root and then recover all containers.
  err = m.createContainer("/", watcher.Raw)
  if err != nil {
     return err
  }
```

```
klog.V(2).Infof("Starting recovery of all containers")
err = m.detectSubcontainers("/")
if err != nil {
    return err
}
  ...

return nil
}
```

The collection process is performed by the m.createContainer(..)
function and Figure 18-12 shows what is created.

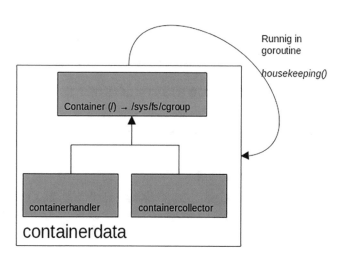

Figure 18-12. *The createContainer function process*

Basically, what it is doing the following:

- Creating a containerData struct that is populated with container-related information. In this case, it's populated with information regarding the /sys/fs/cgroup directory.

- Creating a ContainerHandler and CollectManager that will handle everything related to this particular container (in this case /sys/fs/cgroup) and collecting all the necessary metric information.

- Once all structs have been initialized successfully, it will call Start() of the containerData struct to start monitoring.

From the steps above, it is clear that cAdvisor is monitoring activities that are happening inside the /sys/fs/cgroup directory. As you learned in Chapter 4, this directory refers to cgroups, which is the cornerstone of Docker containers.

cAdvisor also monitors the subdirectories of /sys/fs/cgroup, which are all treated as containers and will be monitored the same as the main /sys/fs/cgroup directory. This is performed by the detectSubcontainers(..) function, as shown here:

```
func (m *manager) detectSubcontainers(containerName
string) error {
  added, removed, err := m.getContainersDiff(containerName)
  ...
  for _, cont := range added {
    err = m.createContainer(cont.Name, watcher.Raw)
    ...

  }

  ...

  return nil
}
```

Once all the subdirectories of /sys/fs/cgroup have been processed, it adds those containers to be watched by Container Watcher. This is done by the watchForNewContainers() function shown in the following code:

```
func (m *manager) watchForNewContainers(quit chan
error) error {
    ...
    for _, watcher := range m.containerWatchers {
        err := watcher.Start(m.eventsChannel)
        if err != nil {
            for _, w := range watched {
                stopErr := w.Stop()
                ...
            }
            return err
        }
        watched = append(watched, watcher)
    }

    err := m.detectSubcontainers("/")
    ...
    return nil
}
```

After all containers have been set up to be watched, cAdvisor will be informed about any changes to them. This job is done by the goroutine shown in the above code snippets. In the next section, you will look at how cAdvisor uses inotify, which is provided by the Linux operating system to let applications to be notified if any activities are detected for the directories that are watched.

Monitoring Filesystem

cAdvisor uses the inotify API that is provided by the Linux kernel
(https://linux.die.net/man/7/inotify). This API allows applications
to monitor file systems events, such as if any files are deleted or created.
Figure 18-13 shows how cAdvisor uses the inotify events.

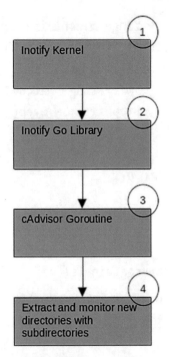

Figure 18-13. *inotify flow in cAdvisor*

In the previous section, you learned that cAdvisor monitors and listens
for events for /sys/fs/cgroup and its subdirectories. This is how cAdvisor
knows what Docker containers are created or deleted from memory. Let's
take a look at how it uses inotify for this purpose.

The code uses the inotify library that listens to events
coming in from the kernel. The cAdvisor code uses a goroutine to
process the inotify events. This goroutine is created as part of

the initialization process when watchForNewContainers is called.
watchForNewContainers calls the Start function inside container/raw/
watcher.go, as shown:

```go
func (w *rawContainerWatcher) Start(events chan watcher.
ContainerEvent) error {
  watched := make([]string, 0)
  for _, cgroupPath := range w.cgroupPaths {
    _, err := w.watchDirectory(events, cgroupPath, "/")
    ...
    watched = append(watched, cgroupPath)
  }

  go func() {
    for {
      select {
      case event := <-w.watcher.Event():
        err := w.processEvent(event, events)
        if err != nil {

          ...

        }
      case err := <-w.watcher.Error():
        ...
      case <-w.stopWatcher:
        err := w.watcher.Close()
        ...
      }
    }
  }()

  return nil
}
```

The w.processEvent(..) function takes care of the received inotify event and converts it into its own internal event, as shown:

```go
func (w *rawContainerWatcher) processEvent(event *inotify.
Event, events chan watcher.ContainerEvent) error {
  // Convert the inotify event type to a container create
  or delete.
  var eventType watcher.ContainerEventType
  switch {
  case (event.Mask & inotify.InCreate) > 0:
    eventType = watcher.ContainerAdd
  case (event.Mask & inotify.InDelete) > 0:
    eventType = watcher.ContainerDelete
   ...
  }

  ...
  switch eventType {
  case watcher.ContainerAdd:
    alreadyWatched, err := w.watchDirectory(events, event.
    Name, containerName)
    ...
  case watcher.ContainerDelete:
    // Container was deleted, stop watching for it.
    lastWatched, err := w.watcher.RemoveWatch(containerName,
    event.Name)
    ...
  default:
    return fmt.Errorf("unknown event type %v", eventType)
  }

  // Deliver the event.
  events <- watcher.ContainerEvent{
```

```
    EventType:    eventType,
    Name:         containerName,
    WatchSource:  watcher.Raw,
  }

  return nil
}
```

The function converts the events received into internal events that the code understands: watcher.ContainerAdd and watcher.ContainerDelete. These events are broadcast internally for other parts of the code to process.

Information from /sys and /proc

In Chapters 2 and 3, you learned about the /sys and /proc filesystems and what kind of system-related information can be found. cAdvisor uses the same way to collect machine information that is reported as part of the metric information.

Manager takes care of collecting and updating machine information, as shown in the following code snippet:

```
func New(memoryCache *memory.InMemoryCache, sysfs sysfs.
SysFs, houskeepingConfig HouskeepingConfig, includedMetricsSet
container.MetricSet, collectorHTTPClient *http.Client,
rawContainerCgroupPathPrefixWhiteList []string, perfEventsFile
string) (Manager, error) {
  ...
  machineInfo, err := machine.Info(sysfs, fsInfo,
  inHostNamespace)
  ...
}
```

The primary code that does the collection of machine information can be seen in the following snippet (machine/info.go):

```go
func Info(sysFs sysfs.SysFs, fsInfo fs.FsInfo, inHostNamespace
bool) (*info.MachineInfo, error) {
  ...
  clockSpeed, err := GetClockSpeed(cpuinfo)
  ...
  memoryCapacity, err := GetMachineMemoryCapacity()
  ...
  filesystems, err := fsInfo.GetGlobalFsInfo()
  ...
  netDevices, err := sysinfo.GetNetworkDevices(sysFs)
  ...
  topology, numCores, err := GetTopology(sysFs)
  ...
  return machineInfo, nil
}
```

Here's the GetMachineMemoryCapacity() function and how it collects memory information using the /proc directory:

```go
func GetMachineMemoryCapacity() (uint64, error) {
  out, err := ioutil.ReadFile("/proc/meminfo")
  if err != nil {
     return 0, err
  }

  memoryCapacity, err := parseCapacity(out,
  memoryCapacityRegexp)
  if err != nil {
     return 0, err
  }
  return memoryCapacity, err
}
```

The function reads the /proc/meminfo directory and parses the information received by calling the parseCapacity() function. The raw information extracted from /proc/meminfo looks like the following:

```
MemTotal:       16078860 kB
MemFree:          698260 kB
...
Hugepagesize:       2048 kB
Hugetlb:               0 kB
DirectMap4k:      901628 kB
DirectMap2M:    15566848 kB
DirectMap1G:           0 kB
```

Let's look at another function called GetGlobalFsInfo() (fs/fs.go). This function calls another function called GetFsInfoForPath(..) (fs/fs.go), which is shown in the following snippet:

```
func (i *RealFsInfo) GetFsInfoForPath(mountSet
map[string]struct{}) ([]Fs, error) {
  ...
  diskStatsMap, err := getDiskStatsMap("/proc/diskstats")
  ...
  return filesystems, nil
}
```

It calls getDiskStatsMap(..), passing in /proc/diskstats as the parameter. The function getDiskStatsMap(..) reads and parses the information from that directory. The raw information from that directory looks like the following:

...

```
259         0 nvme0n1 17925716 1726716 2140111562 27153144
9657604 6144332 374398866 10096182 1 7081436 37829936 0 0 0 0
666569 580610
...
253         2 dm-2 728297 0 5837468 252644 2635588 0 21084640
7281316 0 334744 7533960 0 0 0 0 0 0
```

Now let's look at how cAdvisor reads information using the /sys directory. The function GetNetworkDevices(..) (utils/sysinfo/sysinfo.go) shown in the code snippets calls another function to get the information from /sys/class/net.

```go
func GetNetworkDevices(sysfs sysfs.SysFs) ([]info.NetInfo,
error) {
  devs, err := sysfs.GetNetworkDevices()
  ...
  return netDevices, nil
}
```

The sysfs.GetNetworkDevices() (utils/sysfs/sysfs.go) snippet looks like the following:

```go
const (
  ...
  netDir      = "/sys/class/net"
  ...
)
func (fs *realSysFs) GetNetworkDevices() ([]os.FileInfo,
error) {
  files, err := ioutil.ReadDir(netDir)
  ...
  var dirs []os.FileInfo
  for _, f := range files {
```

```
    ...
  }
  return dirs, nil
}
```

The function extracts and parses the information, which looks like the following in raw format:

```
lrwxrwxrwx  1 root root 0 Jun 19 14:09 docker0 -> ../../
devices/virtual/net/docker0
...
../../devices/virtual/net/veth710aac6
lrwxrwxrwx  1 root root 0 Jun 19 12:30 veth98e6a97 -> ../../
devices/virtual/net/veth98e6a97
lrwxrwxrwx  1 root root 0 Jun 19 14:09 wlp0s20f3 -> ../../
devices/pci0000:00/0000:00:14.3/net/wlp0s20f3
```

Client Library

In the repository inside the chapter18 folder, there are examples of how to use the cAdvisor client library to communicate with cAdvisor. The examples show how to use the client library to get container information, event streaming from cAdvisor, and so on.

Summary

In this chapter, you learned about installing and running cAdvisor to monitor metrics of your local machine and Docker containers. The tool provides a lot of information that shows the performance of the different containers that are running on a machine. This chapter discussed how cAdvisor collects metric information for containers and local machines using the knowledge you learned in previous chapters.

cAdvisor provides much more functionality than what was discussed in this chapter. For example, it has built-in support for exporting metrics to a Prometheus, it provides an API that can be used to integrated with other third-party or in-house tools to monitor container performance, and more.

Index

© Nanik Tolaram 2023
N. Tolaram, *Software Development with Go*,
https://doi.org/10.1007/978-1-4842-8731-6

S

W, X, Y, Z

Printed in the United States
by Baker & Taylor Publisher Services